T0227909

Security De-Engineering

Solving the Problems in Information Risk Management

IAN TIBBLE

CRC Press
Taylor & Francis Group
Boca Raton London New York

CRC Press is an imprint of the
Taylor & Francis Group, an **informa** business

AN AUERBACH BOOK

CRC Press
Taylor & Francis Group
6000 Broken Sound Parkway NW, Suite 300
Boca Raton, FL 33487-2742

First issued in hardback 2017

© 2012 by Taylor & Francis Group, LLC
CRC Press is an imprint of Taylor & Francis Group, an Informa business

No claim to original U.S. Government works

Version Date: 20110815

ISBN-13: 978-1-4398-6834-8 (pbk)
ISBN-13: 978-1-138-44038-8 (hbk)

Library of Congress Cataloging-in-Publication Data

Tibble, Ian.
    Security de-engineering : solving the problems in information risk management / Ian Tibble.
      p. cm.
    Includes bibliographical references and index.
    ISBN 978-1-4398-6834-8
    1. Business enterprises--Computer networks--Security measures. 2. Information technology--Security measures. 3. Data protection. 4. Computer security. 5. Database security. I. Title.

HF5548.37.T53 2011
658.4'78--dc23   2011033830

Visit the Taylor & Francis Web site at
http://www.taylorandfrancis.com

and the CRC Press Web site at
http://www.crcpress.com

Contents

PREFACE   ix

ACKNOWLEDGMENTS   xvii

INTRODUCTION   xix

AUTHOR   xxxvii

SECTION 1   PEOPLE AND BLAME

CHAPTER 1   WHOM DO YOU BLAME?   3
The Buck Stops at the Top?   3
Managers and Their Loyal Secretaries   5
Information Security Spending—Driving Factors in the Wild   7
Do Top-Level Managers Care about Information Security?   10
Ignoring the Signs   12
Summary   14

CHAPTER 2   THE HACKERS   17
Hat Colors and Ethics   17
"Hacker" Defined   20
Zen and the Art of Remote Assessment   25
The Hacker through the Looking Glass   29
Communication, Hyper-Casual Fridays, and "Maturity"   35
Hacker Cries Wolf   38
Unmuzzled Hackers and Facebook   40
Summary   42

CHAPTER 3   CHECKLISTS AND STANDARDS EVANGELISTS   47
Platform Security in HELL   54

CASE Survival Guidelines   58
CASEs and Network Security   60
Security Teams and Incident Investigation   61
Vulnerability/Malware Announcements   63
This Land Is Our Land   65
Common CASE Assertions   67
Summary   68

SECTION 2   THE DE-ENGINEERING OF SECURITY

CHAPTER 4   HOW SECURITY CHANGED POST 2000   75
Migrating South: Osmosis of Analysis Functions to
    Operations Teams   75
The Rise of the Automated Vulnerability Scanner   83
The Rise of the Checklist   89
Incident Response and Management—According to Best
    Practices   93
"Best Practices" in Security Service Provision   98
Tip of the Iceberg—Audit-Driven Security Strategy   99
Summary   106

CHAPTER 5   AUTOMATED VULNERABILITY SCANNERS   111
Law of Diminishing Enthusiasm   115
False Positive Testing Revelations   121
The Great Autoscanning Lottery   125
Judgment Day   129
Automation and Web Application Vulnerability Assessment   132
Web Application Security Source Code Testing   136
Summary   137

CHAPTER 6   THE ETERNAL YAWN: CAREERS IN INFORMATION
SECURITY   143
Information Security and Strange Attractors   145
Specialization in Security   146
The Instant Manager   151
The Technical Track   154
Summary   160

CHAPTER 7   PENETRATION TESTING—OLD AND NEW   169
Testing Restrictions   170
Restriction 1: Source IP Address   171
Restriction 2: Testing IP Address Range(s)   173
Restriction 3: Exploits Testing   175
Penetration Testing—The Bigger Picture   179
Summary   186

CHAPTER 8   THE LOVE OF CLOUDS AND INCIDENTS—
             THE VAIN SEARCH FOR VALIDATION   193
             Love of Incidents   195
             The Love of Clouds   200
             Summary   206

SECTION 3   SECURITY PRODUCTS

CHAPTER 9   INTRUSION DETECTION   213
             Tuning/Initial Costs   216
             Belt and Suspenders?   216
             NIDS and Denial of Service   217
             Hidden Costs   218
             Return on Investment   218
             Network Intrusion Prevention Systems   220
             Summary   222
             A Final Note   223

CHAPTER 10   OTHER PRODUCTS   225
             Identity Management   226
             Security Information Event Management Solutions   231
             Summary   240

SECTION 4   THE RE-ENGINEERING OF SECURITY

CHAPTER 11   ONE PROFESSIONAL ACCREDITATION
             PROGRAM TO BIND THEM ALL   251
             C-Levels Do Not Trust Us   254
             Infosec Vocational Classifications   256
             Requirements of an Infosec Manager   257
             The Requirements of a Security Analyst   260
             Regaining the Trust: A Theoretical Infosec Accreditation
                 Structure   270
             Summary   278

INDEX   285

Preface

Security de-engineering is for anyone with an interest in security, but the focus is on the aspects of security that matter to businesses and how businesses do security.

It is clear that the good guys have been doing something wrong in security. There are increasing levels of fear and insecurity in the world as a result of almost daily news headlines relating to new acts of skullduggery by financially motivated bad guys. Large-scale incidents now regularly make headline news even in financial publications—this is because the bottom line is now being impacted. Smaller-scale malware attacks gnaw at corporate balance sheets and lead to identity theft. These attacks have led to botnetz-r-us criminal gangs surpassing drug cartels in terms of revenue generation.

One can be led to think the world is falling apart with so many credit card fraud horror stories and so on. But are we getting closer to a solution for corporate security? Not really, because we have not yet identified the problems.

There is no secret that the security world and its customers are in something of a quagmire. All large organizations of more than 10,000 nodes will have been the victims of advanced persistent threat (APT) in some form or another. Indeed, most of them are already "owned." In *Security De-Engineering*, I give a simple foundational remedy for our security ills, but in order to give a prescription, one must first make an accurate diagnosis of the ailment. In this respect, *Security De-Engineering* is a definitive guide to the current problems in corporate information risk management. What are the problems? How and why were they manifested? How will they be addressed?

Security De-Engineering is a unique take on the security world from several different aspects. I am not a manager or C-level exec, so my view on security is not from such an altitude that I cannot clearly see the ground. I have worked on three different continents and with close to 100 different Fortune 500s and multinationals—so my perspective is global and also crosses industry sectors. Lastly, my view is independent and objective. I have no affiliations with product vendors and no vested interests.

I started out in security in the late 1990s, and I witnessed some spectacular security failures in these early years. Then into the 2000s, the situation seemed to be getting worse. In the early 2000s, I had seen some serious problems, but I thought maybe I was just unlucky—I sort of hoped that these problems were only localized issues that I had the misfortune to stumble across. But as my career progressed, I came to realize that the problems I encountered were pandemic and global. As if I needed further assurance, I heard of similar stories from many others in the field.

Some of the problems I speak of are becoming better known, but they are not yet mainstream; then there are others that do not seem to be at all well known. I also cover the reasons why these problems have remained underground for more than a decade. In many cases, it is because there is a vested interest in keeping these issues hidden.

At an Asia–Pacific regional conference in 2002, the audience was told, "Security is no longer about people with green hair and facial piercings." Hackers were no longer welcome in the good guys' world, and by 2002, there were very few remaining. At the time it was thought that information risk management programs would succeed—with or without IT skills. Time has proven this assumption to be incorrect.

The root (no pun intended) cause of all of our problems can be summed up in terms of skills, or lack of, and unless we want to revert to the paper office, with filing cabinets and carrier pigeon, we had better do something about it. The title of this narrative is a play on the title of Ross Anderson's famous book *Security Engineering*. Security started out bad, but rather than evolve, it got worse as a result of the removal of critical analysis skills—the security industry was effectively dumbed down or de-engineered. From roughly the start of the 2000s onward, there was a loss of intellectual capital from security that put firms on a collision course with fiends and eroded the capacity of organizations to protect the confidentiality, integrity, and availability of their information assets.

After all the talk of doom and gloom, how about solutions? I agree with many in the field that there are some problems that we will not solve any time soon. Examples would be application security, employee awareness, and malware issues. But if an organization experiences an incident along these lines, does it have to lead to massive financial losses? There are plenty of things that organizations can do to reduce their risk. For example, there are technical means by which they can reduce their "attack surface" and increase the time needed for the bad guys to do them harm. The risk cannot be completely mitigated, but organizations *can* improve their security with "layers" so that they are no longer low-hanging fruit.

If our problems have resulted from a loss of skills in security, then we need to somehow channel the right analysis skills back to the industry. How do we do this? Please read on.

The following is a summary of the main chapters.

Chapter 1: Whom Do You Blame?

Who do we blame for all of these problems? Is it necessarily the C-level execs? Perhaps it is the case that the C-levels have never been well advised in security. C-levels make decisions based on available information, but if the information provided is not accurate, can they be blamed for making poor decisions?

Chapter 2: The Hackers

This is "Hackers" with an uppercase "H." In this chapter, I introduce the Hacker concept as in a set of skills. "Hacker" as a word conjures all different kinds of images, so I need to define what I mean by hacker for this narrative. Chapter 2 is a look at the first generation of security pros and their skills. Much of this chapter is based on my own experiences of working with Hackers in the formative years (late 1990s) of my career.

Chapter 3: Checklists and Standards Evangelists

In Chapter 3, I introduce the second genre of security professional— the checklists and standards evangelist (CASE). Typical skill sets changed radically from the early 2000s onward. The skills sets were reduced down to the level that was needed to deliver lower quality security offerings. The modern-era security professional was effectively defined by the requirements of the modern-era security department, and these requirements were very different from those of the late 1990s. This chapter covers the practices of security departments in larger organizations.

Chapter 4: How Security Changed Post 2000

In Chapter 4, I cover six detrimental post 2000s security changes and how these trends came about.

First I take a look at the common practice of devolving security functions to IT operations and the impact this has on the organization as a whole. Also in this chapter, I cover the introduction of automation into security, the use of checklists as a substitute for analysis, the use and abuse of the phrase "best practices" in security, and finally the all too common security strategy that is aimed at nothing more than base compliance.

Chapter 5: Automated Vulnerability Scanners

Automated vulnerability scanners are tools such as GFI LANguard and "Nessus." This genre of tool is heavily used in the security industry and forms the basis of the majority of organizations' vulnerability management strategies. Some of the problems with autoscanners are starting to become more publicized, but the extent of the failings remains hidden.

The security industry is just not ready for this level of automation. Other industries such as automobile manufacturing slowly phased in automation over a period of years, but even today, there are still plenty of humans employed in automobile manufacturing. The security industry went full automatic at a very early stage in its formation—to the detriment of our economic security.

In Chapter 5, I cover what goes on "under the hood" with these tools and rationalize the differences between the perceived and the actual value returned with use of autoscanners.

Chapter 6: The Eternal Yawn: Careers in Information Security

The previous chapters should have served something of a warning for any prospective security professionals out there, but Chapter 6 paints the vocational security picture in more vivid detail. Perhaps there are people out there who want to go get a Certified Information Systems Security Professional (CISSP) and jump into the field (according to the exam prequalifiers, one must have several years of vocational experience, but in practice, even undergrads can be accredited as being CISSP). In Chapter 6, I cover the security industry in the light of some of the more common drivers for pursuit of a career in security.

Chapter 7: Penetration Testing—Old and New

At the time of writing, most penetration testing projects are sold only on the basis of compliance (organizations need to show that their perimeter defenses have been tested by an independent third party), but the increasing frequency of incidents may have led many security departments to rethink the value offering of penetration testing.

Older style penetration tests were unrestricted, and Hackers defined the methodology. As the 2000s dragged on, the network penetration testing scene changed a great deal, with a dramatic fall in the quality of the delivery.

Penetration testing has been heavily restricted (with the result that it is no longer a simulated attack) and also delivered with more automation, but even if everything is perfect with the delivery methodology, what can we really expect to get from penetration testing, and how should we position it in our information risk management strategies? Chapter 7 gives an answer to some of the more pressing questions over the whole network penetration testing circus.

Chapter 8: The Love of Clouds and Incidents—
The Vain Search for Validation

Many folks in security are inwardly reflective of their lives as CASEs and conscious that the downward spiral of the industry has effectively led to their hands being tied in being able to offer anything of any value to their organizations. This has led to some unfortunate developments in the industry that end up wasting a lot of corporate resources and further damaging the reputation of security departments.

In Chapter 8, I first examine the common premise that in security we need a global incident database in order to "prove" the existence of a threat (when there is some doubt expressed over risks, we can go to some database of collected data concerning past incidents and produce the "evidence") and therefore justify our own corporate right to exist. Do we really need such an entity in order to prove the existence of a threat, and even if we have a global incident database, how much emphasis should we place on its contents?

Secondly, I cover some aspects of cloud computing security and try to answer the following questions: Does this area deserve the extensive coverage it attracts or is moving to the cloud just a change in the network architecture? Is cloud security really a whole new ball game in security?

Chapter 9: Intrusion Detection

Chapters 9 and 10 cover security products, starting with the various different types of intrusion detection. What is our approximate return on investment with this technology? The value of detection is not in doubt, but does existing detection technology give us more of a headache than a solution?

Chapter 10: Other Products

I first take a look at security incident event management (SIEM) solutions in Chapter 10. Again, do we get the sort of return on investment that was promised by the vendor? Is SIEM really such a technological breakthrough? Does a SIEM solution give us a turn-key answer to our incident response issues, or is it a small (but very expensive) piece of the puzzle?

Identity management (IdM) was another modern development in security. Vendors will have us believe that we cannot manage identities unless we invest in a huge, complex software package of the IdM variety. But IdM solutions need some thought. We cannot just buy a product and hope to solve all of our problems in managing complex user account environments.

There will be many cases where IdM products do not really do that much for us. There are very few, if any, cases where IdM can give us centralized user management for all applications and services. If we break up the enterprise into smaller "pieces" such as Unix, Web applications, Windows, and so on, and actually think about what we are trying to achieve, we may find that our pre-IdM architecture had everything we ever needed.

Chapter 11: One Professional Accreditation Program to Bind Them All

Justice cannot be done to the area of solutions in this narrative because a microdetailed view is needed of the different issues we face. Such topics have a fairly extensive real-estate prerequisite, but in writing this book, I did feel a need to avoid talking purely about problems and taking *Security De-Engineering* down the road of being a Book of Revelations for the electronically connected world.

In Chapter 11, I give a simplified view of how I think we might channel the necessary skills back into security—and with the reintroduction of properly managed security artists ("properly managed" is the key here; the late 1990s Hackers were properly skilled but not properly managed), it is hoped that all issues may at least be reviewed within an improved framework.

I hope the reader will not be too gloomy after reading this. That was not my intention. At times, *Security De-Engineering* can read like the most condemning commentary ever written about the modern-day security industry. But I just felt like this approach is long overdue, and as they say, just as with taking out the trash, "someone has to do it."

I hope you enjoy reading *Security De-Engineering*. My comments are based purely on observation, and I waited many years to confirm my own suspicions about the security industry before committing my thoughts to media. My views are somewhat condemning, but I hope the whole experience will not be entirely negative for the reader. As I mentioned before, the first stage of solving a problem is realization of its existence. But also, I hope the reader could learn something while reading about the problems.

Acknowledgments

There are many folks who have made direct or indirect contributions to *Security De-Engineering*, including family and friends, past and present acquaintances, and experts in their respective fields.

First up is family—one that is split over two continents and seven time zones. My wife Suzanna here in Jakarta has shown great tolerance and support while I have hidden myself away in production of this narrative. There is never enough time in a day; 24 hours just does not cut it really. A lot of time that I would usually set aside for home time was eaten into by the production of this book, and I thank Suzanna for her patience during this testing period, and for my mother-in-law for her expertise in the field of beef rendang—I swear her rendition of this famous Indonesian recipe has to be the best in the world. Ibu Ida's overall support has been appreciated in this trying time.

My Mum and Dad in Cornwall endured my presence there in 2010, as the production of *Security De-Engineering* got under way. My parents always did what parents are supposed to do to the best of their abilities. No further elaboration is necessary in this regard, and no words are enough to express my appreciation.

I want to give special thanks to several individuals who shared some of their expertise in the production of this book. They are as follows: Ilya Levin, Senior R&D Engineer at D'Crypt Pte Ltd (Singapore); Fyodor Yarochkin, Black Hat speaker and researcher at the 0th Day Church of Kyrgyzstan; Taweesak Meksikarin, consultant at PricewaterhouseCoopers (Thailand); Kor Kittikorn, manager at PricewaterhouseCoopers (Thailand); Sheena Chin, FSI sales manager, Symantec (Singapore); Scott West, managing consultant at Acumin Consulting (UK); and last but not least Jack Gnyszka, security manager at DHL ITSC Europe and Middle East (Czech Republic).

There were of course many people who I would like to mention from my presecurity days; in fact, there are really too many. From my security days, there are plenty who shaped my career and who inspired me, but my work colleagues from my first security position (the company referred to as TSAP in this book) deserve a special mention for their contribution to my experience, and therefore this narrative. Great thanks go out to Vanja, Vladimir, Anton, Oleg, Mika, and Emmanuel.

In my career, there were various different managers who inspired me in various nontech ways and unknowingly helped to form some of the ideas for this book: Jack, Sowmy, Luke, Pierre, and Pongsak (also known as P'Noo).

I have enjoyed the work of and taken inspiration from these security authors: John Viega, Bruce Schneier, Mark Dowd, John McDonald, Justin Schuh, Chris McNab, Adam Shostack, Andrew Stewart, Steven Levy, Ross Anderson, Elizabeth Zwicky, Simon Cooper, and Brent Chapman.

I have mentioned some names of contributors and reviewers in this acknowledgment, but nobody is to blame for my opinions other than myself. I am open to being corrected on any of my points if a respectful, objective, and logical opinion can be formulated—suffice it to say, I have been wrong before and will be again. I am more than willing to discuss any of the points I have raised in a respectful way: feel free to email me at itibble@gmail.com.

Introduction

This book is only worth writing because of the nature of human beings and the fact that we will continue to commit acts of deception and aggression against each other for at least the foreseeable future.

The main driver behind the undeniable spike in malevolent activity on the public Internet during the past few years has of course been economic. One could be forgiven for thinking that greed is interwoven into our DNA, so I am not sure that I can say that I would prefer a world without greed because that world is a hard one to picture. A world without human greed is a way different world.

Without greed, there would be no raison d'être for a book such as this one, or any other security books, or indeed security itself. So just for now, we will celebrate humanity and greed because without the latter, there would be no information security. That does not mean I celebrate greed—I am just one of the few in security who actually sort of like my job.

There is a consensus among information security professionals that the picture with regard to global security incidents is getting worse. Reports of information security problems are making headline news with increasing frequency. There are of course sources of information on the actual numbers of recorded incidents, such as Carnegie Mellon's CERT Coordination Center, but one does not need to see the numbers (the accuracy or usefulness of incident data in general is discussed in Chapter 8) to be aware of the increasing scale of the problem. Statistical analysis of security incidents has never been a precise science, and why would an organization wish to report an information security incident if it results in a loss of reputation? Other problems exist with the "science" of gathering breach data, and these are discussed in Chapter 8.

I first noticed a major headline in the *Financial Times* (*FT*) newspaper (not a front-page headline, but a major headline nonetheless) in 2006 about IT security incidents and banks in Japan. "Interesting," I thought, because it is a widely known fact that as a percentage, more Japan-located organizations subscribe to ISO 27001 (or its predecessor BS7799) than in any other country. Since that article from 2006, there have been more *FT* articles related to breaches and other problems. There have been more articles and reports from all major news sources and with increasing frequency. Certainly when we consider the *FT* and its target audience, it is interesting that major headlines about security incidents are increasingly a common sight.

The U.K. government's Office of Cyber Security and Information Assurance in 2011 estimated the cost of cybercrime to the U.K. economy at more than US$40 billion per annum.

Incidents in the wild involve attacks against corporations (some of the more common incidents from 2010 to 2011 were related to APT attacks and corporate espionage incidents, the latter of which are usually attributed to Chinese sources) to identity theft attacks against large numbers of individuals. Attacks can be manual attacks by motivated individuals and the more common case: wide scale automated malware attacks. It is really the nature of the attacks that has changed, more than a weakening of security postures. Motivations these days are more financial than before. Back in the good old days, vanity was the more common driver behind malware development efforts.

I would not venture to say that the security posture of networks has improved significantly with time. I do not have the figures because they are not freely available to me, and I do not want to pay for such information, but from my perspective, it seems clear that organizations are now spending more (as a percentage of their IT budget) on information security as compared with during 1998. Does this mean that security postures have improved? Do organizations now have the right balance of risk and spending? The answers to these questions are both "no."

Among other activities on the "dark side," thousands of compromised computers in homes and offices are unwitting components in the propagation of electronic crime. "Botnets," as they are known, are hired out by criminal gangs for those who wish to spread SPAM emails and perform other acts of electronic crime, in such a way as to make the actions hard to attribute to an individual entity. When computers are compromised these days, it is often not noticed by the user because the computer is only used to send spam emails. "Only" used? It sounds like a trivial annoyance—but if it is a corporate computer and it is sending spam, it could result in the organization being blacklisted by other companies.

Organizations on the dark side reportedly exist with management structures and organization charts. There is a supply–demand economic model in the world of selling stolen identities and credit card details. At the time of writing, prices for credit numbers were subject to deflationary pressures resulting from an oversupply of stolen details. According to a Symantec employee: ". . . what can you buy for $10 in 2008? I could buy just under three gallons of gas for my car, which would probably last me a couple of days. I could buy lunch at the local sushi place but only lunch since there wouldn't be enough left to buy something to drink. Or, I could buy 10 United States identities."

In January 2010, Google was subject to an incident that may have led to the compromise of their crown jewels—the source code of their search engine. Later in the year, several tech sector companies (including Google) added new warnings to their U.S. Securities and Exchange Commission filings, informing investors of the risks of computer attacks.

The time of takeoff for the public Internet was around the mid-1990s, and between that time and approximately Q1 2002 (give or take three quarters), information security was the best and most interesting field of information technology. During this period, professionals from different IT backgrounds were attracted to the field. Information security was seen by many as the most interesting IT field. What happened after this period is one of the main themes of this narrative and helped to lay the foundations for the increased frequency of security breaches and identity thefts that we experience at the time of writing.

Many explanations are touted for the rise in occurrence of information security incidents. Most of the explanations that find their way into books such as Bruce Schneier's *Secrets and Lies* and *The New School of Information Security* (Adam Shostack and Andrew Stewart) are perfectly valid, and certainly I can say that unique ways of looking at the problem are described in those books. Also of worthy mention are most of the comments in John Viega's book, *The Myths of Security*. I find congruence in many of the points raised in the aforementioned titles, as well as give my own two cents worth to the industry; I also seek to build on others' comments and give them added momentum—for the good of the infosec industry and therefore the interconnected world in general.

On the aspect of how to deal with the problem, there has also been an increasing volume of big picture solutions—each as revolutionary and incredible as the next, and each composed by management-oriented figures with an approach toward the technical side that borders on disdain. Yes, economics is a factor. Yes, people are a factor (employees in any size of organization must be mandated to buy into a security awareness program and sign off on an information security policy). Yes, we need to improve our "processes" and other factors that have different names but mean the same thing.

The noble efforts of various figures in the information security community to remind the world at-large of these risk-mitigating factors are much appreciated by at least the author of this narrative and hopefully also C-level executives.

Local Stories, Global Phenomena

In my journeys as an information security professional, I have had the privilege to work with some of the best in the industry and the worst of the worse. I have encountered stories from all areas of the spectrum that are not for the faint hearted.

In my work with various Fortune 500 clients, I grew sufficiently acquainted with their business and IT practices that I was able to get to know their personnel issues and see in detail how they went about trying to handle information security.

I have spent weeks, and in some cases months, with clients, mostly in finance, but also transport, insurance, tobacco, electronics, and logistics. I worked full-time with two major consulting firms and one multinational insurance company. My other engagements were as a contracted consultant to a variety of companies, in offices on three different continents.

Over a decade, I have grown to become familiar with some common trends that I see across companies and continents. These are not trends that are particular to a geographic or industry sector. The problems I illustrate are global, and they are, in my opinion, the problems that are the root of all evil in today's information security practices.

Some of the phenomena I describe in this section, and others, will surprise many readers in that they have personally never experienced such phenomena. Some will be aware of some of the problems I describe, but have never witnessed a description of the problems in black and white. Others would see what I have written and be of the conclusion that the problems I describe are subjective and only exist in a limited sample of organizations.

I have witnessed global-scale information security practices across the globe, and I mentioned my vocational exposure so as to re-enforce the point that the observations I illustrate in this book come from similar experiences in *every* organization with which I have been acquainted. And to emphasize again, in case it was not clear before, that is *a lot* of organizations. Given the fact that my observations are common to all organizations, with the possible (but unlikely) exception of a very small percentage, we can say that these symptoms are indicative of an illness in today's world of commercial information security.

In the earlier days of my career, I was shocked at some of the practices I witnessed in supposedly reputable multinationals. I also was under the impression that what I saw could not possibly be symptoms of an industry-wide pandemic. But then as time progressed, I began to realize that what I experienced was in different ways common to all organizations.

With this narrative, I do not aim to shock. If my intention were really to shock readers, I would probably have written a horror story. Some will read this and be horrified by its content, but it was not my intention to keep people awake at night. If some readers have trouble sleeping at night as a result of reading my diatribe, then I most humbly apologize. Let me reiterate: that was not my intention. As I said before, sometimes you have to be cruel to be kind. Of course my book may also have the undesired effect of inducing sleep as opposed to preventing it.

My career as a consultant started out in the Asia–Pacific region. Our head office was located in Bangkok, Thailand. Most of our clients were based around the region in places like Singapore, Taiwan, Hong Kong, Malaysia, and Indonesia, with some smaller involvement in the local Thai market. Later we started to get more active in Australia.

There were a few occasions where I was required to visit our HQ in Herndon, VA. Our U.S. regional office served the needs of literally hundreds of clients across the length and breadth of the United States.

From that company, I moved to work full-time as an analyst with a global logistics giant. Their regional "Information Technology Service Centre" was located in Prague, Czech Republic. During my time as an associate director with a "Big 4" consultancy, with a centralized global support team, I came across many reports and stories pertaining to client audits from just about everywhere that you can imagine. Later in my career, I was based full-time in London as an analyst with a multinational insurance firm.

So from diverse global experiences, I expected to hear diverse stories in terms of client awareness and the level of maturity of security practices. I was totally wrong. In fact, I heard the same stories from all areas. I expected the U.S. clients to be more aware and more risk averse. They were not. The analysts in our HQ in Herndon had the same war stories to tell as we did in Asia–Pacific.

The Devil Is Everywhere, Including in the Details

The overall momentum since the earlier part of the "noughties" (2000 to 2010) has been away from technical solutions and technical people. Many professionals in security see the battle lines as being drawn in the area of employees' security awareness. Granted, this is certainly an area of concern. Companies can implement the most balanced, cost-effective, perfect technical security solution and manage the infrastructure superbly, but if an employee discloses their corporate logon password to the wrong person, the results can be economically catastrophic for the company.

Issues such as user awareness, implementation of international standards, and information security management systems are critical issues that cannot be ignored, but in the architecting of IT security solutions, it should not be forgotten that there is a technical element to the solution. Hackers play on a technical playing field, and for this reason, security professionals also need to play on the same field. Not everyone can be a manager on the sidelines.

Given all the talk of Internet user awareness and so on, one could be forgiven for thinking that the world has successfully negotiated the whole area of technical vulnerability management (and more generally the ISO 27001 domain "Operations and Communications Management"). Make no mistake, the subject of IT risk management is not entirely a technical area, but there are many "out there," some of them security professionals with 10 years or more experience, who succeed in convincing the budget approver that the solutions are entirely composed of "processes" and "awareness," and the solutions can be implemented with minimal, transparent use of technical input.

The processes, management, and the awareness of the "average schmoo" are important elements to consider, but they are not more or less important than the other oft-neglected sides of security.

Security Is Broken

When discussing the information security sector, the word "broken" crops up quite often in blogs and other sources. John Viega is chief technical officer (CTO) of the Software as a Service (SaaS) business unit at McAfee (now Intel), and in his book *The Myths of Security* he says about security: "A lot of little things are just fundamentally wrong, and the industry as a whole is broken."

With today's social paradigms, there will always be someone, somewhere who sees use of "broken" as a descriptor for the security industry as "cynical" or "nonconstructive." Apparently, we need to be more "positive" in our assessment. Such responses are quite often born from insecurity and a defensive mindset, but then there are also those who are permanently in "glass half full" mode.

Others have said that the industry is not broken; it is just going through a growth phase. "Security is *immature*?" The industry *is* immature, but is it also becoming more mature with time? The answer is unequivocally "no."

I discuss such points as drivers for security spending in the first chapter of this book. Are there drivers out there that would lead to better security and more efficient use of corporate resources in information risk management? Right now, I do not even think we can see the problems clearly, and the first step of solving a problem is the realization of its existence. So there are no drivers for improvement at this time.

When you have a poor state of affairs such as this, with no visible signs of drivers for change, then "broken" is a perfectly fine phrase to use.

Leave the Details to Operations?

If we look at a short case study that involves a risk assessment with a database, the nontechnical security staff will see the database according to the dictionary definition, something like a store of logically organized information. They may see the database as being fixed in the network somewhere, but it is not in their mandate to analyze risk using nasty network diagrams, data flows, and so on.

A database is a collection of information that can be represented in successively more detailed layers of abstraction down to bits as in zeros and ones. The data are organized by a software package such as Oracle or MySQL Server—a relational database management system (RDBMS) package. The RDBMS is hosted on a computer (or "server," as in the classic client–server model) that will run an operating system (OS) such as some flavor of Unix or Microsoft Windows.

The server is physically connected to the rest of the network, usually with an Ethernet cable that links to a hub or more likely a Cisco switch (Cisco has a greater market share as opposed to another manufacturer such as Juniper). That switch is in itself a CPU-controlled device with an OS, much like a computer, that can be configured in many different ways.

The switch is connected to a large corporate private network with (hopefully) firewalls and other network infrastructure devices. OK, so you begin to see the picture develop. How do we assess the risk in this case? The *devil is in the details*, as Bruce Schneier has commented. In order to know the risk, we need to know the risk associated with each device in the connection chain from the "outside" (the public Internet) to the database server, and then even on the database server itself—how would a remotely connected individual first compromise the server and then the information it hosts? What are the threats and *attack vectors*? There is in many cases a greater risk from the internal network as compared with external, although at the end of it all, a network is a network.

I think it is clear that in order to assess the risk to the database, the skills required are both technical and diverse, but the stark reality is that in most security departments I come across, there may be one or two who have a background in IT administration, or they "have a Linux box at home." The skills required to effectively assess risk do not exist in the vast majority of security teams in large companies, but it is their mandate to assess the risk.

Some security teams "teflon" (a commonly used phrase, at least in the U.K., which means nonstick) the risk assessment to operations. Yes, the operations teams are more technically versed, but does the skills portfolio of a typical operations team cut it when it comes to risk assessment here?

In Chapter 4, I discuss the commonly held premise that the nasty technobabble stuff can be dumped on IT and/or network operations departments.

There are certain rarefied skill sets that died out in white hat/ethical corporate environments years ago. These are the skill sets necessary to carry out a risk assessment. What are the required skills exactly? Security departments need a portfolio of skills, the contents of which are summarized in Chapter 11.

The Good Old Days?

Since the early 2000s, things did get less "engineeringy" or "de-engineered." Since that time, security did become a nonfunctional waste of corporate resources. But that is not to say that things were perfect in the mid to late 1990s. No, far from it—in fact, there was a major ingredient missing in those days and that was the "f" word—finances. Small details!

So really, all that old technical speak was of no more value than today's IT-free security offerings from corporate security teams.

Whereas the advisories from the good old boys were factually correct, the efforts were misguided, too much or too little attention to detail was applied to every situation, and the whole effort lacked the necessary direction. Just as an artist has an agent to help them sell their work, the Hackers (I introduce the "Hacker," uppercase "H," in Chapter 2) needed a manager who understood business goals, costs, and architecture, who could maintain good relations with other departments, and who could also manage a small group of highly talented individuals (who could walk out of their job and into a new job in a heartbeat). No such managers existed; moreover, there was no identified need for such a job description.

Some could be mistaken along the lines that this book is purely a critique aimed at the nontechnical elements of the new school. It is not. It is the job functions and skills (or lack of) in vocational security that are several degrees off from where they should be, but that is not to say that things were all rosy in the late 1990s.

The Times They Were a-Changing

In Chapter 4, I discuss some of the changes I noticed happening in the industry in the few years since the turn of the millennium.

There are two distinct camps in security, with one being significantly bigger than the other. In the second and third chapters, I introduce the people in security as a necessary framework for the rest of the book. We started back in the mid-1990s with the Hackers and then came the CASEs.

The Hackers came at a time when security departments did not actually exist in the corporate world. In most cases, they were people who worked in IT operations, or they were programmers, and they were motivated to get into security out of a love of IT. There were many actual white hat Hackers in those days that possessed remarkably diverse skill sets, and never really saw any distinction between work and play. Their "private time" was almost the same as their work time. In their private time, they would read IT books and try out new acts of wizardry.

The second wave came as a result of the perceived failings of the first wave. The first wave of security pros was purely technical and became physically ill when corporate business drivers were discussed. The second wave was more "mature," took the International Information Systems Security Certification Consortium Certified Information Systems Security Professional [(ISC)² CISSP] exam, "looked the part" (they wore shirts and neckties), sounded the part (they used buzzwords), and was more aesthetically pleasing to senior management. But the second wave took on a pale complexion and started sweating at the mention of terms such as TCP/IP or "false positive."

One factor stayed common through these formative years in security up until today: *senior managers were never well advised in security*.

The major theme of *Security De-Engineering* is how most of our problems today are borne from a distancing of security professionals from the bits-n-bytes.

The changing of the guard in security from the Hackers to the CASEs has led to a variety of other problems, but the root of all these problems is a certain disconnect—a disconnect between risk management and the information on hard disks, tapes, clouds, and so on. In Chapter 4, I discuss in detail how security has changed for the worse.

Automated Vulnerability Scanners

One of the most detrimental developments in the early 2000s was the widespread acceptance of the automated vulnerability scanner (or "autoscanner" as I will refer to it here). Autoscanners such as Nessus and GFI LANguard came with a promise of finding your server and application vulnerability with the touch of a button; all you need to do is "spend a few minutes" checking for false positives.

The autoscanner seemed at first glance to be like a dream come true for the security world. In the eyes of managers, including our managers in TSAP (TSAP is the pseudonym I give for my first employer in security: a global service provider; I was working with TSAP from 1999 to 2004 based in the Asia–Pacific (APAC) regional HQ in Bangkok, Thailand), the nasty person with green hair and expletive-bearing T-shirt (the multitalented and highly skilled IT professional) could be replaced by a fresh graduate.

In Chapter 5, I outline the impact that the rise of the autoscanner has had on risk profiles, and whether or not the Hacker can really be replaced by a lesser skilled (and therefore cheaper) person who can enter

IP addresses in an autoscanner configuration, hit the enter key, and then attach the automatically generated findings report to an email.

How much value do these tools actually bring to information risk management? A discussion on autoscanners is long overdue because they are so widespread. Popular commercial software tools use an autoscanning engine such as Nessus, and they take center stage in most organizations' vulnerability management strategies.

Mammas Don't Let Your Babies Grow Up to Be Security Analysts

People, be they undergrads or other types of IT professional, usually have some fairly grandiose ideas about what a career in information security may be like. Aside from the discussion about IT operation's relationship to security, in Chapter 6, I discuss the picture with careers in security. I attempt to give a picture of the typical consultant or analyst role, and how it fits with the corporate structure. I give some advice to more technically oriented people who are thinking about getting into information security, and I also give some advice to those IT enthusiasts who are currently working in a security department.

Love of Clouds and Incidents

In the year 2000, there were distributed denial of service (DDoS) attacks carried out against Amazon, Yahoo, CNN, and buy.com. During my time with TSAP from 1999 to 2004, there were very few publicly declared incidents.

Several times, clients had asked us to justify why they should spend on our services—a question that sales and management staff struggled to answer. With the aforementioned DDoS incident from 2000, the managers in TSAP were actually happy to hear of this incident. It was not exactly champagne and cigars, but it was almost. The mindset was something like this: "our invoice amounts cannot be justified because there is really no bad stuff happening in the world—but now there is some bad stuff. You see? DoS is real—it actually happens."

As I will explain in Chapter 8, I do not believe the security industry needs to celebrate incidents in order to validate itself. When the security industry became de-engineered through the 2000s, security managers lost all hope of ever being able to convince the C-level executives of the need for investment in security, other than just passing the audit. But the reality is it is quite possible to change this state of affairs for the better, and this does not involve rewriting the books or reinventing the wheel or moving to another planet.

With a reinfusion of *properly managed* tech resource into the information security game, we would never struggle to justify our existence. We could confidently stand in front of whoever asked, look them in the eye, and tell them what was needed in order to efficiently manage risk. Sounds like I have gone mad? That would not be a surprising reaction to me, and I do not blame you.

Another buzzword has recently been added to the nonstandard, noninternational vocabulary of information security words, and that buzzword was *cloud*. Security pros saw the dawn of cloud computing as an opportunity to find new intellectual capital that would be of some value to organizations, and in so doing, they would feel useful and appreciated again, and everyone would live happily ever after.

I receive on average approximately 10 notification emails everyday from forums and so on that relate to cloud security. There are seemingly thousands of "cloud security experts" now. There are terabytes of drivel in blogs on the subject.

With the cloud security showpiece, there are some slightly new security considerations to take into account, but it is not a radical new model to consider. Regardless of the cloud type, the cloud does not symbolize a new dawn for security. There should not be any need for firms to spend exuberantly on the acquisition of specific cloud security skills. Migration to the cloud presents a security challenge that is not too dissimilar from outsourcing IT operations functions or creation of VPN (virtual private network)-linked regional offices.

Taking cloud security as an example, in Chapter 8, I lament on the desperate search for new intellectual capital in security. It should not be necessary for security pros to have to do this because if one were to look in the right places, one would find plenty to learn that is of *real* value for businesses.

On a separate but related theme, there is this idea that has been afloat from the very beginning about an all-knowing, all-seeing organization that gathers incident data and stores them in a database. The idea is that if we can somehow create a database of all security incidents and categorize them, then after some time, we will have a valid source of evidence (of vulnerability to a threat) to show to the decision makers when we go looking for cash. Again, I do not think we need to go looking for incidents in order to validate ourselves. In Chapter 8, I discuss this point and also the practical difficulties associated with gathering incident data.

Security Products

In Chapter 9, I look at some examples of security technologies and consider them in the light of return on investment.

There is an awful lot of zero-day activity in the underworld these days. Undisclosed malware and undisclosed vulnerabilities are rife. If we are in a situation where we are under some sort of zero-day attack, we cannot detect the attack with pattern matching. We need detection technology that can alert us on the basis of generic indicators (I nearly used the term "heuristic" there, but I refrained; that term is heavily abused by some of the security product vendors).

In Chapter 9, I look at network intrusion detection systems (NIDS) and intrusion detection systems in general. I do not question the value that detection has for information risk management, but I do question the value of the technology currently available to us in security.

In Chapter 10, I look at identity management (IdM) and security incident event management (SIEM) solutions. In both cases, I look at some of the factors that can lead to the vendors' marketing promises being broken.

Especially with SIEM, there are many requirements that firms need to fulfill if they are to see some value from their investment. SIEM should only be considered as a technology that supports incident response, and incident response is more about people than technology. Certainly if there is no incident response capability, the purchaser will not see any value from their SIEM solution, perhaps other than a nice network diagnostics tool for IT and network operations team.

Some of the considerations with SIEM are similar to those with NIDS. There is a sizable initial investment, and then there are on-going operational, maintenance, and initial fine-tuning requirements.

Even for large-sized organizations, IdM products are not necessarily economically viable in every scenario. The organization considering an IdM acquisition must understand what they currently have in the way of user management technology, and which users need access to which resources. Application layer protocols for centrally managing user accounts have been around for a long time, plus many applications may not be compatible with the new IdM solution. In Chapter 10, I take a closer look at the IdM picture. Larger organizations will in most cases already have Lightweight Directory Access Protocol or Active Directory. They need to ask themselves exactly what it is that the IdM solution will do for them on top of their existing technologies.

A Period of Consequences

When I was writing this book and thinking about its content and structure, some famous quotes from history came to mind, and I was reminded of a topic that was similar in some ways to *Security De-Engineering*. The subject was global warming, as portrayed by Al Gore in his *An Inconvenient Truth* road show and documentary.

In *An Inconvenient Truth*, Al Gore quotes Winston Churchill in his pre–World War II warning about rising nationalism in Germany: "The era of procrastination, of half-measures, of soothing and baffling expedients, of delays, is coming to its close. In its place we are entering a period of consequences."

Global warming is related to climate, and the premise that humans are causing global warming is a very difficult one to prove definitively. There is warming (maybe), but is it caused by increasing levels of carbon dioxide? Frankly, climate is too complex for anybody to answer this question or even make sensible estimates.

Corporate information security is complex, but not as much as climate. We can make definitive statements about the relative levels of risk, even if we cannot put numbers to it, and we are aware of the threats. We cannot read the future and say for sure what will happen if we ignore the risks, but we can extrapolate and make educated estimates.

Like many other security professionals, I believe that incidents that result in financial losses are becoming more frequent, and the incidents themselves are no longer just a few malware incidents. The incidents such as the January 2010 Google incident will become more frequent mostly because of the worsening financial climate in the world, and quite frankly, even in a "cool" tech giant like Google, the door was proved to be almost wide-open.

The de-engineering of security departments has led to a situation where corporates are wide-open to attack by automated and manual means, either from "outside" or within their own private networks. Just as with pre-war Germany, we are entering a period of consequences.

Some of the consequences of the current de-engineered security world have already emerged, and I am not just talking about the widespread incidents. In some cases, senior managers have lost their patience with security departments and totally disbanded them. The functions of the security team were passed to IT operations. As I explain in the first chapter of this book, do you blame the managers for this? Personally I do not think you can blame the managers.

From what I have seen of the vast majority of organizations, if they are targeted, they are very likely to suffer major financial losses. The corporate world is now at a stage where we need to make a decision. The drivers for most acts of skullduggery these days are economic, and we are still in a very slow, stagnant period of recovery from the worse recession since the 1930s. There are two choices: we either improve the way we handle information security, or we make a phased migration back to using pens, paper, manual typewriters, and filing cabinets. We either act or be acted upon. If we are acted upon, the situation could be disastrous. Businesses have grown used to the efficiencies that IT allows. Bosses were able to cut staff numbers, and the general public was able to avoid queuing in bank branches and use ATMs instead. What happens if all these innovations are suddenly removed over-night? With the more recent buzz of the threat of cyberwarfare, how safe are national infrastructures from attack?

Another thing that is changing fast is the complexity of software. As software gets more complex, it gets more buggy and open to abuse by fiends. There are endless dialogues on how to get software developers writing secure code, but the efforts are like those of a dog chasing its own tail. Software bugs are here to stay, and the motivations for exploiting them also are not going away anytime soon.

Security Reengineering

The title of this book is *Security De-Engineering* in that the major theme is about how today's information risk management practices have become so unbalanced. The juggling act in security is one of balancing too much or too little technical detail in our risk analysis, while also balancing the costs of safeguards against the goals of the business. Now there is an ever-growing need to shift the balance back to a more analytical approach. So how do we do that? After all, in today's social paradigm, a pure discussion of problems is oh so "negative."

In the last chapter of this book, I do talk about solutions, but although my original plan was to talk in some detail about the solutions, I found that the discussion of the problems already took up a lot of real estate. Clearly we need to identify the problems before we can solve them, so the details of the solutions will need to come at a later date. In Section 4 (Chapter 11) of this book, I do give some ideas on the solutions, although some of the answers will be apparent in the discussion of the problem.

I think the main drive of the solution has to come in the propagation of the appropriate skill sets and an associated structure of professional accreditation (in this book, I do not focus much on the accreditation problems we face today—mostly because I think the problems are relatively well known). Security departments will be quite different under this new scheme, and the tools and products in use will be different, but I am not of the opinion that we need to go back to square one and totally reinvent the wheel. Such disruption will not be necessary.

The ideas put forward in this book may be familiar to some readers. Occasionally, when I comment on the state of play in security, I will get a response to the effect that I was not making a point that was new to the reader. I commented in a blog once on Web application testing, and I got a sarcastic response "thanks for giving us the status quo." Really though, even if what I have written is well known to some people, I am quite sure that the majority are not at all aware of most of the problems, and if they are, nobody has ever hammered out a description of the problems in black and white.

In any case, it is clear that the decision makers and C-level executives are not aware of the problems, and we, as security professionals, have to make them aware. Right now, they probably will not listen to us (and I do not blame them), but I believe the drivers for change in our industry are coming soon. They will most likely come from new regulations and then auditors. How we change is important. Businesses cannot afford to change just for change's sake.

In the best case, what you are about to read is something you have known for a long time, but are not willing to admit the truth to the senior managers above you in the food chain. But for the sake of everyone's principles and, ultimately, at the end of the day, their sanity, it is time for us to come clean with the decision makers and budget signatories.

With *Security De-Engineering*, I hope to be able to get us on the same page in terms of problems. Just talking about problems is not cynical or nonconstructive in this case. It is the first step to solving the problems—and that is not nonconstructive, even if it is a double negative.

The book is clearly not intended to be a technical manual or tutorial; in fact, it is very far from that. I aim to talk about principles and ideas that are not too high up in the clouds to be discussed at the senior management level. Some of the content in this narrative is too detailed for senior management (rather, I should say that senior managers' time is too valuable to be spent listening to too much detail), but then there are also plenty of ideas that should be acceptable as advisories in themselves, or at least serve to illustrate an advisory.

I also do not talk about the better-known aspects such as malware and employee awareness schemes, or "how long should a password be?" These are areas that the industry deals with in a standard way, and they are well covered. Anyway, I only talk about problems that I believe can be solved. The problems such as malware and awareness will never go away for quite some time to come, and it seems to make more sense to take the approach "we will get malware problems and other issues resulting from Homo sapiens doing stupid stuff," and then plan for this to happen.

Information security is not the coolest, most enjoyable, most rewarding, or the most prestigious area of vocational IT today, but it should be and it can be. And when we are back at that point when security is a fun place to work again, business will be spending better, and although it may not be obvious to you at this time, the two are connected. There will of course still be problems. Nobody can promise that there will never be any more financial losses from incidents, but there will be a high level of trust that senior management has in their information risk management strategy and the people who carry it out. Doesn't that sound better?

Even if we cannot address any of our problems in our lifetimes, at least I hope you can learn something from this book. If nothing else, I hope you enjoy reading *Security De-Engineering*.

Author

Ian Tibble was an IT specialist with IBM Global Services before entering into the security arena. His experience of more than 11 years in information security allowed him to gain practical risk management expertise from both an architectural IT and a business analysis aspect. His experience in Infosec has been with service providers Trusecure (now Verizon) and PricewaterhouseCoopers, and also with end users in logistics, banking, and insurance. He has been engaged with security service delivery projects with close to 100 Fortune 500 companies and multinational financial institutions in Asia (Indonesia, Singapore, Malaysia, Taiwan, Hong Kong, and Australia) and Europe.

SECTION 1

PEOPLE AND

BLAME

Bonobo monkeys in the Democratic Republic of Congo, along with most other primates, have opposable thumbs. Bonobos also show a whole different range of emotions in a similar way to humans. It is also believed that some other animals (such as some ape species, bottlenose dolphins, and elephants) have the capability of self-awareness and show signs of being able to regard themselves.

Self-awareness gives one the option to choose thoughts being thought rather than simply thinking the thoughts that are stimulated from the accumulative events leading up to the circumstances of the moment. Self-awareness gives us the potential to change our habits. Without this, there would be no need to write a book such as this. Hopefully, in information security, we will eventually prove our humanity by fixing our ways.

Stephen Covey is a world famous author and recognized expert in too many fields to be listed here. Master of business administration (MBA) students regard him as something of a deity. If I had to sum up the best way to describe his field of expertise in one word, the word I would choose would be one of relationships or humanity. His book titled *The Seven Habits of Highly Effective People* was one I read while commuting to the office on the Prague Metro, and I would strongly recommend it. In a survey of *Chief Executive Magazine* readers, for the "Most Influential Business Book of the Twentieth Century," *Seven Habits* was tied in the number one spot for seven successive years.

The first of the seven habits described is "Be Proactive," and as part of the build-up, Mr. Covey focuses a lot on the ability to take responsibility for solving a problem and the human ability to choose one's response to a stimulus. As humans, we have the capability to choose our response, and in so doing, we are effectively taking responsibility. Taking responsibility is an enabling factor in being proactive, and being proactive is one of Mr. Covey's seven main habits that make us more effective.

So along with opposable thumbs and the gift of self-awareness, the ability to choose our responses to a stimulus is what sets us apart from the animal kingdom and supposedly makes us human.

We are capable of changing our ways in information security, but at this moment in time, I do not even have reason to believe that there is any acknowledgment of shortcomings in our information security practices.

1

WHOM DO YOU BLAME?

It goes without saying that human beings are responsible for all of our problems in information security, and we have to hold our hands up and say, "we are responsible for the world's information security problems."

Each and every one of us has the potential to change the world in terms of how we manage information risk—by taking responsibility to do so. But as to why information security is such a mess these days, should we attribute blame to some parties more than others? Is there a corporate position that holds more responsibility than others in information security? Is there a single person to whom we should direct our primordial wrath?

The Buck Stops at the Top?

The tendency for most security professionals such as consultants, lower-to-middle tier managers, and analysts is to blame the board-room for all of our problems—and in so doing, we lose our effectiveness in being able to solve the problem. There is the stimulus that is "information security is in a mess," but rather than take responsibility for cleaning up the mess, we choose to pass the buck to the higher echelons of management. We can choose to take responsibility for the mess, and I sincerely hope that this book can help us, as security professionals, to at least identify the problems.

Naturally, we assume that all the problems in the world are the responsibility of senior management and governments—which, to some extent, is an assumption that is not without foundation. Of course, with the lines of authority, and the fact that the guy (or girl) at the top is the one who vetoes all decisions, anything that is ordered by the top boss is final, and those who disobey are fired (subject to there being sufficient evidence of underperformance to avoid violation of labor laws). But we all have the potential to influence decision-making without directly going against the views of our superiors. Everywhere is the possibility for a win-win scenario (from Covey's fourth habit of the seven).

The economic crisis that some called the "credit crunch" started with falling U.S. property prices in 2007 and then dramatically accelerated with the domino effect of the Lehman Brothers liquidation of September 2008. Many economists refuse to write off the possibility of a "double dip" scenario, with the first dip occurring in March 2009.

The crisis was based on the unscrupulous trading of debt, mostly from U.S. property mortgages, which resulted in the buildup of enormous debt positions with the financial institutions at the top of the chain. Lehman Brothers was one of these, but all of the major investment banks and many of the high-street retail banks were millions of dollars in debt and billions in some cases. The overall debt position (in U.S. dollars) of the U.S. financial sector was a number that would not fit on the liquid crystal display of my calculator.

When there was a loss of confidence in property markets, there was also a loss of any confidence that the debts would ever be repaid, and so started a sell-off in global equities that, with the collapse of Lehman Brothers, took on record-breaking proportions.

According to Ben Bernanke (chairman of the U.S. Federal Reserve), the financial crisis has gotten to be so severe that, in September 2008, the financial system in the United States was close to collapse, and indeed, if not for a federal bailout of US$700 billion, he warned, "If we don't do this [bailout], we may not have an economy on Monday."

Overall, the U.S. government and the U.S. Federal Reserve have committed US$13.9 trillion to offset the decline in consumption and lending capacity, from which, as of June 2009, US$6.8 trillion dollars had been invested. And guess what? Eventually, who will pay back the majority of this debt? Of course, it will be the taxpayer.

The public needed a scapegoat for the crisis that is still ongoing and was the worst financial crisis since the Great Depression of the 1930s. Some blamed the government, whereas others blamed the bankers. There was real anger in the United Kingdom against bankers, stirred up by the media, which turned to scenes of violence in London's financial district, "The Square Mile."

But really, is it not the case that anyone who was borrowing beyond his or her means was to blame? There were many cases of citizens in western countries acquiring mortgages at levels that were ten times their annual salary. If you earn US$30,000 as a salary and you live in a house worth US$400,000, is there no instinct that says "there is something wrong with this picture?"

Whereas I sympathize with anybody who ran into financial problems (who, in most cases, were shunned by the banks and left out in the cold), I do not think we can always blame those in authority.

There were several government figures from around the world that blamed the U.S. government for the crisis, but they were heads of state in countries that had some of this U.S. debt as investments that formed part of their sovereign wealth funds. Were they not aware of the precarious nature of the U.S. property market, especially as prices had been declining as far back as mid-2007?

Senior managers, chief executive officers (CEO), chief information officers, directors, and anyone who sits on the board of directors of any organization are all mere humans. They are not superbeings who are all knowing and omnipresent, and they cannot travel in time or magically heal any injury. Whereas there may be witch doctors, there are no superbeings at board meetings.

How much blame can we really attribute to the higher levels of management? I think we have to look at ourselves as consultants and analysts before we blame others. CEOs are human and use a laptop and/or desktop personal computer. They are just like most other citizens—they are aware of at least antivirus issues and spam, especially as it is quite likely, given recent trends, that they have been negatively affected by malware in one way or another.

Managers and Their Loyal Secretaries

A common practice is for the seniors to give their log-on password(s) to their secretaries. This draws much dismay and actual physical pain to many security people who cannot believe that a senior manager "would be so stupid." But then again, think about it from the manager's perspective (part of Stephen Covey's fifth habit is about empathy and "putting yourself into other's shoes" and trying to see it from their perspective)—if you trust your secretary, why would confiding your password with your secretary be so bad?

There is also the small matter of why managers revealed their password to their secretaries. There has to be some benefit here, and it may not be just the case that managers cannot remember their password. Furthermore, if managers cannot remember their password, chances are that there is a problem in the company's password strategy (à la "at least 14 characters with at least 1 uppercase, 1 number, 1 punctuation mark, 1 unicode Chinese language character . . . "—you get the point).

I should clarify at this point that the problem with the manager/secretary password issue has nothing to do with the secretary being easier to manipulate or more vulnerable to social engineering—this may not be the case. I am discussing the manager/secretary anecdote purely because I am led to believe that it is a common practice and a rather neat example of how managers "interface" with security (or not).

Many larger organizations now have adopted security awareness programs, wherein staff are allocated to "spread the word" among employees about some basic dos and don'ts. This can come in the form of classroom-based interactive exercises, online/Intranet-based exercises (not recommended by most awareness campaigners), a list of the "eleven commandments," or poster campaigns (also not recommended by seasoned veterans in the field).

Kevin Mitnick was one of the more famous cybercriminals, and many of his unauthorized activities involved what is now known as social engineering. Social engineering, in the information security sense, is the art of manipulating people into performing an action (such as revealing sensitive information) that would be useful to an attacker.

If managers confide in their secretaries to keep their passwords, does this not present a severe crack in the armor of the organization's security posture? Skilled social engineers can easily find out the name and contact details from the secretary, and then the next step would be relatively trivial—especially as is often the case, the password is in a text file on the secretary's computer or in the secretary's memory.

Do we attribute blame to the manager in this case? If neither the manager nor the secretary has been subjected to an effective awareness campaign, can we blame them for divulging sensitive information?

"Not really" is the answer. As I mentioned previously, when it comes to awareness about security matters, managers (and their secretaries) are ordinary citizens. We have awareness campaigns because the average schmoo does not realize that giving out a password to strangers, or writing it on FLYN (Fair Little Yellow Note) (or in one case I heard of, the ceiling board above their desk), is necessarily a bad thing.

Therefore, no, we cannot blame managers in this case. Managers are human beings, and when it comes to security matters, they are as clueless as the next. It is our job as security experts to explain things in a financial perspective to decision makers. Managers need to be fed information with which they can relate before they can make a decision on budgets. For various reasons, which hopefully will become clearer in this book, we as security experts have failed to do this.

Information Security Spending—Driving Factors in the Wild

Of the subject of attributing blame to managers, it helps if we try to see the security picture from their perspective. In this sense, we need to take a look at the most base-level driver for spending on security. For various reasons (which I will cover later), the issues to do with actual technical risk will be ignored, even if there has been a related security incident that had a financial impact. So after all the nonsensical (from the manager's view) talk of information technology (IT) risks, vulnerabilities, and threats has been dismissed, what is the residue? What are the drivers that managers absolutely cannot ignore?

In most cases, the main driving force for information security spending by organizations is regulatory compliance. Taking the finance sector as an example, a central banking authority can impose penalties on a bank if it fails to meet specific information security goals. During my time with Big Four (in this book, I will refer to this company merely as "Big Four") in 2007, our only clients for information security were banks (and telcos to a lesser degree) because the banking sector was the only sector under a compliance mandate (from Tanakan Haeng Bpratet Thai—The Bank of Thailand).

Other companies with large work forces focused on nothing more than antivirus and antispam, with maybe a default-configured firewall here and there, although some of them were multinationals with "remotely controlled" security (their head office handled detection and monitored policy compliance). Certainly there was no market for Big Four outside the banking sector and telecommunications. This was not because we were too expensive (which we were)—there was actually *no market* for any security service provider, as in no demand whatsoever for any corporate information security services.

Another driving force for security spending is the good old "what are my competitors doing?" factor. Going back to the early 2000s, on professional service engagements, TSAP clients would demand to know how their security posture stacked up against firms in the same industry sector, and they asked for the statistics to be included in the report.

There was one project I remember clearly because of the difficult nature of the client. I was leading an Incident Response and Management service engagement with a large Singapore-based transport firm—that had suffered several major incidents (which were not announced publicly). My initial report was 200 pages in length, and it was compiled after several weeks of site visits, teleconferences, and interviews with staff members. A lot of work went into the assessment, and then the report.

The client never had any real problems with the report content in terms of its factual correctness. There was one particular individual who handled the report review and revisions on the client's side. Basically his undisclosed goal was to reword the report and re-create it to make it his own—thereby taking the credit for the report. Additionally though, much of the report content was actually removed. What was once a 200-page report was stripped down to a meager 70 pages—because the other 130 pages did not have any relation to what other firms in the industry sector were doing.

My view on this grand scale strip-down was that we should stand our ground, have some self-respect, and leave the actual structure and summarized findings intact. I was OK with the client playing with grammar, changing a few words here and there to satisfy the requirements of ego—but I was not OK with removing critical findings, which, if ignored, could very well lead to a severe financial impact down the road somewhere. Anyway, our management team decided to sell the firm's soul to the devil and just pamper the client on this first date, supposedly because it would "lead to a massive revenue stream in the future."

I became more aware of some of the politics behind this "industry sector comparison" while I was in Prague in HELL. (HELL is the pseudonym I use for a large logistics firm with a major IT service center in Prague, Czech Republic. I was a consultant in HELL from early 2005 to late 2006.) A big four consultancy (actually the same Big Four that I later worked with in Thailand) that also did audits for other logistics firms conducted our external audit. During a review of their findings, a meeting in which all but the top two levels of management were present, there was a heated debate about one particular finding to do with network segmentation. Our managers were briefed on the issue and they were quite aware of the problem, although because of the costs involved with risk mitigation, there was some reluctance to raise the issue with the next level up in the food chain.

There was some heated debate on the network segmentation issue in the meeting, with our managers demanding that the finding be removed from the report. Then there was an interjection from one of the Associate Directors on the auditor's side. His point was that our competitors had all passed that particular criterion of the audit. The atmosphere in the meeting changed noticeably as a result of this. The discussion was taken off-line. Two months later, our network operations team had compiled draft network designs, and I began to work together with them to hammer out some final designs.

The big fours gain a lot of their power from off-line meetings with clients' senior management on golf courses and so on. In many countries, they also have the mandate to audit certain government departments.

The Directors and Partners in the big fours are very socially oriented. They have very many large-sized client firms in their portfolios and have all sorts of informal gatherings with higher level managers of their clients. Hence, there is a kind of underworld where, regardless of the ethics of the situation, there is a potential for information to be passed about competitors in the same market sector. So if a big four has audited you, and you failed some parts of the audit, the news of your failure may well end up in the hands of your competitors.

Thus, along with regulatory requirements, another more subliminal driver is basically just "keeping up with the Joneses."

Do Top-Level Managers Care About Information Security?

Judging by the way that so many of us talk, you would think that CEOs were never concerned about security. To be honest, I think it is very unlikely that CEOs would be as irresponsible as that. One does not need to be a technical wizard to understand that information in electronic form is the core of most organizations' businesses, and that there could therefore be associated financial risks with loss of confidentiality, integrity, or availability of that information.

Many security experts are aware that any larger company's CEO, regardless of whether their firm's shares are public or privately owned, cares first about its shareholders. From 2010 going into 2011, there were a few incidents that had an undeniable impact on the victims' stock prices. However, as of Q2 2011, there were still only a small number of incidents for which you could connect a loss of market capitalization; with this in mind, the uber-cynic would be led to believe that no CEO would ever be interested in anything to do with information security, and this is why things are as bad as they are.

Another comment I have heard about management is one along the lines "there is a physical part of a company that is like buildings and tables and stuff, and they're happy to pay the insurance premium for those, but then there's information in electronic form—and because you can't touch or feel it, the risks are passed over by the powers that be." Again, I really do not think that this is the case. Whereas information security is complex and information in electronic form can seem intangible, you only have to pick up a newspaper to know that threats exist.

As I have said, for most senior managers, their only concern with security is regulatory compliance, but I am aware of some cases where top managers have taken it upon themselves to dig deeper into ground-level security practices.

One particular case I remember was during a TSAP client engagement for a transport and logistics firm at their headquarters in Sydney, Australia. I was helping the client to formulate a global baseline information security policy. During the wrap-up at the end of the week, the CEO interrupted our meeting. He wanted a summary of what had been concluded and what it meant to the business. Was this not real concern on behalf of senior management?

If we want to assess whether managers "care" about security, we can also ask ourselves whether there has been evidence of a threat over the last decade or so. Aside from events that may have occurred within their own company, perhaps there have been newspaper reports covering security issues.

What is the history with media coverage of security incidents? Going back to the heady days of the "dot com boom" of the last decade of the twentieth century, from my perspective of living in Asia, information security was sort of an exciting area, but there were very few top-level managers taking it at all seriously. Interest in the subject was entirely at a kind of "romantic fascination" level. The bad guys were certainly active. There were reported incidents, but they were few and far between and did not get much media coverage.

Moving onto the early 2000s, there were a handful of incidents that made big news, such as the distributed denial of service attacks against Amazon, Yahoo, CNN, and buy.com in 2000. As the decade moved on, just from the point of view of a passive observer who skims daily news headlines, there actually seemed to be even fewer incidents, but from 2009 to 2011, there was news about major incidents on a regular basis.

After an incident with Google in 2010, several tech sector companies added new warnings to their U.S. Securities and Exchange Commission (SEC) filings informing investors of the risks of computer attacks. So the world of computer crime is now mentioned in SEC listings!

Even the *Financial Times* newspaper had run several reports from 2009 to 2011 about information security incidents. Therefore, we can say that it is very likely that information security was on the CEOs' radars at least for the past two to three years, and probably longer.

I pictured a scene of how CEO conversations manifested themselves with regard to information security. Throughout the 1990s, there would most likely be nothing to speak of. Then perhaps moving into 2000s, it could be something like "What's all this security stuff about? Should we be doing something about it?" Then later, "I saw in the FT, these firms are having problems, can you update me on what we're doing about this stuff and how much we're spending?"

Recessions can also put security on the radar of C-levels. At the height of the recession in Q2 2009, I was aware of two cases in the UK where C-level executives had reviewed an information security budget for the first time in six years, completely shut down the security department, and merged the information security function into IT operations.

Overall, I have seen enough evidence to suggest that C-level executives *do* care about security. The evidence of a threat is clear. The reason why security strategies get dumbed down to the level of base regulatory compliance is rarely because C-levels dismiss the risk. The actual reasons seem to be related to the information being passed to the C-levels from lower levels—and this is a topic that I will cover in Chapter 4.

Ignoring the Signs

If we as security professionals have confidently given clear warnings to management about threats, but if they ignore the warnings and an incident occurred, then, of course, management is to blame. But security professionals do not give clear evidence to managers about threats. We get tied up in looking for evidence such as past incident data and so on (I discuss this quandary in more detail in Chapter 8), when actually we should be able to *confidently* talk about qualitative risks based on assessment of vulnerability. For various reasons (covered in later chapters), the security pro that reports to management has no confidence. Therefore, the vain search for incident data begins, and when nothing is found, the risks are not reported. In this case, we absolutely cannot blame managers for ignoring threats because no evidence of a threat was reported to their level.

What happens when threats are ignored? History tells us that perhaps in the past, throughout the 2000s, security pros could have slept easily at night even though they lacked confidence in their security architecture. However, things do seem to be changing in this regard.

As a classic facet of human behavior, we have reacted too late to a threat many times in our history because we were waiting for absolute proof of the existence of the threat before we would do anything about protecting ourselves from it. In many cases, the absolute proof that I speak of was the resulting damage from the theoretical threat becoming a reality.

If we are talking about cases from the corporate world of ignoring warnings over threats, the case involving BP's (by the way, this is no longer an acronym for British Petroleum—the company name has been "BP" for more than a decade now) offshore oil drilling disaster in the Gulf of Mexico is a good, but unfortunate, example.

On 20 April 2010, there was an explosion on a deep-water drilling platform, Deepwater Horizon, which was contracted out by BP to Transocean, a Swiss-based contractor. The rig was 40 miles offshore from Louisiana. Eleven men lost their lives in the incident.

Aside from the tragedy of losing lives, the incident also resulted in the rupture of the underwater well and the consequent spilling of oil into the Gulf of Mexico. Two months after the explosion, an international response team had stemmed the flow of oil to some degree; however, huge volumes of oil were still being released. The oil out-flows threatened wildlife and tourism, and many other business ventures based on the coastlines of Mississippi, Alabama, Louisiana, and later Florida.

The financial impact on BP was projected forward at the time of writing to be of the order of US$40 billion gross. Nearly 50% of the company's market capitalization had been lost. There was talk of BP's U.S. operations being forced into liquidation—with the U.S. market making up one-third of its reserves and one quarter of its global production.

In mid-June of 2010, two Democratic lawmakers said in a letter to Tony Hayward, BP chief executive officer, "In spite of the well's difficulties, BP appears to have made multiple decisions for economic reasons that increased the danger of a catastrophic well failure." The investigation report uncovered instances in which operational decisions were made that appeared to violate industry guidelines and that were made despite warnings from BP's own personnel and the contractors that it employed.

Conspiracy theorists would argue in terms of BP not necessarily being too concerned about the disaster because of its deep pockets and it being handed an opportunity to offer shares at a bargain price. There are such horror stories occurring on a daily basis in the greed of the capitalist world, but conspiracy aside, there is no way that BP would have allowed this disaster to happen given a choice. Even if the company directors have no humanity whatsoever, they would not want to be blocked from exploiting the U.S. market.

With information security incidents, there is the potential for considerably more damage to be inflicted as compared with the BP case.

Companies' "crown jewels" are held in electronic form on storage media. Given recent incidents and the state of our information security world, a real disaster that is worse than the BP case is just around the corner.

Management in BP allegedly ignored warnings about the potential for disaster. Worryingly in information security, bigger dangers are real and prevalent—but the managers are not getting the warnings. Reasons for this are several and they are the major theme of this book, but first we need to introduce the people in security—because, ultimately, security professionals are to blame for all, yes *all*, of our problems. The people are introduced in the next two chapters.

Summary

It is not hard to justify comments to the effect that security, as it is practiced by large organizations today, is broken. But whom do we blame for these problems? There is a natural reaction for corporate people to try to find a scapegoat whenever something goes wrong— and that scapegoat is usually the person at the top.

Is it wise or justifiable to blame a C-level executive for all of our problems? The final decisions are made by C-levels, but their decision-making is based on information supplied by the security department and chief information security officer (CISO). Considering security managers in firms that suffered major incidents, I wonder how many of them reported that risk levels were acceptable.

Many security pros will tell you that CEOs do not care about security. Although it is entirely subjective, given that security incidents make the front pages of nontech publications on an increasingly frequent basis, and that share prices *have* been impacted by security incidents, we can say at least that CEOs are likely to be aware that there are challenges *out there* somewhere.

C-levels can only act on information passed to them by their security staff, and to be perfectly honest, in various different ways as described in this book, the security industry has de-engineered itself in an almost deliberate phasing out of critical analytical skills from the industry. If the analytical skills are not there, and we rely on full automation (in an industry that has never been ready for even partial automation—please see Chapter 5) and meaningless checklists (see

Chapter 4), then how can we know the severity of the risks, or even whether they exist? How accurate is our reporting to C-levels going to be if we are not in a position to perform any kind of accurate analysis in areas such as vulnerability assessment?

The de-engineering of security took on various different facades, as will be covered in this book. Private networks of large organizations are essentially wide-open to attack, and the most disappointing aspect is that security professionals in some cases knowingly brought about this predicament. We cannot blame the upper echelons of management because the hard reality is that the C-levels have thus far *never* been well informed with regard to information risk management.

2
THE HACKERS

The term "Hacker" (with a quite deliberate upper case "H" so as to distinguish from any other usage of the word *hacker*) was used long before the public Internet existed. Throughout the 1950s and 1960s, the term was widely understood in a positive light, but then the perception was malformed (sorry) by the media into a term having negative, criminal connotations.

"Hacker" as a term invokes some highly emotional responses from many people in information security, and there are fundamentalist views on the usage of this word. So, for the purposes of this narrative, I will first outline how I intend to use this phrase.

Hat Colors and Ethics

A full picture of what is meant by "Hacker" in this book becomes clearer as this chapter progresses, but just for now, given the heightened state of tensions over the word, it seems almost mandatory to at least make clear what I do *not* mean by "Hacker."

When the term Hacker is used these days, most uninitiated people will think of a criminal—mostly because whenever there has been a high-profile act of computer crime reported by the media, the perpetrator is always referred to as a Hacker.

Ethics is a word that is used in security more often these days, as compared with the early 2000s, partly because of the inclusion of a prequalifier for the International Information Systems Security Certification Consortium (ISC)² Certified Information Systems Security Professional (CISSP) (at the time of writing, the CISSP qualification is the most widely recognized and sought-after accreditation in the industry) that is a mandatory acceptance of the CISSP Code of Ethics.

Ethics is discussed heavily in some of the CISSP textbooks, and it gets a lot of emphasis on other professional accreditation training courses. There is also the Certified Ethical Hacker (CEH) professional accreditation. The proud holder of a CEH certificate has supposedly demonstrated competence in nice, legal, conforming, and effective network penetration testing.

Use of the word "ethical" introduces a new and more emotional dimension to the discussions. Many would talk about ethics as being connected to morality and good and evil. So an ethical Hacker is a moral, good person. An unethical Hacker is an immoral, evil person.

Talking about the law and acts of computer crime in reference to hacking is somewhat inappropriate because in so many cases where someone has been arrested and that person has allegedly done something uh . . . bad, there is a good chance that he or she is not going to be prosecuted for reasons too complicated to discuss here.

I think the new information security world has got it wrong with its use of the e-word. One tends to think of an ethical person as one who is also trustworthy, and this was also presumably the intention of the security industry with its use of the word. So for example, if a security service provider offers "ethical penetration testing" as a service, then what they are really saying is "we do penetration testing and oh, by the way, we won't do anything bad!" For the service provider then, how much benefit is actually derived from the use of the e-word? This seems to be an attempt to tell their client that they are trustworthy. I don't know about you, but I always thought that trust had to be earned.

I will talk about penetration testing methods in some detail in Chapter 7, but just from the perspective of the uninitiated customer of a security service provider, if I am paying for network penetration testing services, I do actually want a simulation of a real attack, then is it really going to be a simulation if the assessment is done in an ethical way? How many actual attacks that resulted in financial losses were done in an ethical way?

From the perspective of the outsider, the use of the e-word does not really benefit security companies or professionals in any way; moreover, it gnaws at the credibility of the industry.

I don't know the origins of the hype over ethics in infosec, but I suspect it was born out of a need to portray a certain image of innocence and conformity. Outsiders could think that I am a criminal if I say I perform information security assessments and I fail to qualify that I am ethical in my practice—people might think I am a Hacker—and that is bad.

There is a slightly more disappointing side of the ethics thing. From what I have experienced from meeting information security professionals, it seems that the ethics brush is also used to draw a dividing line between the more technically oriented so-called Hackers and the information security professional who specializes in checklists, security management standards, and "best practices." There is a tendency to use ethics as a stick that can be used to beat the more technically gifted professionals and enthusiasts in security as in "we're ethical, they're not, and therefore we're better than them."

I am sure there is a genuine concern on behalf of, for example, security service providers who offer penetration testing as a service to put over an angelic image when potentially they might be gaining access to highly sensitive information. But there is also the usage of the e-word in creating an unfortunate dichotomy in security.

So for the purposes of this book, I will refer to a more technically oriented infosec professional as a Hacker, but there will be no connection with ethics in the classification whatsoever. A Hacker is not ethical or unethical before the law has passed judgment.

There is also a phenomenon of hats in security, as in white hat, black hat, gray hat, and even some others such as Microsoft's blue hat.

Again we find relations to ethics here. White hats are supposedly the good guys. White hat people who specialize in penetration testing will not do anything bad, and in most cases, they will not do anything good either. As for black hat penetration-testing experts—who knows what they might do? Scary stuff.

The Black Hat Briefings are a series of conferences held annually in widely varying global locations. The speakers at these briefings are carefully selected to bring something new to the security world in the way of new testing software, demonstrating new exploits (such as a demonstration of an ATM hack at the Abu Dhabi briefing of November 2010), and occasionally, some whole new train of thought is introduced. Most of the material presented bears some real practical benefit in preserving the confidentiality, integrity, and availability of information assets—and from this, *economic security* is also benefitted.

When I look at the home page of the Black Hat Technical Security Conferences, I notice some "sustaining sponsors," and included in there are some nice ethical names such as IBM and Microsoft.

If Black hat speakers are honest law-abiding citizens, then maybe there has to be a blacker-than-black category for those who have actually been convicted of a crime.

White hat is supposedly the ethical side of security. We hear mention of "white hat security testing services" and so on, while gray hat is not really worth mentioning here.

The following brings further ridicule to the hat color saga: early in 2011, U.S. federal criminal charges were brought against two self-proclaimed "white hat Hackers" who allegedly grabbed the email addresses and SIM ID numbers of 114,000 AT&T 3G customers.

Security researchers who find vulnerabilities and write exploit code for those vulnerabilities can be said to be in the white hat category, but then it depends to what ends the fruits of their labor are used. Is a researcher who writes a white paper on antiforensics a black hatter, white hatter, or just mad hatter? When the new material is presented at a Black Hat Briefing, the speaker can say that their work is purely for the benefit of the universe and not to be used in any criminally related activities—thereby adding to the folly associated with hats and security.

In security circles, there was first the black hat, and as a reaction to the potential of any negative judgments that might arise from the name of this class, the white hat was later created.

The whole phenomenon of white hat, black hat, and whatever other color carries with it the baggage of being a precursor to either negative or positive judgment depending on which hat you have. Whatever happened to one of the mythical pillars of modern democracies—the Presumption of Innocence, as in *innocent until proven guilty*?

So in summary, here is another thing that a Hacker (in the context of this book) is not. A Hacker in this book does not possess a specific color of hat. Moreover, as I mentioned above, he or she also is not subject to any judgment with regard to ethics. I let the legal establishments do the judgment here.

"Hacker" Defined

Much of my writing in this book is based on my own experiences, and I have read and heard reports from others in the field that effectively corroborate my experiences over the years. In the next few sections, many of my comments are based on my experiences from working with Hackers throughout my career.

A service provider hired me as an analyst in 1999, and this was my first vocational security position. I will refer to this company as TSAP in this book, and it was at TSAP that I had my first encounter with the marvels of the Hackers' world. I have fantastic memories of these first years of my security career.

When I read the book *Hackers: Heroes of the Computer Revolution* by *Wired Magazine's* Steven Levy, I was struck by the similarities between his 1950s Hackers at Massachusetts Institute of Technology (MIT) and my TSAP friends. But of course, in this book, I will relate the Hacker ethic in a more modern perspective.

In contrast to the image portrayed by many in information security these days (and especially the media), the Hacker ethic deals with the idea that individuals are performing a duty for the common good. Some would draw analogies to a modern-day Robin Hood, but in all cases, that analogy strains credibility. A Hacker *is* someone who is seen by many as being rebellious or one who is more prepared to take a risk than most "normal" people.

One of the common points of discussion through Mr. Levy's book was about freedom of access to information, such that it may be used to learn about systems (and the world in general) to create more useful and accurate knowledge and systems. Open source was liked, whereas the community frowned upon blockage of access to information, and in many cases, the community would work to subvert access controls to such information in a benign and therein unnoticeable way (mostly).

While reading Hackers, I did find many analogies with my former work colleagues from TSAP and other Hackers I have met over the years. The Hacker ethic is one of the symbioses between man and machine. It is about lack of proper nutrition and, in some cases, lack of personal hygiene. There is a certain disconnect between personal finances and welfare. As long as the fridge is not empty, all is well in that department. The Hackers' goals are related to performing some act of programming acrobatics that can involve as many as twenty uninterrupted hours with a keyboard, followed by a few hours of sleep . . . repeat *ad infinitum* until the job is finished. The job may or may not have anything to do with ongoing business interests, and there could have been as many as twenty miniprojects underway simultaneously.

I mentioned in the previous paragraph about the miniprojects and "may or may not have anything to do with ongoing business interests." Actually, from the view of the Hacker, the activities "absolutely were totally" related to business interests, and I could sympathize with this viewpoint in most cases. Managers, however, were in many cases at odds with the Hackers' views (more on that in various later chapters).

The Hackers' computers invariably either ran FreeBSD or some Linux variant as an operating system, and the machines were configured in VGA console mode. This was essentially a display configuration with no graphical user interface (GUI) in the way of a multiwindow display with buttons, menu bars, icons, and so on. However, this was not the same as the display on a personal computer running purely MS-DOS that many readers may have seen. The resolution in VGA console mode was higher, and a multidisplay capability existed with keyboard-initiated display switching.

In his book, Steven Levy mentioned about programming code, and to the Hacker, if the code was aesthetic, innovative, and as minimal as possible (did not waste memory space), then the code could be considered artistically acceptable. The usage of Linux boxes in VGA console mode typified this particular Hacker ethic. A GUI with windows (this was usually X Window with BSD based operating systems), plus the windows manager (with Linux, this could have been the KDE or Gnome managers), and other collateral did occupy some considerable disk space, and when loaded in memory, it consumed a lot of random-access memory (RAM).

On the point about resource utilization and efficiency, the older Steven Levy observations were based on a real lack of available memory and CPU time (with the time sharing systems used in the good old days), but even today, with bountiful resources available to us (just recently, I have installed an Apple iMac from a USB thumb drive), the Hacker will still take great pride in using as little resources as possible in programming stunts.

There was also the issue of being as minimal as possible that was related to security concerns. Apart from the fact that X Window binaries and libraries were considered "buggy" and "full of [security] holes" by the Hackers, there is a general principle of installing as little software as possible so as to remove the possibility of having security compromised as a result of a successful exploit with that software. Of course, to lead to a security problem, a piece of software does not need to be running in memory as a "listening" network service waiting for incoming connections. Even if a program is not acting as a server in the classic client–server model, it may be used in a "local exploit" scenario to elevate privileges (this concept is fairly basic but not at all well understood in the industry), leading to the compromise or "ownage" of the host computer.

Everything that the Hacker needed to achieve on his (in this case, I can safely use "his" without fear of imprisonment because all of my TSAP Hacker colleagues were of the male gender—as far as I was aware) computer could easily be achieved on their VGA console Linux machine, and the "base install" of the Linux machine was around 50% of the disk space usage of some of the default installs, depending on the designated purpose of the machine. This did not stretch as far as performing "adult" tasks such as writing reports and so on because reports were mandated to be in Microsoft Word format (Hackers generally refused to use Microsoft Word for various reasons). Electronic mail was handled by use of an open-source program called Mutt, an open source, non–user-friendly Lynx-handled Web browsing; in fact, according to my colleagues, "everything that needs to be done on a daily basis can be done in VGA console mode—who needs Windows?" and "not being user-friendly does not mean being user-hostile."

The Hacker ethic is not something that was carved in stone or written on paper for all to see. There is no Hacker Website that could be seen as a central authority on what it is to be a Hacker. The Hacker ethic is what Hackers will follow involuntarily without any influence from others. The ethic is driven by the habits of highly skilled and talented people who all share the same traits in their love of computers, programming, and the aesthetics of beautiful, efficient programs. If a certain piece of open-source code is not perceived to be doing what it should be doing, or it lacks efficiency, the Hacker will think nothing but immediately correcting its perceived flaws, even if the task takes several hours, at the cost of almost everything else, including but not limited to eating, showering, or "focusing on business objectives."

In information security, especially when the Hacker is employed under the guise of a professional security analyst, performing remote (and occasionally onsite) security assessments, there were (the use of past tense is quite deliberate here—the major theme of this book is one of the loss of human ingenuity in security) often clashes between the Hacker ethic and the business ethic. The business ethic was about doing things as fast as possible, and making as much money as possible, even if that means that the job is not necessarily done right. The business ethic was about potentially allowing quality to drop to dangerous levels if it meant making a faster buck. For the Hacker, the perpetration of a deliberate act that results in a loss of quality is a capital offense. So there were often clashes between the managers and the Hackers. Indeed, as I will detail later in this book, from around the turn of the millennia, it was clear that at some point in the near future, they would cease to coexist.

From my own experiences of Hackers, from a security perspective, I think they can be defined along the following lines: highly skilled IT professionals with a penchant for fast learning and creativity, highly familiar with the configuration and security aspects of most popular technologies in commercial usage (software packages such as Oracle's database management system, various flavors of Unix, Microsoft Windows, Cisco devices and firewalls), and do not see a boundary between work and that thing that the capitalist world seems to find ever more ingenious ways to take from us—"free time."

Hackers seldom can be found in offices these days (at least not physically), but in all cases, they have computers at home (in some cases, with all the IP-capable devices and virtual machines, a class C subnet—254 addresses—is insufficient allocation for their home network) and are doing things like breaking stuff, and then writing exploits is something that is enjoyable. When you consider that there are millions of ways of accomplishing even a relatively simple programming task, such as sorting a list of 100 random numbers, then programming really is creative and an art form—and generally people like being creative.

In this book, I try to relate the Hacker ethic to the "skill sets" as identified by the IT industry, and in that respect, I try to relate the story in a more specific way that, in most cases, goes something like this: the Hacker knows everything. The Hacker is both a network and

IT operations staff member. From the network operations viewpoint, the Hacker knows Cisco, Juniper, and firewalls in more detail than is necessary to carry out the duties of the network operations staff. The Hacker knows Webservers, database servers, print servers, and all kinds of servers . . . in fact, think of a server and the Hacker will know it. How it comes to be that Hackers know so much is partly because of the methodology deployed in older-style penetration testing, which I will discuss in the next section and also in Chapter 7.

A Hacker lives and breathes IT, and so the timetable of the Hacker is not from nine to five, five days per week. Think in terms of 12 hours per day, 365 days per year. This is a lot of time to learn stuff.

Zen and the Art of Remote Assessment

In this section, I will give some examples based on my experiences of the capabilities of the Hacker in remote security testing—in particular, remote penetration testing. With my illustrations here, I do not intend to blow the reader away with amazing feats of hacking acrobatics. My intention is only to give an indication of the levels of skill that were actually deployed in the penetration tests of days past.

Much of my book is a lament of the loss of analytical skills in security, but with modern-day tests, even if more appropriate skills are deployed, the tests are so restricted (please see Chapter 7) that the whole exercise tends toward insignificant return on resource investment.

The vast majority of post-2000 penetration testing has been performed merely as a requirement of regulations (please see Chapter 4) as in "we need an independent third party to carry out a penetration test of our perimeter," and if the test is passed, the organization gets a tick in the box on the auditor's score sheet. The testing will be carried out with use of automated vulnerability scanning tools (see Chapter 5) with as little analysis as possible. The service provider line management and analysts' key performance indicators will be geared around executing tests as fast as possible, and if they do not meet their targets, end-of-year bonuses suffer. There is no incentive to be analytical because for various reasons, for both the service provider and their client, basic economic pressures outweigh the benefits of unearthing vulnerability—or so it may seem.

So given that penetration testing has been a no-show for at least a decade, and the Hackers were never big on documentation, from where will newcomers be able to find information on practical, effective penetration testing skills and techniques (i.e., techniques that are actually used in real-world testing and compromising)? Newcomers to the penetration testing arena will find extreme difficulty in finding anything but theoretical testing techniques, many of which will never have been successfully put into practice. Some of the "hacking" techniques covered in text books (and other media) represent completely unrealistic testing scenarios because of practical realities or just the simple fact that in real-life testing, there are more rewarding and easier attack vectors to attempt.

From the perspective of the good guys, penetration testing is sort of a lost art. No wonder then that the U.K. and U.S. efforts to recruit for cyberwarfare initiatives have failed to bear fruit.

During the late 1990s, penetration tests as performed by Hackers were not so much of a methodical remote assessment of network perimeter defenses; they were from the Hacker's perspective a test of their capability to penetrate a network—a challenge, a laying down of the gauntlet, a chance to show off a vast arsenal of weaponry in the way of Hacker skills. The Hackers wrote the rules on penetration testing methodology, and the rule was basically that there are no rules. There were no restrictions on attempts to compromise networks. When it came to penetration testing, the gloves were off.

I will give a few real-life scenarios here without putting them in context. There will always be some Hacker somewhere who has a claim of more amazing stories to tell. I am really just trying to give at least a small insight into real-life, unrestricted penetration testing. This also serves to illustrate the Hacker mindset and skills as a precursor for later content.

One of the earlier tests I can remember was for a South Korean telco. The essential parts of the testing (I do not cover obvious steps such as port scanning and so on—I only cover the highlights as in the essential steps that led to hosts and networks being compromised, and many of the technical details are omitted) were as follows: port scanning and then network mapping (remotely building a "map" of the network external infrastructure by tracerouting and firewalking) led to the discovery of some upstream/downstream Cisco routers, but connection attempts to these devices were being blocked. One of the Cisco device configuration files was found by Googling, and this configuration had some aspects that were the same as other Ciscos— including the Access Control List that prevented connections to the device Simple Network Management Protocol (SNMP) (and other services) other than from some specific source IP address. The next step was to modify the snmpwalk program (used for querying and setting configuration of a device over SNMP) to send spoofed source address packets that instructed strategically chosen routers to send their configurations to our Trivial File Transfer Protocol server in our lab in Bangkok. Having compromised routers (full administrative level 15 access over telnet and the private community string was compromised—all devices used the same string), it was then possible to "tunnel" network traffic in such a way that packet sniffing was possible. From this point, multiple critical passwords for key "gateway" infrastructure items were compromised, and given the lack of effective internal controls, compromising other targets was trivial.

A bank in Malaysia had deployed a mail server in their demilitarized zone (DMZ) on a Microsoft Windows platform (although I do not recall which mail server product was used). One of the Hackers used some reverse-engineering techniques in development of a custom (zero-day) exploit during the two-week testing window. The mail server itself was compromised, although little progress was made in the two-week window with regard to other internal client targets.

Custom-made, zero-day exploits were used in a later test also, this time with an Internet service provider (ISP) in Thailand. The service in question was a Web-based mail server, but little was known about the underlying operating system—not exactly a "blind" exploit situation but nearly. In most cases, it is critical to know the operating system architecture in order to write exploit code, and a lucky guess was made to the effect that the operating system (OS) was Linux (compiled for Intel x86). Anyway, within the two-week testing window, an effective exploit was developed, and the server was compromised.

Staying on ISPs in Thailand, and also with a Web-based email system, a "file inclusion bug" was manifested on the server where the Web interface would allow the user to attach a file. The way the file processing was handled on the server was by use of a temporary file, the name of which was included in the user interface in an Hypertext Markup

Language (HTML) hidden field. Cutting some detail, it was possible to have the /etc/passwd (on some Unix systems, this file will include both user names and password hashes) mailed to you if you registered a mail account. Passwords were enumerated in a matter of seconds, and these passwords were used to gain access to other targets—Secure Shell access was not blocked by firewalls.

A Taiwan client, involved with the manufacture of semiconductors, exposed their Lightweight Directory Access Protocol (LDAP) service to the world. From this service, user details were freely available (as part of the design of the protocol as opposed to some sort of attack result), which led to around 20 File Transfer Protocol (FTP) user names and passwords being compromised (email addresses were gleaned from LDAP, which enabled a more "targeted" brute force attempt for FTP access). Unfortunately for the client, the FTP default landing directories were under their main Web server's document root directory. From this point, it was possible to upload a script by FTP that could then be executed under the Web interface. Execution of the script led to the opening of a shell when connecting to a specific port on the server. (As a common oversight, the firewall failed to block access to ports, which were not bound to a listening service. In this case, there were many ports available to which a shell could be bound.) Additionally, IBM AIX systems were compromised by first gleaning lower privileged user names from SNMP, then elevating privileges by use of previously undisclosed local IBM DB2 exploits.

There were many such stories as the aforementioned from around two years of penetration testing. Many of these test scenarios involved recoding/patching open-source tools on the fly during testing windows. There are many such situations where there was a need to quickly familiarize oneself with new products during a test window or tools need to be adapted to do something they were not originally designed to do—and clearly, there is no training material that can come to the aid of a novice in this precise situation. The penetration tester needs to have extensive programming experience and a good all-round knowledge of various different software packages and security testing tools.

Many books such as Chris McNab's *Network Security Assessment* will give a decent enough "script kiddy" introduction to network penetration testing in that the tools and exploits mentioned can help to gain a "foothold" on a network, but the next stages in actually compromising a network need some considerable ingenuity in many cases. Finding code such as local exploits for locally executed binaries on a DMZ server, for example, can be very hard or impossible. So other approaches are needed, and this is where the ingenuity comes in.

In the way of Hacker/penetration testing skills, it is worth mentioning security testing tools and exploits. Many budding security enthusiasts will just slap a keyword on their CV when they apply for a penetration testing position such as Hydra (a multi-application layer protocol network login brute-forcer tool) without realizing that these software packages have their own little nuances; they are badly documented, and in some cases they are buggy. Although they are great tools, one just does not instantly know how to use the tools effectively.

Also with exploiting services using other developers' code, it is rarely the case that you can just download the binary or script and run it and get your result. Very often you have to go through the source code to figure out command line options, and in some cases, it will not be clear what the coder actually intended with the exploit (e.g., if the code binds a shell, is there a "reverse telnet" situation in play?). Other times, the exploit was coded for some specific machine architecture other than your own, so you need to compile it for your target architecture, and this can lead to problems for the uninitiated.

I am not really sure from where, or for what reason, the term "script kiddy" was invented—I mean, it is a derogatory term from the 1990s invented by the hacker community and is aimed at novice hackers, but from what I have seen, it is not really possible for a computer novice to take up penetration testing and get results from day 1 by port scanning and Web searching for exploits. At least we can say that the "script kiddy" approach does not really work in terms of being an effective penetration test.

The Hacker through the Looking Glass

Thus far in this chapter, I have discussed the information security practitioner of yesteryear, whom I have labeled "Hacker" (upper case "H") for the purposes of this book. With the old-style Hacker, you have a human being who has combined extreme levels of ingenuity with extreme levels of diligence to create a fusion reactor with enough energy output to break any network security defenses given sufficient time, and with some of our Asia–Pacific banking clients in 2000, that would be about 20 minutes or so.

The nuclear fusion reactor outputs a huge amount of energy, but is it a replacement for burning ever more scarce fossil fuels, the burning of which results in the emission of greenhouse gases? For many, the answer is no because just as with Hackers, there is a *but* in this argument; in fact, there are at least two *buts*. The spent fuel is highly radioactive, and also there is the question of reliability over the reactor design. If the nuclear fusion reactions are allowed to perpetuate unchecked, then the unthinkable can occur. Nobody wants to see a repeat of the Chernobyl disaster from 1986 or the more recent Fukushima events (as a result of an earthquake off the coast of Japan in March 2011).

TSAP's meltdown in the Asia–Pacific region came about by failing to find a balance in our security offerings. In the beginning, we just delivered raw technical expertise with no emphasis on business goals. Later on, the company followed the path taken by the industry as a whole—they completely removed the Hacker element from service delivery. So what exactly were the problems with the Hacker ethic?

For the first two years or so of farming out Hacker expertise, roughly from 1999 to 2001, clients were flabbergasted at what we had to offer. They had become slowly aware of the whole buzz surrounding security but did not know if they should do anything about it (on top of what they were already doing). Clients were in the situation where in most cases they did not have dedicated security departments. IT operations staff members were responsible for security, but not surprisingly, they had limited exposure to this area (it was not previously part of their job functions). They were aware that they needed to do something about viruses and malware, and they invariably had installed firewalls on their perimeter, albeit badly configured; there was no "segregated subnet" for Internet facing resources (or "DMZ") to speak of.

Remote network security tests (also known as network penetration tests—often abbreviated to "pen tests") with regional clients invariably turned up glaring misconfigurations and bugs in the late 1990s and early 2000s. Access to an internal Oracle database at a major multinational bank was gained in around 15 minutes in one case.

After the testing, we would struggle through language and cultural barriers to compile a report of our findings for the client. There would be the cursory quality analysis by peers, including management, and then the report would be hastily sent off to the client.

Two weeks after delivering the report, the in-country sales rep would follow up with the client, and the Hackers would receive verbal congratulations; everyone was happy, we were fantastic, amazing, "best in the world," etc. However, I always thought it was strange that clients never responded back to us with any technical queries. Our reports always gave great detail on how to address the security problems we discovered, but putting myself in the shoes of our clients, I think I would still have great problems in actually knowing how to address the findings within a complex production environment. Some of the security problems found were labeled "high risk" and were specified as being easy to exploit. High risk and easy to exploit—doesn't that sound alarming? But there were never any questions.

In one case, a Hacker from Kyrgyzstan and I were engaged on a large onsite project with a big bank in Taiwan. The point of the exercise was to assess the security of operating systems in the bank—predominantly Unix-based machines, but there were also some Cisco IOS devices in the assessment. Overall, there were more than 100 devices assessed, and the whole onsite engagement lasted for three weeks. The project formed a major part of a portfolio of services delivered to the bank. I was told the overall cost to the client was something in the order of half a million U.S. dollars. Again, after we delivered the report of our findings (the report comprised 200 pages), there was a long period of silence from the client.

Some months later, the Taiwanese banking client contacted us again. The bank had retail and investment operations in Hong Kong, and they needed to satisfy the information security requirements of the Hong Kong Monetary Authority (HKMA). The client only contacted us because they suddenly had a clear mandate to address our findings, and it was clear that our report had thus far not been given any attention whatsoever. They asked us to summarize our findings in "ten pages max" and then fly to Taiwan to discuss the findings with their CISO and IT operations representative. The fact that the client only reacted to our findings in response to audit requirements, although I could not see it at the time, was a sign of things to come in the industry and is a matter for a later chapter in this book (please see "The Tip of the Iceberg—Audit-Driven Security Strategy" in Chapter 4).

The meeting in Taipei was the first such meeting with clients that I could remember in more than two years. One of my Hacker colleagues and I, together with our line manager, tried to fumble our way through the misdirected questions from the client. Suddenly the client was under a strict mandate to actually address the problems raised in our report. To that point in time, they did not feel compelled to pay attention to a complicated 200-page report.

As an example of one of the findings from our report, Oracle's database management server has a service that listens for incoming connections called a TNS listener. Oracle leaves open the option for administrators to apply a password challenge for clients connecting to this service. Failure to apply a password, among other problems, leaves open the opportunity for attackers to gain access to different kinds of information that can help them to stage a compromise of the database. We saw this as a serious problem, and we thought it should be easy to address the problem—all that was required was simply changing a configuration file and restarting the Oracle database manager, right?

The Hacker element does not see the real challenges facing the client (and by the way, our line manager was none the wiser). Even the part that involves restarting the server process could not be easily implemented by the client in a highly complex production environment consisting of multiple islands of highly valuable information assets and highly important applications.

Many questions arise from what may seem like a simple security change. What are the risks exactly? Given my network architecture, how easy would it be for an attacker (external or internal) to take advantage of an open TNS listener? Does the application of a password mean that all client connections to the database must now be authenticated (thereby affecting not only database administrators' connections but also all application clients that connect to the server)? Does the need to supply a password mean that DBA's lives are now more difficult and it can take longer to fix problems with the database? When one actually engages with operations staff members that know how the pieces of the jigsaw fit together, one realizes that there are rarely any security fixes that can be applied in a nondisruptive manner.

Then of course there was the most important element that should drive all decisions related to security: what are the numbers? What will it cost us in terms of time and materials to address the findings in your report? Why should we spend that amount of money? What are the real risks given our network architecture and multiple other factors? The Hacker generally takes a haughty stance with clients when the latter dares to suggest that security fixes are not easy to make. One case I remember was a security fix that involved the installation of a patch to an online gambling company's Apache Webserver. The Hacker sees the client's Webserver in the same way as their Linux test box. Even a very junior administrator can be walked through the required steps with ease, but what if the Webserver hosts an application that takes 600,000 hits and generates US$75,000 in income daily, plus there are dependencies on other islands of administrators and developers in the organization? I recall from working with customers that the change management system record for doing something as "simple" as restarting a database instance would require reams of information on the steps involved and a "roll-back plan," and the record had to be approved by numerous other departments.

Bruce Schneier's comments about the complexity of security suddenly rang true to me at the first instance of a client actually paying attention to our report findings; but try getting the Hacker to even think about costs. In fact, at that time in security, there were very few people who really understood that security was as much about business analysis as it was about technical assessments and recommendations; anyway, the costs versus risks balancing act was something that the Hacker avoided at all costs—the thought process was something repulsive to the Hacker. For the Hacker, all recommendations related to security improvements must be implemented and costs are not relevant or irrelevant—there is no actual concept of *cost* as such.

We fumbled our way through that meeting in Taipei. The meeting took all day, and at the end of it, was the client any closer to understanding how they should go about meeting the HKMA requirements? Not really. Neither party understood the nature of the challenges involved. The challenge was not purely technical; it was also a business challenge, and the costs of implementing an effective information risk management program can come from a variety of diverse sources, not just from hardware and software costs.

What are the security challenges for a company doing research and development in pharmaceuticals? Apart from the protection of personal data that many companies will face, their main concern would be the protection of intellectual property in the way of research findings. So identification of the client's internal assets that relate to research is, in this case, a good place to start an information security risk management program—but the Hacker will ask to see a network diagram and then will recommend a myriad of firewalls, virtual private networks (VPNs), and highly disruptive (and therefore highly expensive) changes based purely on a technical viewpoint. The Hacker's name will be on the report of findings sent to the client—so there will be an issue of ego if the client is later hacked, and the Hacker's name is associated with the safeguarding of the client's network. What if the Hacker's esteemed colleagues from the Hacker community somehow discover that the client was hacked? With these points in mind, Hackers take the view that their recommendations are easy to understand, and there is "no reason whatsoever" why the client cannot just implement them immediately without any problems in less than 10 minutes.

Problems with communication with the Hacker element are better known. Hackers speak to each other in an abbreviated language that the non-Hacker, even the IT administrator with years of experience, will find hard to follow. So what happens when Hackers are left to explain how they exploited security vulnerability and compromised a client's network? The outcome is invariably glazed expression, and in one case, "I really like your analysis, the guy is a real genius—by the way, what does he mean by temporary file name enumeration?"

The Hacker element in security provided (again the use of past tense is quite deliberate here) a compatible level of technical expertise compared with the risks faced by interconnected large organizations. But there was never an open check given to IT departments for fixing security problems. Business has never had an affinity for unfiltered technical advice, based on pride and ego, poor communication, and absolutely zero empathy.

There was a growing realization at the time (based on my experience and the general consensus—it was roughly around the end of 2001 going into 2002) that the Hacker-led approach to security was flawed, but as one of the major themes of this book, the way that the security industry responded to this problem was to make the Hackers the scapegoats, which has turned out to be not just a minor misdemeanor—it has effectively removed the tools needed to counter information security problems. The Hackers left the corporate security arena through the exit door and in less time than is needed to say, "How are we actually going to implement these security policies?", highly sensitive data left by the upstream link.

Communication, Hyper-Casual Fridays, and "Maturity"

Corporates such as security service providers who had hired Hackers made many mistakes and generally wound up completely failing in their attempts to people-manage Hackers.

Another side of the Hacker paradigm that was seen as negative was the lack of any willingness on the part of the Hackers to do anything that they did not want to do. The happy-go-lucky type of behavior with Hackers from the very birth of security service provision just did not sit well at all with managers.

Security service providers perform assessment services for their clients, and their findings are passed on to clients in the form of a Microsoft Word format report or Adobe PDF format file. The report is supposed to give clients as much information as possible about the nature of the problem found, how it was exploited, an indication of risk (high, medium, or low), and recommendations of how to address the vulnerability.

As my first taste of life in TSAP, I was asked to perform a quality analysis check of a report in raw form from the Hackers after they had performed a remote penetration test for a banking customer in Malaysia. Aside from the fact that the report was already two weeks late, what was handed to me was a text file (completely unformatted document compiled with the Unix vi editor) with headings like "description:" and then "criticality:" and so on. As an example of a recommendation for addressing a buffer overflow problem, there were three words: "patch the system!!" (the double exclamation mark was in the report).

It was commonplace to see smiley faces, expletives, "ASCII art," slang, Russian words (our clients expected reports in English), lower-case acronyms (e.g., snmp instead of SNMP), and total lack of punctuation. Furthermore the report was always lacking detail in such a way that no single living person other than the writer could interpret its meaning. It was not the case that the reader had to be at a similar level of skill as the writer in order to understand the report—it was just that there was no actual information in the 3-kB text document that took four weeks to produce.

Reports from the Hackers were clearly off someway from what they needed to be. For myself, as a native English and Hacker speaker, I was in a position to bridge the gap between what our clients needed and what the Hackers produced (worthless drivel)—but it did mean writing every single report produced by TSAP all by myself.

Before I arrived on the scene in TSAP, managers were spending literally hours in workshops in a vain attempt to convert the text forwarded by the Hackers into something that had at least a semblance of value for clients who were paying in the order of tens of thousands of U.S. dollars for a two-week penetration test. Our regional CEO and his cohorts were probably losing sleep over the whole reporting issue.

I had read a report from a year before I joined TSAP. Honestly, as a technical person, even I could not make any sense of it. It was really a hopeless effort, and much of it was either just plain wrong or tragically lacking in every aspect. There were the unmistakable signs of a nontechnical person trying to interpret the ramblings of a Hacker who lacked any communication skills.

Other activities that were not so pleasing to the eyes of TSAP managers included but were not limited to: claiming all kinds of expenses with no receipts, asking to go to overseas conferences with no real justification, asking for software licenses with no real justification, and asking for "test boxes"—you guessed it right: with no real justification. The list goes on. Our local office manager in Thailand had a hotel management background, and the irregular working hours and other Hacker habits did not sit well with him. He was able to show remarkable patience though, as long as the clients kept paying.

What evolved in TSAP was the separation of the Hackers from others in the company. It was an actual physical separation—with the Hackers on one side of the building (initially our office was a residential town house with Ethernet cables passed from office to office around the outside of the building and so on) and the rest of the staff on the other side of the building. There was no actual communication between the two sides unless there was an on-going client engagement. One side was a noisy, smoky, dark environment, whereas the other side was actually what you might expect from an office environment.

There was a physical separation, but also a logical one. There was a rather unfortunate distinction drawn between one side and the other that was deliberately designed by TSAP managers from around the region. One side was supposedly composed of mature adults, whereas the other was not. Through the days where Hackers still had a place in information security, this was actually quite a common insult against the Hackers in other companies, not just in TSAP.

Another area where the Hackers did not blend in well with the modern corporate world was the dress code—and I am not talking about casual Friday dress code here. Anyone who has ever been to a Black Hat conference will know the dress code of the Hacker fraternity. This was also the dress code employed by at least one of our TSAP Hackers at various times both in the office (which was OK because the Hackers had their zoo cordoned off behind closed doors) *and onsite with clients in locations such as Singapore.* One of our crew, in particular, wore different T-shirts while onsite with clients—I think it was a different theme for each day of the week—which varied from aiming expletives at a famous software house to others with scary images from metal bands. By the way, the unorthodox appearance facets were not limited to T-shirts; there were also unnatural hair colors, piercings, tattoos, and steel toe-capped military issue boots.

Our managers tried in vain to prevent this practice of showing up onsite "inappropriately dressed," but in reality, they were powerless to prevent this without actually firing the Hackers.

Singapore was a place I visited a lot during my years with TSAP. The Monetary Authority of Singapore (MAS) had a mandate that required us to be onsite with the client, even when we were performing a "remote" penetration test from outside the client's perimeter firewalls.

I do not really know from where the idea stemmed that Singaporean society was especially conservative—some would say draconian society; but anyway, I was personally a bit wary about our clients' reactions to my colleagues' informal dress code. However, what actually emerged from our Singapore client visits was pleasantly surprising. Instead of disapproving of my colleagues' appearances, the communicative T-shirt thing actually seemed to work well for us. Singapore clients, and as it turned out, those from everywhere else, were OK with the T-shirts because "this is what a Hacker looks like." TSAP managers thought we would appear less professional as a result of our appearance, but in the eyes of the bill-paying clients, we looked *more* professional than an analyst who shows up onsite in the robotic suit and tie. In our debriefings with clients on the final day of our assessment engagements, I was in my suit and tie, and my colleagues were at the other end of the formality scale. Regardless of how articulate and confident I was while briefing clients on our findings, questions would invariably be directed at my Hacker coworkers, not myself, even though the information being communicated was totally unintelligible.

Clients were getting the real, authentic security assessment circus that they expected with TSAP, but our managers, like so many others in the industry at the time, were not at all happy with what was being delivered, and they were especially not happy with the "type of person" doing the delivery.

Security in the late 1990s really was the biggest vanity fair in town, and TSAP managers just had to be a part of it. I do believe that managers felt somehow left out of the whole security show, and this was the main reason behind the constant stream of objections being aimed at the Hackers. In security in general, from around 2001 onward, the managers in security along with the self-declared "mature" elements of the security world were waiting on the sidelines for their piece of the action and any excuse to remove the Hackers from the picture. Don't get me wrong; as I have explained in this chapter, there were some problems with the Hacker element—but the problems were only cosmetic.

Hacker Cries Wolf

We have spoken so far about Hackers and what I think are fairly easy people management problems to deal with. A more serious problem is about overstating risks in security. There are a couple of example cases in this regard that I have come across several times, and I will give a brief insight here.

One classic example is the old adage about Secure Sockets Layer (SSL)/man-in-the-middle attacks (or like Ross Anderson in *Security Engineering*—we should probably say "middleperson" attacks) in that if a remote Website does not issue an SSL certificate, it is possible that a fiend between you and the server could "packetsniff" your traffic and capture everything sent between your Web browser and the remote Webserver or impersonate the remote Webserver.

If there is a business application requirement for the transmission of sensitive data (such as personal identification data or passwords for example), then it is advisable to configure SSL certificates in the encryption of the transmitted data. The certificate identifies the remote Webserver (if the certificate has been signed by a "reputable" certificate authority such as Verisign) and is used to encrypt traffic between your Web browser and the server.

But oh so often the risks are overstated. Several times I heard Hackers talking in the way "yes—very easy to capture your passwords if there is no SSL—I can do it very easily." In one case, actually with an insurance company, there was a DES-encrypted certificate used instead of a DES3-encrypted version, and the Hacker was telling the management at the firm that this was a "really severe problem" and it needed to be fixed "immediately," adding, "I can hack that very easily."

First, the payload traffic was not even highly sensitive data, and second (and I am cutting out a lot of technobabble here), even if you have "owned" the ISP through which the traffic is routed, or managed to "ARP cache poison" someone on the same subnet, actually capturing the data and decrypting it is not going to be a simple 10-min task. Possibly if the data is encrypted with a weak key, it could be a lot faster, but it is not a simple or quick attack to stage successfully.

There are other potential security problems with sending weak-encrypted traffic over the Internet and other ways in which "you could be hacked," but none of them are as straightforward as the "leet"-speak Hacker would have you believe.

In really sensitive situations, there are a series of recommendations to follow, and these are important for banks and such firms who deal with corporate clients or big-portfolio investors. Where the identities or transaction details are such that a Hacker would feel warranted in spending some considerable time to stage an attack for considerable financial gain, then yes, this is a situation where extensive safeguards need to be on the table and the business case considered. Typically in these situations, the bank will set up their client with a client-side certificate/two-factor authentication (although this is not related to packet interception/middle-person attacks).

In application security, it is important to consider how, at a mathematical level, is the encryption being facilitated, but more often than not, the real risks will be with key management (keys need to be stored, transferred, expired, reissued, and so on, and obviously, if an attacker has a key, the traffic can be decrypted if one of the more common encryption algorithms is used) and what happens at the two ends of the network transaction. If an attacker, or the National Security Agency (NSA) (for example), wants to capture sensitive information from a target, it is far easier to use social engineering or install a keyboard sniffer on their computer rather than try and break the encryption in their network traffic—but I often heard Hackers talking to the uninitiated (and sometimes those who make decisions on security budgets) in a way that is like "yes I can break the encryption, no problem."

Certainly if you compare this interception/middleperson type of attack with the complexity of most successful attacks that are actually reported these days, the real, modern-day attacks are much easier to stage and less complex in nature. Of course, I am not talking about wireless 802.1-variant middleperson attacks. This is a different story entirely, and it is something that is so often ignored in wireless security reviews—however, it is a little off-topic.

Of all the Hacker traits, the trait where dangers are overstated is the one that I find most problematic, and it is the one that can lead senior management to mistrust advice from highly skilled security experts. However, while this does pose a more difficult problem to solve for the Hacker's line manager than the other problems I have described in this chapter, it is a problem that is not impossible to solve, and given a bit of flexibility, it is a problem we are quite capable of solving given a slight reworking of the skills and job description of a security manager (I talk more about solutions in Section 4).

Unmuzzled Hackers and Facebook

Another one is that favorite topic—Facebook. This is another area where the unmuzzled Hacker will put the fear of God into the uninitiated with use of scary-sounding phrases like "clickjacking," and I have heard Hackers telling people that doing the wrong thing within Facebook can lead to the contents of their hard disk being sucked into the ether—including bank details and passwords— with the real intention of letting the listener know that they (the Hacker) can do this in Facebook. Yes, this scenario is possible and has occurred many times, but the key point is that it is not possible *directly* from within Facebook with "one wrong click." Generally the user would need to be directed to another site first, from where they can inadvertently download malicious code, install the code, then the user's machine is handed over to the underworld. Clicking on the wrong link can also lead users to another site wherein they are fooled into entering credit card details (for example). But did you notice that there are several steps involved here? The Hacker would have you believe that just opening a Facebook page can lead to instant identity theft.

From within Facebook, you can click on something you should not click, and you wind up posting embarrassing things to all your "friends" (and isn't it amazing how many friends people have—2000 friends of which 200 are people they have actually physically seen with their own eyes), or your friends can have their accounts hacked and weird things can ensue; but the real nightmare scenarios will take several steps and redirection(s) in order for the user to end up in trouble.

Security in Facebook gets a lot of attention because as of March 2011, there are approximately half a billion users, and even now, many users find the "Privacy" settings to be a little confusing. Users can leave huge holes in their profiles making them open to everyone, and they are in many cases easily duped into accepting "friend" requests from people they have never met. Generally, Facebook is going to be a juicy target for fiends wishing to gain access to personal information. But is Facebook an inherently more insecure application than others? There have been some public-declared server-side issues relating to cross-site scripting and cross-site request forgery problems, but these have been fixed quickly and given both the complexity of Facebook and the intense scrutiny it is under, the frequency of occurrence of these problems is surprisingly low.

The risks within Facebook are no more than the risks from general Web browsing and any service that requires you to enter personal information, and to be honest, even the most astute and security-aware can at least be embarrassed or inconvenienced. The main difference is only with the attention that comes from a user base of half a billion people, all of whom enter personal details. In fact, the ideas here are similar to those in the old argument about malware and Windows versus Mac. Windows can seem to be more vulnerable to these malware issues, but one needs to remember that Windows is still far more widespread (I did not say "popular") as compared with Mac—and therefore more juicy a platform from which to seek unlawful financial gains. As Mac gets more widespread in homes and offices, no doubt there will be proportionally more malware issues with Mac.

Summary

The purpose of this chapter and the next chapter is to introduce the people in security, and when we are talking about information security analysts and consultants, there are two distinct types. The first, as introduced in this chapter, will be referred to in this book as a Hacker, and the Hacker has a very different skill set from the second type, who will be introduced in the next chapter.

The Hackers roamed the security plains first, back in the 1990s, when organizations first tentatively dipped their toes in the ocean of information security risk management.

For most organizations with a newfound awareness in security, their first steps were to get someone from IT operations to set up a border firewall and install antivirus software on computers. Then as the 1990s progressed, actual security experts started coming out of the woodwork, and new information security service providers recruited many of them. These individuals were the Hackers, and it was the Hackers who shaped the first major era in information security.

The Hacker was generally a highly gifted IT professional, with extremely diverse knowledge, that covered all of the major IT technologies in use by large organizations at the time. The Hacker was a pure IT enthusiast who saw no real distinction between work and play because both involved doing what they loved—programming, tinkering, analyzing, re-engineering, breaking things, writing exploits, malforming, overflowing, poisoning, enumerating, and so on.

TSAP was my first employer in information security, which was a service provider with a head office in Bangkok and clients around the Asia–Pacific region. Each country where TSAP operated generally employed a sales rep and a local security analyst, supposedly for the purpose of providing support to clients who spoke the same language and understood the culture. The local security analysts were far from being Hackers. In fact, in most cases, they had no actual interest in IT whatsoever. So whenever TSAP had to deliver a project for clients outside of Thailand, it required Hackers to fly to that country, stay in hotels, and run up expenses that were seen by many as adding unnecessary costs to projects. Naturally, the response of some of the regional managers was "can you train our local analysts so we don't need to fly you down here to deliver a project?", to which the response from the Hacker lab was "if you want to be able to deliver these services, do your usual nine to five, then spend six hours every evening to learn security for the next 10 years." The response was greeted with a great deal of suspicion and frustration—but in all honesty, the situation was exactly as depicted by the Hackers. There has to be a certain mindset in place before one can even begin to assimilate oneself into the matrix of the Hacker, and then once that enthusiasm has been found, a *lot of work* is required from that point.

The older style of penetration testing involved some technical acrobatics, the likes of which cannot even be imagined by most IT professionals, even those with ten-plus years of experience in the field. Many of the techniques used by Hackers have been described at some level in theory, but the vast majority of people reading the theory would not even know the first steps of actually performing the act. An attack such as SNMP spoofing has been described in theory, but when it is actually used in a penetration test to compromise a device, it becomes clear that the theory falls way short of actually doing it in practice, and the theoretical attack is usually only one stage of many that are involved in actually compromising a network. Hackers also may not know everything before going into a penetration test, but they are adept at learning on the fly what is required—this is not something that can be taught. I suppose it could be possible to learn how to learn faster (so to speak), but there comes a point, if you are trying to train someone to be a Hacker, where you have to draw a line and say "you can either do this or you cannot."

The Hacker understands the security threats faced by large organizations in sufficient detail to know how to counter the threats, but of course, there is a problem—organizations face business challenges in security as well as technical challenges. Every organization needs to balance the cost of security safeguards against the risks. The situation where an organization has an open check for addressing security problems simply does not exist.

Security challenges are complex, and even organizations in the same industry sector face radically different challenges. Hackers love IT and have never had an interest in even their own business objectives, let alone those of their customers or employers—and to be fair, they cannot really be expected to have such interests (their managers should help in this respect). Hackers will look at a client's network and recommend every possible security change they can think of—regardless of costs. Every device in the network must be hardened to the hilt—regardless of the maintainability and scalability challenges faced by IT operations in such a venture. According to the Hacker's plot lines, the network must have countless subnets with rigorous network access control between the subnets; furthermore, each firewall and switch must be doubled up in hot-swap mode for redundancy and denial of service protection.

Security topics such as International Standards Organization (ISO) information security risk management standards represent the height of boredom for the Hacker brethren. There are many areas in management standards and audit programs that the Hacker would not touch with a barge pole, but these do at least provide a decent framework, or checklist, for companies to follow.

The other boring roads that the Hacker will not pass are any kind of documentation, "acceptable dress codes" (even casual Friday dress codes are unacceptably formal for most Hackers), and many other facets of corporate life, which TSAP managers deemed to be "requirements of mature adults."

I recall an incident from 2003 when two of my Hacker colleagues from Kyrgyzstan and I were onsite giving a presentation about application security with a Taiwan bank. The older, slightly more mature guy who specialized in cryptology and application security (as well as many other areas—personally, I never met anyone who knew Microsoft Windows security to the same level) was detailing a specific type of vulnerability and gave an example. The other, younger chap disagreed with some minor point that was raised and began quite loudly voicing his disagreement in Russian. Ego was strong with these guys, and the younger guy was questioning the authority of the older one. Voices got louder, and then the younger party began imitating a monkey. *The end result was a fistfight.* Always in Taiwan, whenever we did any kind of presentation, there was an army of people attending, ranging from very senior managers to junior operations staff.

So basically, there were many facets of the Hackers' behavior that just did not sit well with the modern corporate world—but they provided a level of technical expertise that was at the very least not incompatible to the security challenges faced by networked organizations.

The Hackers were "immature" in the way of dress codes and report writing, and yes, they did not understand the challenges faced by clients, but the answer was never to remove the Hackers from the scene altogether just because of these cosmetic issues.

I will talk more about solutions in Chapter 11, but in brief, what was missing from the time of the Hackers was effective people management. The Hackers needed an "interface" between themselves and the other inhabitants of this planet they had landed on. The answer was never for the capitalists to cast the Hackers adrift on the ocean. After all, who knows where they might end up?

3

CHECKLISTS AND
STANDARDS EVANGELISTS

"Security is no longer about people with green hair and piercings," so the message from our regional operations manager went at our incredibly expensive regional conference hosted in a five-star hotel in Bangkok, Thailand. It was Q3 2003, barely a fortnight since three of my Hacker colleagues had been fired by TSAP. The big boss had been flown in business class from the U.K. There were several members of the Australia office crew on show who had been flown in from Sydney and all put up in the same five-star hotel. Others had come from Hong Kong, Indonesia, Singapore, and Taiwan to absorb the pearls of wisdom from our management team. Overall, there were 35 regional employees at the gathering, 30 of whom were from outside Thailand, and it was intended to boost our regional sales by infusion of sales and technical knowledge.

While in silent mourning over the loss of my colleagues, I had been tasked with giving a presentation on wireless security for this regional forum. I had diligently prepared the slides only to have my presentation hijacked by my line manager who fancied a bit of the limelight—of the 35 attendees, more than half were female and under the age of 40. Most of the slides were skipped, and the only message coming from the presentation was that wireless security was all about "war walking" and if the client had access control on their wireless access points, then they were just fine. Needless to say, regional sales people went away dispassionate about our new service offering, and we did not get even a sniff of interest from clients for this service.

"Security is no longer about people with green hair and piercings." Hmm, OK. Well what is it about then? By 2003, it was becoming clearer what was happening to the industry. My Hacker friends at TSAP had been cast aside by the capitalist world to go out and find their own way in life—and being the talented people they are, they did not

47

have to wait long before other opportunities came along. What opportunities though? Of those three, and the string of others who were "phased out" before them, only two remained working with reputable firms. The others? After a few months of trying to make contact, and being greeted with general discomforted shiftiness, I stopped asking. This was a common story from the mid-2000s and beyond. Having lost their comfortable "seat" in the capitalist world, the unemployable/ unmanageable, undesirable, un-everything were not daunted. They quickly found their seat in another world, which sometimes carries the label "underworld." In fact, there are now seats in "the underworld" in the same way as there are comfortable seats on the light side of the fence. Criminal organizations, performing such business activities as trading personal data, now have hierarchical organization structures, with CEOs and internal departments specializing in different areas such as corporate spying, botnets, malware, and identity theft.

TSAP had fired most of their experienced staff, and the quality of their service had dropped to such levels that the company had become to be known in the United States as the "McDonalds of the security world." After my colleagues were fired, we had lost nearly all of our competitive advantage in the Asia–Pacific region, and the quality of our service had dropped almost to zero, but our prices had increased. We were surviving on the trust we had gained from the previous two years of service provision in the region, but that was not a bottomless pit—in fact, it was only another 18 months before the Bangkok office was dissolved and the company was "merged" (read: "acquired") by a bigger fish, with only the operations in Australia and one junior analyst (who was then also required to wear a sales hat and work an 80-hour week) being retained in each of the other countries.

TSAP's case was a tragic one, and at the time, mainly because of the company's long history of failures in people management, I thought the firing of technically gifted people was something unique to us. What I came to discover over the next five to six years was that this phenomenon was, in fact, a global epidemic.

When we look at the reasons for the poor state of information security in the world today, there is an unmistakable knock-on effect that was brought about by overcompensating for the lack of business savvy in the pre-2002 Hackers era—but I do not think this tells the whole story.

I do believe it is important to talk about the characteristics of the security professional who acquired the Hacker's seat because, after all, these people are the ones responsible for putting us where we are today, and when we talk about problems in information security, it is important to try and understand how and why those problems came about.

The second class of security professional succeeded the Hacker, and I will refer to this corporate entity as a checklists and standards evangelist (CASE)—the origin of the acronym will become clearer later in this book; please bear with me on this.

I would like to clarify that the emphasis in this chapter is on the skills sought by the industry in the post-Hacker era and the practices of modern security departments. There is no criticism of individuals in security here. To pass negative judgment on a security pro just because they do not have a background in IT makes no sense at all. The wrong skills have been channeled to the industry, and anyone caught in this wave should not be blamed for being washed ashore—there are powerful forces at work here. The security industry as a whole created a fashion out of poor management decisions; companies were losing valuable intellectual capital, but this was very much the trend—everyone was doing it.

So certainly, if I were to point a finger at anyone (which I do not), I would first acknowledge that we all have some stake in the blame, but also one does not usually blame the foot soldiers and cannon fodder (the CASEs—that I will discuss in this chapter); one blames their superior ranking officers. However, it is difficult to attribute blame because it is difficult to generalize on what went wrong with management decision-making. Valuable human resource was lost, in some cases because of vindictive political reasons (and I can bear witness to a handful of such cases), but I would not like to generalize on the motivations for these HR decisions. In other cases, the decision was down to plain old-fashioned incompetence in security management. In yet more cases, there was no logical reason at all.

With regard to the typical make-up of the CASE, in some cases, the security pro will have an extensive IT career behind them, but their security team does not actually practice IT-oriented security. There are personal behavior traits in security that have a negative effect on the business world as a whole—I have experienced these a number of times, and I have reason to believe they are commonplace in the industry. These points are worthy of criticism—but again, we all make mistakes, more so because security is still a relatively young field.

In this book, I am merely trying to explain how the industry came to be in the dire state that it is in today, and in so doing, I am obligated to discuss something about *people* in security because decisions made by human beings shape where we are today. The business world today finds different ways to avoid talking about individuals when a problem needs to be addressed, but the result of this is often just confusion. Sometimes political correctness does not work for us—it works against us. In this book, I will talk clearly in plain English about clear, unmistakable behavioral traits and skill sets in the security workplace. In our professional lives, various pressures act on human beings to do things that we know are wrong.

A large proportion, roughly 60% or so, of information security consultants and analysts that I met since roughly 2002 had no vocational technical experience in the way of programming, system administration, network administration, or any kind of technical experience. The other 40% did have a background in IT but left that behind when they started a dedicated security position.

My experiences are based on my own experience first with TSAP, then with a company which I refer to as HELL in this book (a large logistics firm—I was working as a contractor security analyst based at their Europe and Middle-East Information Technology Service Centre in Prague, Czech Republic), then with a big four consultancy (which I will refer to simply as the "Big Four"), and then with a multinational insurance firm (which I will refer to as Q). I have worked with more than 90 client organizations in my time with both TSAP, Big Four, and through my own freelance engagements.

Many of my peers in the industry have given me similar reports to my own over the years, and from what I have read in online forums and blogs, I have seen enough to suggest that my own experiences are far from an isolated story.

The reason as to why security departments need to be technically oriented may not be clear to many. That will become clear later in this book (please see Chapter 4). Just for now, I need to introduce the CASE as a framework for the rest of the book.

As I mentioned in the Introduction, the security industry started out being purely technical. The security professional was the Hacker who I introduced in Chapter 2. Then in the reaction to the perceived shortcomings of the Hacker ethic in security, the balance was shifted too far the other way. Today's security professional is, in most cases, the opposite of the Hacker. Like matter and antimatter, I did consider calling the latter-day security professional an Anti-Hacker, but it does not seem informative enough.

Many CASEs enter the security field with a background in business analysis and a master of business administration (MBA). The genre that enters security with certifications from Microsoft or Cisco is definitely the minority these days.

I have seen some tepid signs of the industry starting to try to shift the balance back to a more technical standpoint. In the U.K. job market over the past few years, some companies have been looking for more technically oriented security professionals, but quite understandably, they just wind up being confused about what requirements they should pass out to recruitment agents. A common requirement is something like "security expert with 10 years experience who can work in operations configuring Cisco devices and firewalls," so they want a person who wears two hats: a security and an operations hat. In the U.K., I doubt the number of candidates that *truthfully* meet this requirement would be as much as a three-digit number.

Overall though, at the time of writing, the security space is still very much nontechnical, and moreover, there is no real sign of a momentum shift away from this situation. I see increasing signs of frustration from security practitioners themselves, and others who have had to deal with security departments, about the lack of any really useful input from security—but these frustrations themselves will not lead to change in the industry. We still seem to be some way off even taking our first step toward improvements.

The CASE culture is defined by the activities of modern security departments, so it will help to explain the CASE tenet if I describe these activities. In the current era at the time of writing, with a CASE-oriented team, what actually does a security department in a large organization do? Well, mostly, as the acronym suggests, the team specializes in checklists and information security management standards, guidelines, and policies.

Most firms these days have a baseline information security standard that is something like the ISO 27001/2 standards, which specify at a low level of detail what an organization needs to cover and then how to implement the standard as a living process. Having developed their own version of this standard and called it a "baseline standard," they will ask senior management to sign off on this document, thereby making it a binding resolution that a security department can use to terrorize every other department in the company.

From the baseline standard, other more detailed standards and guidelines are formulated that link back to the baseline. For example, the baseline standard will state that all computing devices need an inactivity time-out on login sessions of 300 s (i.e., if the login session is idle for more than 300 s, it must be automatically closed, thereby reducing the risk of hijack by an unauthorized party), and then Unix, Windows, custom applications, Cisco, and other standards will follow this requirement and state what the actual detailed configuration should be on those platforms.

Security standards are owned by the organization as a whole, but the security team is responsible for ensuring compliance and maintenance, and if the standards cannot be followed for whatever reason (typically the reasons are not really reasons), then an exception is raised and signed off by the relevant department head.

The "security standard" is really a *checklist* of items that need to be followed, and a 200-page document that is supposed to be a Red Hat Linux security standard can be reduced down to a two-page checklist of configuration requirements.

The security standards form the bedrock of all security team activities. Other activities can be related to dealing with internal and external security auditors, responding to security incidents, implementing new products in line with the standards, and many other activities that make up an information security risk management strategy.

The security service provider is an outside party who helps their clients to meet their standards and internal/external audit requirements. This can involve, for example, remote penetration testing, performed by an independent third party, supposedly to help the organization demonstrate that perimeter security measures are sufficiently effective. This is usually a requirement of auditors.

In reality, as I will explain in Chapter 4, it is the external audit that really drives the whole shebang in security. This should not be the case, but it is in most cases. In HELL, it was the external PricewaterhouseCoopers audit that drove our entire strategy, and in Q, somewhat surprisingly, it was the internal audit that line managers cared most about. Most of my clients in the past six years or so have cared more about external audits than anything else in security.

Also in Chapter 4, I will talk about checklists in security, but just for now, the checklist is the "C" in CASE.

To further illustrate the CASE ethic in security: taking an example of security team activities, what does a nontechnical CASE do in the situation where they need to ensure Red Hat Linux security standard compliance? Because they do not have a background in Unix, they will not have been granted rights to access the Linux computers; so how can they check for compliance? To check for standards compliance, they will need top-level administrative rights, and personally, I am only aware of one case in my 11 years in security where a root password was given to a security team. Can software tools help? Remote assessment tools, such as automated vulnerability scanners and vulnerability management solutions, are ineffective (I will explain this point in Chapter 5). So all the CASE can really do is just pass the checklist to the IT operations team and hope for the best. The IT operations team will look at the list, and if they do have some sense of responsibility, they will have numerous questions and objections related to the requirements. What can the CASE do in response? The answer is, of course, not very much at all. The IT operations team will be asked to sign off blindly on the list, and the Linux boxes will not have been secured in a cost-effective way, if at all.

In many cases, the security team will just use an automated tool, organize a time window for scanning, and run the tool against the target computers and other devices. They will swear by this method as being totally effective, but in reality, it is anything but (it is actually a horrendous waste of resources, as I will explain in Chapter 5). A non-IT savvy staff member can run the automated tool. The autogenerated report from the scan will be sent to the operations teams, but the report file will be deleted without even having been opened. There is nothing vindictive about this—it is just that operations will not see any benefit in analyzing the report contents.

What should be happening in this example of Linux policy compliance is that the security team understands both the business goals of the company and the challenges faced by development teams and IT operations, and they have at least one member who knows Linux to the level of being able to do third-level support. They should also know the attack vectors against Linux, and they should personally have a track record of remotely and locally compromising Linux servers. In such a scenario, the security team can give IT operations the checklist, but then, rather than hiding in a corner and playing the silent tough guy (or tough girl), they can talk to operations in the same language (the language of IT as opposed to the language of buzzwords and ISO standards) and reach compromises on what can be achieved in line with business goals.

Platform Security in HELL

As another scenario that serves to detail the CASE paradigm, in this section, I will cover my experiences of [trying] to implement Linux platform security in HELL, and there will be some background information regarding network architecture and risk assessment.

For the time frame of mid-2000s, HELL's story is typical for a firm that was not subject to regulatory compliance. HELL's security departments (there were more than one of them) were CASE teams. HELL was a global organization with data centers in Prague, Scottsdale (AZ), and Kuala Lumpur. Their security organization top layer was a global security team who were supposed to coordinate security initiatives globally, but there was not much coordination going on as far as I could tell. Then there were local security teams in each data center. I was a contractor engaged as a security analyst in the Prague data center.

Prague security was made up of security professionals from varying backgrounds. The global team was quite frankly almost completely inactive. When I arrived in the company, I asked a few people what the global team was doing and got blank expressions as an answer. Their role seemed to be to initiate policy development but not actually contribute anything to that initiative other than sign off on policies at the final stage of review and take all the credit.

There was a member of the global team in Kuala Lumpur who had initiated the development of a Linux security standard. Upon completion, the first draft was sent to myself for review. Without wanting to be too critical, let's just say I had to rewrite most of the content and then add some material relating to critical aspects of Linux security. The final policy was predominantly the one I had written with no further amendments after my review, but my name was omitted from the list of contributors. Of course, it could be that he just forgot to include me—I always try to give the benefit of the doubt in these cases.

The network architecture at HELL was not unlike the model set by many multinationals, including many financial institutions. The network was a DMZ with external and internal firewalls (with hot-swap backup firewalls for availability reasons), and then the rest of the network was essentially a private, ten-dot addressed internal network, with no internal security segregation. Implementation of internal network security segregation can be disruptive and expensive, but also has huge long-term advantages in terms of cost savings in security. Furthermore, as time marches on, internal threats from malware and social engineering are becoming more prevalent (U.S. consulting firm HBgary in 2011 spoke of the "advanced persistent threat" in security—an older phrase related to intelligence gathering), and internal network access controls are consequently ever more critical (i.e., "layers" are needed; if there has been a compromise of one system, hopefully it would not transparently lead to the compromise of everything).

The Prague data center served many other countries in the region, and there were no firewalls between countries and the data center. Many of the country networks had no security whatsoever, apart from outdated antivirus software. So it was possible to sit in an office in Moscow and connect directly to an Oracle database in the Prague data center (and database security was another story—just for now, I will say it was bad and leave it at that).

One of the consequences of this open network architecture was that if one internal device was compromised, the whole network would be wide open to attack. If there was a worm outbreak in the office in Algiers, it could easily propagate to the entire internal network.

The network architecture was a problem that we were aware of, and also external auditors had raised it as a highly critical issue. Many companies globally have serious network architecture problems such as these, and in more than 90% of cases, decision makers have not been given a solid enough business/risk case for phasing out these problems—so naturally, they just leave it alone/sweep it under the carpet. To be fair, it is also a very complex, disruptive, and expensive problem to solve in most cases, and hence, there had better be sufficient justification for change.

One item of security where we had some influence was platform security, and of course, with such a wide-open network, it was critical to take a look at this area.

Aside from the architectural point, the Linux security program was important not only because external auditors told us we had to bridge the gaps, but also from the more down-to-earth perspective that more than 70% of all existing applications were hosted on Linux, all new applications would require a Linux server build, and there was an overall drive in the company to migrate to the commercial open-source operating system of Red Hat.

There were more than 500 instances of servers running Linux in Prague—all of them wide open to untrusted networks and hence the criticality of the Linux security program. I got talking with the network infrastructure team members first, and then IT operations came later. I had developed sufficient trust to get a root password (root, or super-user, is the most privileged user account in Unix systems) and kicked off the assessment program. Later on, I compiled a report of my findings from the assessment.

The network infrastructure team managed a series of Linux machines that were in production for Web proxy-ing, Lightweight Directory Access Protocol, and a variety of other purposes—they were fairly critical devices for HELL. I was informed, however, that I was the first person in security since the start of the operation in Prague to have engaged with the network team.

Prior to my involvement in Linux security in Prague, the IT and network operations teams had made their own security fixes. They were very knowledgeable, conscientious, and enthusiastic IT staff that all had at least some interest in security. In some cases, they had overdone the security hardening; in most cases, there were some gaping holes—but generally, operations teams cannot be expected to know enough about security to efficiently meet the challenges in security by themselves (I will talk about this point in more detail in Chapter 4).

Network operations staff told me they learned a great deal from the security program, and from that point on, whenever they were planning changes in infrastructure, they would come to security rather than the usual situation wherein security has to chase other teams, who over the years had become experts in security department evasion tactics.

IT operations were at first a very difficult team to deal with mainly because there was a mistrust that came from several years of security teams just blocking developments without really understanding the business or administrative challenges faced. But once again, when it became clear that we could speak the language of technical security and we were all on the same side, changes in Linux standard operating system builds and existing platforms went ahead smoothly in phases. Again, I had been given a root/super-user login, and I was able to monitor everything myself.

With these two Linux projects, a very rare phenomenon was witnessed—a security department was actually doing something useful. No time-wasting automated scans were performed, people in operations were inspired by security rather than annoyed by it, and no expensive snake oil products were purchased. Security initiatives were documented and implemented that would last into the future, and the overall cost to the company was only the labor cost for myself and a few operations personnel—with the project lasting roughly six weeks.

What happened when the global team discovered that we had actually met some of our audit requirements in Linux security? Let us just say it was very far from cigars and champagne in the global security team area on the fourth floor of the Prague Information Technology Service Center (ITSC). Because we had actually achieved something in the local security team, we had raised the bar, and in a relative light, the global team saw themselves as being under pressure to rise to the challenge of security. They were not happy at all, but of course, it was inappropriate to voice concerns openly.

A few weeks later, there was a time when our local security team manager was away. The ITSC security manager was almost the most senior manager in the Prague global team contingent, and oddly enough, he volunteered to step in for our line manager for our weekly team meeting. During the meeting, he addressed the whole team, but the comments were aimed at myself: "we do not go around the data center logging into servers and making people's lives difficult," and later "you had better look after your seats"—so here was a not-too-subtle threat of being fired if we continued to address security concerns in a cost-effective manner, a warning that was aimed at all of us. Some of the more junior team members were visibly worried about this.

I have witnessed acts of cowardice like this from CASEs, driven by insecurity, many times in my career. This is unfortunately a common phenomenon in the industry, where CASEs actually work against security initiatives.

There was one member of the Prague global team who had come into the team from a technical background from a major local bank. When we were kicking off our Oracle security program, I spoke to him because I was aware of his background. He quite rightly told me that there are no tools out there, even commercial, that can really do the job for you in Oracle security assessments—you have to piece together your own Structured Query Language (a language used for administration and for running queries on databases) script. He clearly did know something about Oracle security, but we did not get any support from the global team for our program. This is another common CASE story—even when someone does come into the company with some technical knowledge, they stop being a techie and start being a CASE, sometimes because of peer pressure, other times because of a lack of motivation to actually achieve something in their job (this is not unique to security and there is a catchphrase for this situation— "how can I soar like an eagle when I'm surrounded by turkeys?").

CASE Survival Guidelines

As the name suggests, the CASE specializes in checklists, and in most cases, they will know their own internal security standards and policies, and perhaps some international standards—which are all effectively checklists in themselves. Their main job function is to assess future and existing infrastructure for the purpose of policy compliance, but as I have explained, the degree to which they are in a position to assess the security of *information* is somewhat hampered by a lack of experience in *information* technology. The thing is: CASEs are aware of this conundrum themselves.

CASEs are all educated people. They all come from university or at least some sort of higher educational backgrounds—and it does not take much intelligence to know that if you are employed to help maintain the confidentiality, integrity, and availability of information processed and stored by computers, then your job function at the entry level has to have some sort of IT component to it (I talk in more details about careers in information security in Chapter 6), at least some component that is more than passing checklists to other departments, quoting standards, running automated software tools, and dealing with audits. It is this self-awareness that we humans possess that tells the CASE that something is wrong with their job function. I have come across many cases where security pros have openly shown signs of frustration with their job function, and many are just plain bored. There were a few who told me that they like their jobs but could not tell me why.

In all cases, there will be some insecurity with CASEs that comes from the knowledge that they carry a negative perception in the eyes of other departments (especially IT operations, networking teams, and development crews), and also from their own reflective viewpoint—but open shows of insecurity are guaranteed to condemn you to eternal damnation when it comes to judgment day. There is the old adage about "how can others respect you when you don't even respect yourself?" But in information security, it can be hard to find respect for oneself just from your job function—or lack of a job function.

Obviously not something that is unique to security is the way that corporate people handle situations in which they are expected to give an answer, but they are not in a position to give one because of a lack of background knowledge in the case at hand. Generally, the response will be a lack of response—but it is still possible to say a lot without moving one's lips. The key is the manner in which you are silent. There is a certain *je ne sais quoi* with being silent that all who have become managers will have learned at an early stage—and it is really just the duplicity of learning how to *appear* dignified and confident, even though you are anything but.

The skill of duplicity and maintaining an air of confidence when being silent is critical in the CASE world. When you are handing the development project team a corporate policy mandate that says their application must have two-factor authentication, but you are unable to justify this potentially resource-intensive requirement, you need to know how to counter the protestations of the development team who, to be honest, were aware of the two-factor requirement anyway (but rightly or wrongly, they do not see a significant risk if two-factor authentication is not deployed). Usually, the CASE will deal with this just by being silent and neutral—and in order to progress up the ladder in security, being neutral is a great skill to possess. Some would say neutral, others would say stubborn and unhelpful, but by being silent, the CASE hopes to convey that they do not need to answer the protestations of the other departments to whom they are blindly imposing "mandatory" standards "signed off by senior management."

What I have just described to you sounds like a grim portrayal of corporate information security life, but I can assure you, it is endemic in information security departments. If you are skilled in the art of appearing confident while not answering emails, never contributing anything in meetings or teleconferences, not answering phone calls, and generally being neutral (as the British would say, "keeping a straight bat"), then you have a promising career ahead of you in information security.

You may be thinking, how does this work? Surely with such behavior, it will not be long before you are looking for a new job. But what if your line manager and their line manager are also CASE-oriented and experts at being silent? You see, this is a contagious disease. If you come into a silent security department such as the one I have just described, you will find yourself under pressure to conform to the code of silence or you will be seen as treading on toes and generally you will not fit in. If you start trying to actually improve security, you will experience something akin to what I experienced at HELL as I described earlier in this chapter.

CASEs and Network Security

The way that modern security departments deal with network security issues (such as firewall configuration) is another example of the CASE modus operandi.

"Technical" has been a four-letter word for most security professionals for more than a decade now, but there is no mandate carved in stone in any organizations' list of commandments that says that the information security department team members will not spend any time in a freezing machine room and will not get involved with nasty computers and command shells, and there are not even any subtle hints to the effect that IT operations will do all the technical work in security. There is nothing in a company's manifesto that says network operations will be responsible for configuring firewalls and intrusion detection systems (IDSs)—it is just something that oozes out of the rather wide cracks of the security department.

Frankly, the skills do not exist in security departments to handle matters such as configuring firewalls. As an independent consultant, I have seen documents passed to network operations teams from security, supposedly to give them guidelines on the firewall rules configuration. In the vast majority of cases, the document was actually worthless—just loosely stating guidelines copied and pasted from Wikipedia—something along the lines "the firewall must have a default-deny policy and not permit any unneeded ports or addresses."

Generally speaking, even if the security department does have some level of knowledge in networking and firewalls, it is unfamiliar with the network architecture or applications, and so is not in a position to make a detailed review of a firewall configuration.

Security Teams and Incident Investigation

The CASEs ruled the waves for the past decade in security, and during this time, there had been some interesting developments in the way that firms handle incident investigation. Incident management and forensics serve as a further illustration of the activities of modern security departments.

Most of the time, security department managers are skilled politicians, and they are quite often able to "teflon" IT-related tasks to other departments, with some loose arguments about the task not actually being related to security.

For new people coming into IT operations who have yet to discover the joys of working with the security team, there is one area that really does at first appear to have security's name on it—security incident investigation. There is a snag though—because security teams do not have an abundance of IT skills, they will not have been granted access to IT resources such as computers and routers, so how can they do the investigation themselves [and although some firms have deployed a log correlation solution from the security information event management (SIEM) product family, it is usually the IT or network operations staff who have responsibility for the management and monitoring of SIEM]?

To be fair, there are some security pros who do know something about security incident management and investigation, and in firms who are lucky enough to have such people on their books, you will quite often see initial attempts by security at remotely managing the incident (hands-off) while directing other departments in the case. However, this approach does not work. There is a language incompatibility between modern security departments and operations. Communications break down, and operations handle the incident independently.

In the blame game that follows an incident, this is one area in which security is usually unable to dodge the bullet because senior management will see the word "security" in "security incident." As a result of this, in recent years, there has been an increase in requirements sent to recruitment agents for people with skills in "forensics" or candidates with the word "incident" on their CV. Indeed, a U.K. recruitment agent recently told me, "We have seen broad growth in the forensics and investigations space, where over the last 18 months there have been a number of acquisitions and the growth of specialist consultancies focused purely within the forensics area."

The results of recruitment agency searches for forensics experts are varied. In most cases, there was insufficient expertise on the side of the potential employer to know what type of candidate would work for them, candidates only have generic security accreditations (I will talk in more detail about accreditations in Chapter 11), and there is always a lot of confusion and "last-minute dot com" changes in requirements.

Generally, the results of going to head hunters and looking for forensics experts are varied. Some pros that I met knew EnCase inside out, but had no systems expertise, and they were missing the finer aspects of actually managing incidents, gathering evidence, dealing with the computer incident response team (if one exists), and dealing with operations teams. Then there were those who knew the theory but not the practice. Also, there were those who knew very little about anything. I do not want to put numbers to these categories at this stage because I have already painted enough doom and gloom in this chapter.

Security is a young industry, and there is no internationally accepted framework for defining what is needed in incident management and investigation—so it is hardly surprising that organizations have gaps in their response capability, but certainly deploying an individual in incident response with little or no IT experience is not the way to go.

Probably the best solution is to use a security analyst for this area (one who knows penetration testing and major core technologies such as Windows, Cisco, and Unix). The specialized forensics/incident handling knowledge acquisition is not a great stretch for experienced analysts with a broad IT background. Anyway, I will cover the skills aspect in Chapter 11.

Vulnerability/Malware Announcements

Another fine example of the dangers of inappropriate skills deployment in security comes in the area of handling recently discovered software vulnerabilities.

Many security departments and service providers will monitor for security alerts such as vulnerability and exploit announcements from Packet Storm (http://packetstormsecurity.org), vendors, and other sources, and then coordinate a response with other departments—usually IT and network operations.

I can relate one case with a CASE department in a major global bank that illustrates what can go wrong when inappropriate skills are deployed in this area.

Cutting some detail, around 2006, there was a Microsoft security announcement regarding vulnerability with most popular flavors of Microsoft Windows at the time. The global security team was composed mainly of compliance-oriented staff. The CISO asked the only chap who had any technical experience to formulate an email and circulate it globally. Quoting the email about this vulnerability: "Please inform your NOCs to watch closely port 4444 for potential attacks by the new exploit to MS06-040 vulnerability. I already spoke to [censored] and they saw some suspicious connections on this port and they are currently investigating it. Please let me know any updates on this topic."

Problems with this are numerous. First, the "attack" was actually against the Windows Server Message Block (SMB) services via port 139 TCP (among others) and the service with Common Internet File System (CIFS) support on port 445 (TCP). If the exploit is successful, there will be a "backdoor" listening on port 4444 TCP. So really, *if there has already been a successful attack*, there could be a connection attempt to port 4444 (i.e., if there is a "suspicious" connection, as it said in the email alert, to port 4444, then the server has already been compromised).

Now, in theory, although not very likely, this email could be vaguely useful from the point of view of detection—as in, we can now tell our IDS (more on intrusion detection in Chapter 9) to watch out for connection attempts to port 4444. But really what is missing is how to prevent this attack in the first place (by the way, to this point in time, Microsoft was yet to release a "patch" for this vulnerability), and given that not even a CASE-oriented company allows connections from the public Internet to ports 139/445, and that there is no vulnerability if anonymous connections to SMB services are disabled (the SMB services permit unauthenticated connections by default—also known as "NULL sessions"), then it is quite possible to use technical means to work around this vulnerability.

There is a fixation with port 4444 TCP in this case, but the port number used can be any port above 1024 (depending on the privileges gained as a result of a successful exploit). The attacker can remotely "port scan" from outside the network and detect "closed" but not "filtered" ports (i.e., ports for which there is no active listening service, but also the firewall does not block access to said port). The attacker can then change the binding port number in her "shellcode" accordingly, so that incoming remote connections to her backdoor may be possible from "outside" the private network (although in most cases, it will not be possible to make a direct connection—unless there is some network address translation (NAT) in place that facilitates routing to the target from "outside" the network).

So in the aforementioned case, the really critical part of this security problem was missed, and that can pose what will be in most business cases an unacceptable risk.

This Land Is Our Land

Another relatively common trait with CASEs is one of disputes over territory as in "security is 'ours', not yours, hands off!" From more than 10 years in security, I can personally bare witness to several exhibitions of chest beating and territorial claims.

The arrival of the CASE in security was born out of two major factors. One was the aesthetic appeal of the CASE, in that they wore suits and ties and they fitted in to modern corporate environments. The CASE is a talker, not a doer, but in the early days after the end of the Hackers, senior management was happy to have the CASEs around; after all, they looked and sounded the part, and they were supposedly more trustworthy—whereas the Hackers they succeeded would quite happily swear at a senior manager because he or she was using a laptop with a Microsoft Windows operating system rather than some open-source Unix variant.

The other factor was about territorial disputes, and in these battles, the Hackers were guaranteed to lose mainly because they had no interest or motivation to play political games.

From my own experiences and from combing various media sources, several points repeat themselves when CASEs talk about technical input in security, and many will openly criticize the Hacker fraternity, labeling them as "geeks," "IT bods," or "propellor heads." The agenda of many CASEs I met was secretly, or sometimes quite openly, to exclude the more technically oriented from the security picture in their company, with some pretense about a lack of any need for technical input in security. There was also a commonly quoted adage that was repeated with minor variations: "security is all about awareness and standards, there is no threat from outside the network, the only threats are from inside" (if this is the case, then is there no need for external firewalls?).

Additionally cryptology is a stick that is often used by the CASE to beat the Hacker. There is a common slur aimed at Hackers: "amateurs study cryptography, professionals study economics." This line is actually a chapter heading in *The New School of Information Security* (Shostack and Stewart), but I do not believe the authors intended any criticism of Hackers. Without really knowing why, the CASE has become aware of the decreasing significance of the mathematics of crypto algorithms. Usually in real-life business situations, public crypto algorithms such as triple DES will be used, the business challenge of encryption is really in key management, and who cares about the math behind it all (although this is a real concern for application security specialists in highly sensitive situations where a custom algorithm has been used)? If an attacker is going to gain unauthorized access to private data, there are usually easier ways of doing it than brute forcing/exploiting holes in crypto algorithms and so on and so forth.

The thing is, though, I have never come across a Hacker who even once ranted about mathematics and encryption algorithms, so who is this mythical Hacker who is less in touch with reality than his or her CASE counterpart?

As a further illustrator of territorial claims: there was an article on the securityfocus.com Website from 2007 from a chap with a square head and a stern grimace. The article was basically about the lack of the right to exist for the Hacker. "We," meaning mature, adult consultants, "have access" to "upper levels of management," whereas (according to the author) Hackers have severe problems with ego, talk like children, and must be prevented from having access to senior management. "We" can do everything, we can talk, and we can also talk to senior managers. This is our land, not the Hackers' land. There was a real anger in the article directed at Hackers and their supposed ego problems (this last part is not without foundation, as I stated in Chapter 2, but ego was also the motivating force for the author's outburst).

It is true that CASEs have access to senior management whereas Hackers do not, but a look at the state of infosec today should indicate that perhaps this unique privilege granted to CASEs is not benefitting our economic security.

From my experience, Hackers do have ego, but it is usually (not in all cases) a positive ego—one that pushes them on to learn and achieve more. With the CASEs, ego has a destructive edge. It is an ego that works against others in their own organizations, and it serves only to divide the security world into two camps—good guys and "bad guys," "white hats" and black hats, ethical and "unethical," adults and "kids," "felons" and law-abiding citizens, and so on. The same ego has worked to reduce the Hacker camp to its current-day population of less than 10% of the whole. It is this ego that is partly responsible for the de-engineering of security over the past decade.

Common CASE Assertions

There are many assertions from CASEs that you will hear repeatedly in some form or another.

A common scenario is one where you have several security analysts with similar time-served numbers in security—and there are one or two analysts in the team who came from a technical background. The CASE element in the team will proclaim themselves to be more senior than the other contingent—they are "more of a manager," even though the word "management" does not appear anywhere on the list of their roles and responsibilities.

A CASE is also often a self-proclaimed Hacker, "but I grew out of it." The reality, however, is usually one of, in the words of a Hungarian former work colleague, "[he] has never seen a command prompt in his life." Of course, it is only the senior manager, and more generally any non-Hacker, who will get to hear this line about "I was once was a Hacker." Security managers are especially adept at convincing others in the company that they were, and still are, an IT expert with enough knowledge and experience to get back into IT at the drop of a hat.

One CASE (a security analyst) I can remember from HELL was mostly involved with business continuity and he felt there was no need for any technical input in this area (more on this in Chapter 6). He told us he was an HP-UX (Hewlett Packard's flavor of Unix) administrator earlier in his career but could not tell us which version of HP-UX he was familiar with, or even for what purpose the company was using HP-UX. He saw himself as a manager and got quite angry whenever anyone started using the language of IT in meetings—his assertion was that such talk was a waste of time and that security was all about management and "processes." The technical side of security was, according to our colleague, something which "I used to do and can do today easily—it's a job a monkey can do."

In my team I was one of two security analysts with technical experience, and between us, we had facilitated good relations with IT operations and other IT departments—a relationship that allowed us to meet audit requirements and keep my line manager in a job. However, our esteemed colleague felt we had no right to be in his team. His main line in this regard was another common assertion from CASEs in security and that is that anything technical to do with security is an area for IT operations (I will go into this in more detail in Chapter 4).

Recently, I have seen an article from a leading figure in the U.K. information security scene. In his article from 2010, he was bemoaning the fact that security functions are heavily devolved to other IT departments, and the other departments call the shots on areas such as firewall configuration, IDS configuration, log management, identity management, and most other areas for that matter. Whereas this is an observation I would concur with, and it is encouraging to see someone else identifying this problem, I am not sure if he was aware that it was actually security departments who engineered this situation themselves, and given the current lack of relevant skills in security departments, this devolved model is really the only way of doing security for at least the near future.

Surely it is understandable that security functions are migrated to other IT teams. Picture the following scene: there is a network operations staff member who has responsibility for firewalls and IDS. A security staff member comes to her and asks for administrative access for the devices she manages. Naturally enough, she asks for evidence of management experience with those devices. Her firewall is a checkpoint firewall, and she rightly demands to see a checkpoint certificate. The security staff member has no such accreditation. She rightly refuses access to her machines. She may be making up the rules herself, but she is taking the correct stance nonetheless, and fair play to her.

Summary

In Chapter 2, I covered the characteristics of the Hacker, and on a similar vein, in this chapter, I have covered some examples of life in modern security practices, so as to illustrate the characteristics of the CASE.

It is difficult to generalize the CASE skill set, but roughly speaking, it is defined by the activities of modern security departments. In many cases, CASEs do not have any background in IT at all (and as I have I said, this is purely subjective; there is no shame in this); in other cases, they do—but this is irrelevant. The practices of the modern security department are not technical or analytical in nature, so who cares if the entry-level security pro comes from an IT background?

Maybe the CASE does have a significant IT background (in fact, when you see requirements sent out to head hunters for open security positions, you will often see reference to technical skill requirements such as Cisco certs and so on), but the mandate of the security department can lead to CASEs abandoning their IT careers for a career in the security world of today (the two are mutually exclusive). There is no real mandate for security departments to be too analytical in their approach—so they will not be analytical.

Information security is still in its infancy, and mistakes will be made in the earlier years. We can make an analogy with biology and natural growth, but I tend to agree with a growing number of people in security who believe we have at best gone sideways and that security is "broken."

The late 1990s saw the first actual dedicated infosec departments in some of the bigger organizations (which were composed mainly of people from IT operations who had at least some interest in security), and many of the new security service provider firms were hiring Hackers as network penetration testers. So the first security professionals were heavily technically oriented—I referred to them in Chapter 2 as "Hackers," and that is the name they go by in this narrative.

What happened after that, partly as a result of the perceived failings of the Hacker ethic, was an overcompensation in the way of almost totally removing *information* technology skills from the business of protecting the confidentiality, integrity, and availability of *information* that is critical to businesses. This was the beginning of the de-engineering of security.

I can hear many readers saying, "So what actually is the problem with removing technical skills from security practices? There are technical experts in IT operations teams and other IT departments. Security is not all about IT. Can't security just *manage processes* and let the others in IT handle the technical work?" The short answer is yes, you can do this (and the majority of large organizations do exactly this), but the result will be a failure of the information security department to manage information risk because it will have lost its ability to support governance with information assets.

Can IT operations staff handle security effectively? Operations staff generally have very different skill sets than the late 1990s Hackers—and I will detail in Chapter 4 the gaps between the skill set of the typical IT operations practitioner and the skills that are needed to efficiently manage information security risk.

Roughly from 2001 onward, the CASE started to increase in number in the security arena. CASEs now occupy over 80% of all seats in the global information security professional arena.

The function of modern security departments and hence the role of the CASE can be approximately summed up as follows: the team specializes in checklists and information security management standards and policies. The team creates security policies, which are really just checklists, and uses these to enforce security controls, and then it attempts to monitor policy compliance using tools such as vulnerability management software and others such as security event correlation tools. There are other areas that a security team may be responsible for, such as coordinating with internal or external auditors.

While the aforementioned roles and responsibilities sound like they could form an effective baseline from which to manage information security risk, there is a problem with just administering checklists to other departments in the organization. As Bruce Schneier has stated, "security is complex." Organizations face complex business and technological challenges. Costs can come from unexpected areas. Security teams really should not be just blindly handing out checklists of *mandatory* standards requirements without understanding the challenges faced (I will talk in more detail about checklists in Chapter 4) by other departments and the business as a whole.

Parrot-fashion recital of checklists to development teams and operations is not something that can inspire a security analyst to greatness. They are aware that they are causing other departments a great deal of frustration when they are blindly asking them to implement security controls. The analysts are not in a position to explain why the controls are needed, or how they might be implemented, and they are not in a position to discuss compromises or workarounds on security issues. Inwardly reflecting, this situation causes a lot of frustration with many security pros.

The CASE phenomenon was born from a combination of two factors. Compared with the scruffy Hacker who had no sense of dress code, communication, or any respect for authority, the CASE was aesthetically appealing and trustworthy in the eyes of senior management. The other factor was the territorial claim of the CASE, and in many cases, political arguments were used to oust the Hacker. In any political case, Hackers will always lose because they have no political motivations. This claim of territory is not common to all CASEs, but it was sufficiently prevalent to contribute in splitting the security world in two, with the largest part (today it is more than 80% of the pie) occupied by the CASE. Partly as a result of this dichotomy, some other divisive terms and phrases were born in security such as good guys and "bad guys," white hats and "black hats," ethical and "unethical," adults and "kids," "felons" and law-abiding citizens.

CASE security professionals are invariably coming into security with university degrees or some sort of higher education qualification, and most CASE security pros are very unhappy with their jobs. They are aware themselves that their hands are tied in the way of really being able to contribute anything useful. Indeed, even if the security department hires a highly skilled technical expert, various political pressures will prevent them from being effective in risk management (I gave a brief account of my own experience in this chapter whereby I was threatened with dismissal for facilitating a cost-effective solution for Linux platform security in one of my previous lives).

I realize I may have come over as painting a bleak picture in this chapter and for that I apologize, but sometimes you really cannot find a way to transform a bleak picture in a rosier one, or a half-empty cup into a half-full cup. Even in the Hacker era, security was never a pretty picture, and it probably will not be for some time to come yet.

At the bleakest end of the scale, I am sorry to say that some security departments only exist because an external big four auditor has told the company there should be a security team with a manager and people who perform distinct roles. In these cases, the ineffectiveness of the security department is something that has come from way above the clouds, from a C-level up there somewhere. Their mandate is that just like the old adage with little children, security should be *seen and not heard*, and, in other cases, "just get us through the security audit without blocking anything that makes us money."

Suffice it to say I do sympathize with the majority of CASEs in security. Many of my work colleagues over the last decade were

CASEs, and they were a pleasure to work with. The majority did not know what they were in for when they signed up for a life in security, and then, when they had already started in security, they knew they did not really want to take a CASE career path; but various pressures from within their professional lives, and some from their personal lives, made them feel helpless to make a vocational change—so admirably they just "got on with it."

The post-Hacker agenda for security was put in place by powerful forces, and once started in motion, it quickly gained the momentum of a freight train. People entering the security world at this time would almost be forced into the CASE agenda, and in most cases, there was little they could do about it other than resign.

The security world has so far got it wrong with the skills it thinks are necessary to facilitate cost-effective information risk management—but the end is not nigh. We are not done yet. Things can improve, hopefully they will, and preferably in our lifetimes.

SECTION 2
THE DE-ENGINEERING OF SECURITY

4
HOW SECURITY CHANGED POST 2000

In the introduction and also the previous two chapters I have written briefly regarding changes in security over the past decade and more, I have introduced the security professionals involved: the Hacker and the Hacker's successor—the CASE.

To better understand the problems in modern information security risk management, we need to understand how and why the problems were introduced. Back in the pre-2000s Hacker era, security was very far from perfect, but the changes that took place roughly from 2002 onward certainly did not lead to improvements; instead, things seemed to get worse, with organizations spending increasingly more on security products and personnel, with little or no return.

In this chapter, I cover some of the most detrimental changes in security practices in recent times.

Migrating South: Osmosis of Analysis Functions to Operations Teams

A common scenario in modern-day corporate information security practices is to pass off any technical analysis work to other IT departments, in particular, IT operations. Under the remit of many IT and network operations teams are tasks such as vulnerability assessment and mitigation, firewall configuration, secure network design, policy compliance activities, security information and event management (SIEM) configuration and operation, intrusion detection system (IDS) deployment and configuration, antivirus deployment and management, and others.

I was a security analyst at HELL between 2005 and 2006, and several times in my department, CASE team members tried to engineer a situation where actual analysis work that involved nasty computers and networks was passed off to IT operations. In these cases, it is rarely clear what the real motivation behind these devolvement issues is. Do the people involved really believe that it is in the interests of the organization to pass analysis functions to IT operations? Or is something else going on? There is little doubt in this—the answer is the second option. CASEs may not understand what benefits are brought with analysis functions such as vulnerability assessment or application security assessment, but the least that is understood about these functions, the least qualified the person is to be able to say for sure that another department should be carrying out these functions.

In HELL, with several analysts, the real agenda was to rid their department of any activities that made them look underqualified. The illusion that was created in order to help them realize their goal was to the effect "security is a management" function; IT-related activities were activities for more "junior staff" and should be handled by IT operations. The security department was self-labeled a service management function and should handle "processes" (whatever that meant), "governance" (?), and disaster recovery/business continuity planning (DR/BCP)—these were supposedly functions for managers—even if they are handled by entry-level security analysts.

This smoke-and-mirrors approach to power devolvement in security departments has been widespread for at least eight years. Of those responsible for fobbing off analysis functions to other IT teams, very few can honestly say that they were doing it "synergistically" in the best interests of the organization. I mean there is no science in the decision-making. CASEs behind these decisions are unsure of the potential fall-out from handing over all IT-related tasks to nonsecurity staff—but they are prepared to take the risk anyway. The benefits outweigh the potential risks, at least from the point of view of their own personal risks, as in the risks to their career.

There is no narcissism in this discussion about skill sets in security compared with other IT departments. Anyone can learn anything. An IT operations staff member may be a Hacker (in the Chapter 2 sense) in disguise. But for the sake of this book, we need to talk about typical skill sets that are found in larger organizations such as Fortune 500s and multinational banks. In the case of most "developed" places, certainly in the case of the U.K., the typical skill set is that covered by the administrators' training course. Certainly from what I have seen in the U.K., if there is no training course, there are no skills. If there is no training course, there is an arms-crossed approach that says, "If I haven't had the training, I can't do the job." With this in mind, we can use the framework of the training course material to discuss "typical" skills in IT operations departments.

There is also no territorial dispute here. If the right skills exist in IT operations to be able to manage risk in sync with business goals, then that is fine; let IT operations handle the whole security function. We are just talking about *typical* names of departments/service provision unit (SPUs); the name is not important—but the business as usual (BAU) activities of the organization as a whole *are* important. If a C-level has ambitions of scrapping the security department (which actually did happen in at least a handful of cases after the onset of the 2008 recession), that is fine by me—but certain functions need to remain that are critical to all large organizations, and many small/medium sized enterprises (SMEs) to boot.

Of course, the main drive of this section is to describe the differences between typical IT operations skills (system administration and support) and the skills required to implement and maintain a cost-effective information risk management program. I am not lamenting the passing of security functions to IT operations, in fact far from it; with the current status quo and CASE security teams, IT operations staff are better qualified to handle security analysis. Moreover, when security issues are uncovered in vulnerability assessment, IT operations are best placed to address the issues because of their intimate knowledge of complex production system dependencies (there rarely is such a thing as an easy fix in security). But there is a big difference between typical IT operations skills and the security skills that *should* be present.

If a security team has a notion of passing security analysis and administration functions to IT operations, from the C-level perspective, such an idea may not at first appear to be so flawed. I mean systems administrators *do* know something about security, and they are "IT'y."

A typical Unix system administrator understands issues such as Unix file permissions and ownership. Unix administration course material will have a section on security that is particular to that flavor of Unix. Likewise Microsoft administrators will cover new technology filesystem (NTFS) permissions and other less-important areas, Oracle database administrators (DBAs) will know about Oracle security features, and Cisco experts will have covered areas such as privilege levels, password encryption issues, and so on.

I mentioned earlier in this section about devolvement of the vulnerability assessment function to IT operations from security. With today's status quo in security, operations are better placed to handle vulnerability assessment, but there are nonetheless some shortcomings in the typical portfolio of skills in IT operations. Looking at an example scenario whereby a Cisco device has been the subject of vulnerability assessment by an IT operations team (by use of an automated assessment scanner): a Web HyperText Transfer Protocol (HTTP) and telnet service were discovered, and the autoscanner reports the classic eavesdropping issue with plain-text telnet. The autoscanner also reports vulnerabilities with the HTTP service, and some time later, IT operations will pass the report to network operations. Network operations know that the HTTP service is never used, so they happily disable it without raising a change record—and this is OK (I never heard of a case where the Web-based interface was used to perform admin tasks). What about the telnet service? There will be some questions about this. Most network ops staff will know that secure shell is a better alternative (one that offers encryption) to telnet, but also secure shell places a performance hit on network devices, and also some slightly older versions of Cisco IOS (the "operating system" used by most Cisco network devices) do not even support secure shell. At any stage here, will there have been any contact with the security team, perhaps to discuss the risks/threats involved? No, because in most cases, the security team will not be in a position to address technical queries or address any related concerns. More generally, the security team will not be in a position to tell operations staff anything they do not already know (the pearls of wisdom from security will in most cases be something along the lines "telnet is a plain-text protocol and *best practices* suggest it should be replaced by secure shell").

The outcome of the aforementioned telnet vulnerability analysis is unpredictable and can vary from organization to organization. Most will just leave the issue alone, but there will be some who go ahead and implement secure shell even if there is a significant performance trade-off. Some will spend extravagantly to upgrade their entire network infrastructure to both support secure shell and also implement a secure shell public/private key encryption architecture with negligible performance trade-offs—and the recommendation to do this will have come from the head of network operations (nothing to do with the security department). The change record/project initiative will have security sign-off after a cursory glance over by a CASE analyst lasting approximately 10 minutes; there will be no objection from security, and the project will be implemented with nice, unobstructed involvement from the security department.

I have just described what actually happens in most real scenarios, but what *should* happen? This depends on several main factors. There is certainly no definitive answer here as to which of the three example options works best. Sometimes it can be perfectly fine to do nothing—but it is important to ask the right questions and get educated answers. That did not happen in the case study covered here. When teams that typically deal with IT support and administration handle security functions, bad things are likely to happen.

Remembering the Schneier mantra about complexity in security, there will never be a "right answer" for this problem because there are many thousands of variables in the equation—but with knowledge of some of the more influential variables in the equation, we can at least cut down some of the risk without spending too much.

The main variables of the risk mitigation decision-making process are not covered by standard IT administration course material. Take Unix as an example; the typical administrator will have knowledge of Unix file ownership and permissions, but which files and directories need special attention when it comes to file permissions? Again this depends partly on the threats, and security threats are not covered in Unix administration training courses. IT operations staff will not (by default) have any knowledge at all about how an attacker raises local privileges in an attempt to "root" or compromise the computer.

Attackers may have used a previously undisclosed vulnerability/exploit to gain a local shell "presence" on a business-critical Oracle Solaris (a flavor of Unix) server. What they will do next is find ways to elevate their privileges to that of "root" (although it is not always necessary for an attacker to gain root privileges in order to achieve their goal)." The standard approach is an intelligence gathering operation to look for privilege escalation opportunities. This will usually involve finding anything owned, or running under root privileges, as well as a variety of other things such as "world writable" directories, scheduled job permissions, and password hashes from the /etc/passwd file.

"Setuid root" privileges are especially interesting for Hackers in these local privilege escalation cases. The setuid bit for a root-owned program gives the program root privileges when it runs, regardless of which user executes the program. So, in brief, if an attacker can exploit vulnerability with the setuid root program, they can gain local root privileges. Not many IT operations staff will be aware of this local privilege escalation vector. Some programs need setuid permissions in order to function, whereas others do not. Earlier versions of Oracle's database management software came with many setuid binaries, many of which did not need setuid at all. Some of them were setuid under a default-installed "oracle" ownership, which perhaps does not seem so dangerous until you consider that the database server process will (when the software is installed with default options) run under the same "oracle" account ownership. If you can exploit one of these setuid oracle programs, you have compromised the database (you can run database administration tasks) without necessarily even needing to "root" the server.

Likewise with Unix administrators, the typical Unix administrator will know that "world write" permissions on directories (i.e., those that are open for write permissions even for completely unauthenticated users) are a bad thing, but because security threats and local privilege escalation attacks will not have been covered in the standard Unix training course, the admin will not appreciate the extent of this problem. From the beginning of a Unix server's production life, the admin may have stripped off world (or "other") permissions from as many directories and files as possible, but what happens when a developer or project manager requests world write permissions on a particular directory as a "pressing business requirement"? The request will be granted 99 times out of 100 because the knowledge required to make a technical (and consequently a business) argument as to how such a change impacts the organization's security posture is not a typical component of the arsenal of the IT administrator, and as I described earlier that it is unlikely that the admins will contact the security department over the issues (unless there is actually a Change Management System change record involved—in which case, security will review the case and quickly approve it or merely ask the project team to sign a risk exemption form).

What should happen in the previous example? A security analyst should know how critical the particular directory permissions are in terms of the security posture of the server and the network architecture (and other safeguards) and can pass this information to their security manager. An effective security manager knows exactly how "pressing" the new project is for the business and can therefore make a call on accepting or denying the project manager's request. The security manager can also go back to the security analyst and ask him or her for workarounds or alternatives to making critical directories world-writable (and usually in this case, it is possible just to create groups on the server and add write permissions for the group—and everyone gets to live another day). Probably also, the security analyst knows some of the developers personally and can try to find the real reason behind their request in terms of the application details.

On the subject of Unix, there are many local privilege escalation vectors that IT operations staff will not be aware of—and there is no criticism in this because it is not in their roles and responsibilities to know such things. The same can be said for Microsoft Windows and so on, but these are only operating system–related local attacks; what about network and application security issues? And then there is the bigger picture to do with network architecture and business objectives, as in "how likely is it, given the network architecture and other safeguards on the network, that an APT type of attack can succeed, and even if it can succeed, what are the financial implications?"

With security there are the smaller issues to do with operating system configuration (for example) and the myriad of threats that a typical Hacker is aware of, but then there is also the bigger picture that first connects the little bits of the network (servers, switches, routers, databases, applications, etc.) into a network diagram, and then the even bigger picture that is "why are we all here?" and "how does all this stuff relate to our business objectives?"

So I hope it becomes clearer as to what is missing from the IT operations arsenal of skills in terms of security. IT ops teams in most cases are not aware of the security threats to operating systems and applications, let alone be able to draw a picture of financial risk, taking into account network architecture and the business importance of information assets, subnets, and applications.

Handing over IT security analysis tasks to nonsecurity IT teams with no further input from security will result in either overspending (but not necessarily reduction of risk) or underspending in security. It is true that there is no right answer in terms of the budget size, and even with an open checkbook? for your security budget, you will never be able to cover all of the risks anyway (I feel a "silver bullet" phrase attack coming on); but with the right skill sets in security, you can certainly add some considerable time on most attack efforts against your information assets, and not necessarily by spending more. In fact, as of 2011, many firms are spending too much (more on that in Incident Response and Management) while leaving the door wide open for budding perpetrators of APT attacks.

As it stands as of 2011, the gap between security and other teams in most firms is miles wide. In practical terms, it is infinitely wide. As a freelance consultant, whenever I come across a new client, my introduction will be with the security team, but if I want to know what actually happens in security management, I have to talk to operations, and usually operations will not want to talk because of the history of failed cooperation between operations and security. It can be especially difficult to get a meeting. Constant badgering and desk visits are required, and when a 5-minute window of opportunity presents itself, one has to have their "game face" on in order to take advantage.

I recall in one case in a London-based insurance firm: IT operations had gone very far down the road of rolling out a remote user support/administration facility that involved passing all traffic through a "trusted" third party (that was actually a privately-owned U.S.-based Internet facility) to the user's corporate laptop. Cutting some detail, when I questioned operations about the need for passing unencrypted corporate traffic through an unknown third party, they seemed shocked that someone from security was even questioning them about this. Once the tension died down a bit, we started talking about the potential for just using direct VPN connections, to which the response was "how are the users going to know their IP address? If they can't give us their IP address, how can we connect to them?" There are several different means of setting up a Windows XP user laptop such that the IP address is easily "visible" even to the most unsavvy user, and IT operations were also aware of this. But the thinking was something along the lines "this guy is from security so he's probably a clown, we can fob him off with any old excuse."

In the previous case, operations were not aware of the threats and the potential business impacts from these threats. They were aware that it was perhaps a bad idea to pass unencrypted private data through a third party's network (and even if it was encrypted, this is still a bad idea in most cases)—the security posture of which was completely unknown. But they were not aware of the extent of the risk. Sure, if legal agreements are used to cover different eventualities, this is better, but the bottom line was, there is no cost saving with this idea, and it is not even necessary to use this third party plan.

Such stories are commonplace. Even if security does raise an objection to a project/change, other teams can easily swindle a CASE security analyst, and the operations teams are rarely aware of the real risks involved.

The example I gave in Chapter 3 about Linux platform security in HELL serves as an example of what can happen in security when the right skills are deployed. Suddenly there will be an actual working business relationship between IT operations and security. Basically operations staff are looking to learn something from security. If security can give that to them, it is a good start, trust is earned, and later on down the road, security initiatives will run smoothly and transparently. If security can understand the challenges faced by operations and the business in general, great progress can be made in information risk management, and "synergy" will not just be a word that looks good on PowerPoint slides—it will become reality.

The Rise of the Automated Vulnerability Scanner

There are technical reasons (which I will detail in Chapter 5) as to why one should not rely on total automation in vulnerability management—but this is exactly what the majority of larger organizations are doing these days. How did it come to be that security departments and service providers would choose to handle vulnerability assessment in this way, and so severely neglect information risk postures?

The idea that the automated vulnerability scanning tool is not all it was cracked up to be is just starting to come to the surface in security, but really even the negative reports about automated vulnerability scanning tools fall some way short of painting an accurate picture.

Most of the large Fortune 500s have built entire vulnerability management strategies around the use of remote automated vulnerability scanning techniques, in the form of very expensive software suites that are a little more than a nice graphical wrapper to what used to be a free genre of tool—in the same genre as Nessus (probably the most famous: The "Nessus" Project was started by Renaud Deraison in 1998 as an open-source project and then later was subject to proprietary license from Tenable Security). I should clarify at this point that my dialogue here is not a criticism of the functionality of Nessus or any other automated vulnerability scanner. The tool functions more or less according to the specifications as laid out by the designer. The criticism is with the over-reliance on automation in security.

For a few years, back at the dawn of dedicated security service provision, end users such as banks would have to pay a security service provider to conduct a test of their external security controls within a "network penetration test." The details of the methodology in these tests are a subject for Chapter 7, but just for now, I will talk about how remote testing changed from the late 1990s until now—specifically from the automation point of view.

Many firms still undertake network penetration tests mostly because external or internal security auditors require them to do so. Central banking/monetary authorities require financial institutions to prove their infallible security by having a network penetration test conducted against their network by an independent third party. If the target can show a report with green colors to the auditor, everybody can live happily ever after.

Ignoring the requirements of auditors for a moment—taking a fictional situation where a CISO is concerned about his firm's perimeter security—the actual benefit that comes from doing a remote penetration test, even if it is delivered impeccably, is not as much as one might think. It is certainly very far from being a decent indicator of the security posture of the organization (I will cover this topic in more detail in Chapter 7), but anyway, if a penetration test is going to be delivered, it is in all of our interests to get some value from the exercise that is more than just passing the audit. Imagine if your organization could pay for an audit, and as well as passing the audit, you also get some return on investment in the way of improved security controls (!), but this is a topic for Chapter 7.

The earlier penetration tests were usually conducted by a team of up to six security analysts (but usually the number was four), and the time frame could be up to three weeks (but it was usually one or two weeks). I do not think Asia–Pacific is a good reference for global prices in this area, but I remember that back in 2000 at TSAP, a 40 man-day (four analysts for 10 business days) penetration test would have set clients back roughly US$35,000–40,000.

The type of manual penetration test that I discussed in the previous paragraph would give clients a feel for their perimeter security. Unless there were a huge number of "visible IP addresses" (testing targets) to scan, clients would generally get fairly useful feedback on their external security profile from the malicious Hacker's perspective.

Almost inevitable was the introduction to the security arena of a piece of software that supposedly automated the manual penetration test. Allegedly, all that was required of the user was to give the software the IP addresses for your targets, hit the enter button, and away it goes. The software automatically generates a list of vulnerabilities found and formats them in a nice report. Some, if not all, of the vulnerabilities reported may not really be vulnerabilities; they might be what the industry calls *false positives*. So what is needed is to have a security analyst spend some considerable time sifting through the scanner output to decide which vulnerabilities are real and which are not. Of course, the analyst's ability to do this depends on his or her experience in the field—in fact, to do an effective job, the tester must be an experienced penetration tester. There are some vulnerabilities found by these tools that a novice can verify, but their number is less than 10% of the full list of vulnerabilities in the scanner's database of available vulnerability tests.

Automated vulnerability scanners were around before the 2000s, but they did not really start showing up in any serious commercial capacity until the early 2000s. Examples of such software were Nessus, GFI LANguard, and the tool that we used at TSAP but which is no longer available: Cybercop Scanner (Network Associates pulled the plug on this in 2002).

Almost inevitably, with the US$40,000 price tag associated with manual penetration testing, from roughly 2000 onward, questions were being asked by end users (clients of security service providers) as to why these automated tools could not be used for their penetration tests (hence reducing the price). Of course, service providers were not going to cut their prices so readily, but all it took was one service provider in the region to cut their price, putting competitive pressure on the others.

By mid-2001, there were a rapidly growing number of clients that were under the impression that manual penetration testers could be replaced by magical new (and free) software. Dissuading clients from this cheaper (and extremely inadvisable) approach to security demanded two major factors:

- Sufficient expertise, communication skills, and confidence on behalf of the service provider to explain why a reliance on too much automation in vulnerability testing was a bad idea.
- A high degree of trust between the end user and the service provider—especially because many boutique security firms started coming out of the woodwork offering "golden truly penetration testing service by top Hacker—yeah [thumb up sign]" for US$100. Other firms in the same industry sector as the client would have started using these cheaper services already—or even doing the testing themselves.

The first point is the key here. There were several problems brought about by the Hacker ethic that I described in Chapter 2. (Prior to 2002, nearly all technical staff deployed in an analytical capacity in service providers were Hackers.) First was that, for the Hackers, automated scanner tools would not have been sufficiently interesting for them to investigate, that is, they perhaps will not have "played" or "monkeyed around" with this software. Then, even if they had played with the tool, could they explain either to their manager or directly to the client about the disadvantages of a fully automated approach?

My TSAP Hacker colleagues had done some testing with Nessus and concluded it to be "fairly useless" for vulnerability testing, but it could have some use in performing repetitive, boring tasks (such as testing for "NULL session" Windows SMB services across a wide range of Windows targets), and so it could be used to slightly increase the efficiency of manual penetration tests—this summary was all that came from the Hacker lab in the way of a statement for our clients.

Clearly this was not enough. What was needed was a business justi-fication for our clients as to why they should go against the market and pay 20 times more than their competitors for penetration testing services. Our regional manager was a former hotel manager and was in no position to spin the Hacker's view into a logical case for "staying manual" in penetration testing. In fact, I do not believe he ever really tried to do this because he himself was not convinced of the virtues of the all-manual approach, which leads me to my next point.

Aside from the trust between the service provider and their client, there was also the issue of trust between the service provider manager and the Hacker—and in this point lies another driving factor behind the spread of cheap, automated vulnerability testing services.

Something I believe was very common in security, and still is to this day, is a lack of trust between the service provider manager and the security analyst (this is a separate problem in itself and in extreme brevity: this mistrust can show its ugly face because when a security manager has no relevant background in security, he or she has no reference point from which to pass judgment on an analyst's ability and experience).

Back then in 2002, if a service provider employed analysts to do penetration testing, the manager will, at some point, have needed to ask the Hackers why automated scanners could not be used to do penetration testing. The Hackers advocated against the use of full automation—unfortunately though, their manager took the position that the Hackers were merely trying to protect their job, and therein lies the reason why it has taken so long for the industry to begin to understand the limitations of the fully automated approach. The only folk qualified to pass judgment on automation in security were sys-tematically being ignored.

For all these years, who has been around to explain the problems? Hacker numbers were growing thinner in security, and those that remained were allegedly only trying to keep their jobs when they spoke out about automated approaches to vulnerability detection. So it was eight years before I finally came across an article in securityfocus .com that spoke of the seven deadly sins of penetration testing—one of which was an over-reliance on automated vulnerability scanners—but this article did not quite portray the severity of the shortcomings with these tools.

For almost a decade now, the automated vulnerability scanner has taken center stage in organizations' vulnerability management strategies, and this has suited CASE security departments very nicely. If all you need to do is click a button to do a scan and generate a nice report (so goes the theory), who actually needs to have an extensive technical skill base? All the security team needs to do is find a way to weed out the so-called vulnerabilities, which are very likely to be false positives, right? In reality, what happens is that in many cases, they do not even bother with false positives checking and explain away remaining vulnerabilities as being noncritical with no business case for fixing the issues.

Many security departments will spend literally hundreds of man hours annoying both themselves and other IT departments in attempting to weed out false positives from the scan reports, but in reality, most of the vulnerabilities reported cannot definitively be tested without performing disruptive manual tests, and in these cases, the tester is almost carrying out a "script kiddy" type of manual penetration test anyway.

Many firms swear by the report findings from these automated methods and invest a lot of time in analyzing the output, testing for false positives, and so on. I can promise all such organizations that this is a very inefficient use of resources. There is also the more critical aspect of *false negatives* (where a scanning tool fails to find actual real vulnerability)—the number that is most often quoted in terms of accuracy in testing is 50% (you will get a bunch of "experts" who will set up a target box with known vulnerabilities, run the scanner against it, and then report on the results). As it will become clear in Chapter 5, this number seems vastly inflated to me, and why is it always 50%? In the past, the number was always 90% to 100% in these tests. Over time, it has shrunk to 50%, but it has been at 50% for a long time now. Maybe this is as low as the product vendors will allow it to go.

There are a number of information security magazines and Websites that publish reviews of security products. Not that I am in doubt of the publisher's integrity, but quite often, you will see golden, 10 out of 10 reviews of expensive vulnerability management suites (that rely on automated vulnerability scanning) right next to a full-spread advertising page for the vendor.

In Chapter 5, I will discuss the technical aspects of remotely scanning for vulnerabilities with automated tools, and it will become clear that the value of the output of these tools tends to be approximately the same as running a simple "port scan" with a tool like nmap. Usually the only valuable finding that comes from autoscanner usage is really just the discovery of open "listening services," and this result can be achieved in a much more efficient way without having security analysts spending hours testing for false positives.

The Rise of the Checklist

There was a theory bouncing around the information security scene in the early 2000s. The theory was based on the premise that everything the Hackers knew could be summed up in a checklist of bullet points, so that really the Hackers were not needed in security any more. Supposedly anything the Hacker could do, the CASE could do better because not only could the CASE reduce the value of the Hacker down to a bulleted list of security requirements, but they also "fitted in" and were generally more pleasing to eye and ear.

Manual penetration testing could supposedly be replaced by a checklist of automated tests (as described in The Rise of the Automated Vulnerability Scanner)—but the infiltration of the checklist extends to just about everything in security, not just vulnerability testing.

Shostack and Stewart wrote a nice piece on checklists in their book titled *The New School of Information Security*, with an example based on encryption that, in summary, reads that the checklist dictates that a certain algorithm should be used in encryption (such as DES3), but it says nothing about the real problem with encryption that is key management. The data might be nicely encrypted, but if the key is compromised, as can be deduced from the dictionary definition of the word, the plain text can be trivially revealed.

The key management issue is a good example. A checklist can specify some principles that need to be followed in key management, but is the checklist by itself sufficient to reduce risks with a real-life key management architecture to an acceptable level?

Imagine a situation where a big bank wants to roll out an ATM network nationwide. The bank needs to set up a long-term key with each of its ATMs and each of the interbank networks that it is associated with. The bank also needs to establish a "key of the day" with each ATM and with each network—to allow customers to use ATMs of other banks, with the transaction encrypted using a shared key with a network such as Visa, Mastercard, and Cirrus, for example. The bank may not know it yet (although it probably will), but it has to maintain a master key for each ATM, plus quite possibly also an encryption key, authentication key, and keys for all banking networks for which it is a member.

Banks in general face a huge key management challenge—certainly ATMs are not their only worry. What about the thousands of online banking customers who may have been set up with a private certificate as part of a two-factor authentication challenge? What about the several thousand employees whose passwords may be encrypted with keys under some Kerberos-type scheme?

The security analyst's checklist will give some loose qualifications under the guise of something that is actually useful. The engineer responsible for the architecture of a key management scheme, as an absolute minimum, has to think about how many keys are needed, how they are to be generated, how they are to be transported/shared over potentially untrusted networks, how long the keys will "live" for, and how they will be expired.

Checklists for the above-mentioned scenarios do not exist, and even if they did, it would be impossible to compose a checklist that could cater for all situations such that an engineer doing the design work no longer needs to think about the security aspects. This is the CASE-held premise with checklists—one that implicitly promises that there is no longer any need to *think* in security. Why are analytical/engineering mindsets even necessary?

There is one real example from my own experience that sort of stands out as being one of the worst situations I can remember, mostly because of the sheer gravity of the case in terms of the impact on the reputation of both service provider and client.

Toward the end of my time with TSAP, the Indonesia office had sold a project with a major bank in Jakarta. The time was around the end of 2004, and without being judgmental (there is a "bigger picture" story here), many of the major banks in Indonesia were still very immature in the way of security controls. The bank in question was in the formative stages of an overall security management framework. If delivered well, the output from said workshop would form the basis of the bank's entire information risk management

strategy and would consequently lead to a lot more business generation for TSAP.

I was personally unavailable for the workshop, but I was aware of
the major aspects of the workshop delivery because I was in regular
contact with the TSAP Country Manager for Indonesia (he was a
local analyst for Indonesia and a colleague of mine during the TSAP
years from 2000 to 2004). TSAP at this time were in the process
of acquisition by another company in Australia, and the managers
there eventually decided to fly a "lead security consultant" up from
Melbourne to deliver the three-day workshop in Jakarta.

What was delivered in the workshop? Were there any network
diagrams requested, and what were the major business challenges of
the bank? Was there any discussion around an international security
management standard framework (such as ISO 27001)? Did the consultant try to get a feel for the most critical information assets and
applications?

What was delivered in the workshop was a summary of a CISSP
exam study guide. For various reasons, prices charged to clients in
Indonesia by TSAP were considerably higher as compared with other
countries (in some cases up to five times higher), so the overall cost
for three days with three analysts (plus expenses) would have been in
the order of US$10,000. For an uninitiated client, the CISSP method
may seem like a sensible approach, but in reality, the client was not
seeing any real value for their investment. Later their own staff would
start taking the CISSP exam themselves and so the folly of the workshop was revealed. To give a summary of CISSP is less beneficial for
the client as compared with just going through the applicable parts of
ISO 27001, but really neither of these is actually based on real problems faced by the client—those that might need the help of outsiders
to solve. What was actually delivered was effectively a checklist that
may or may not have been applicable to the client, and one they could
have quickly found themselves from use of an Internet search engine.

What should have happened in the workshop with the Indonesian
bank? Standards by themselves are checklists, and they are useful—but
only as a framework in security. Highly detailed analysis is applicable in
a first date workshop such as this, but it is certainly not the whole story.
The Hacker lacks the communication or business analysis skills necessary to hold this workshop as a lone gunslinger, but he or she should be

there in support. An architect by my understanding is one who is technically proficient (in today's world probably the best-qualified person to do this is a senior network architect, but not so senior that he or she has not logged into a Cisco switch for three years or more) but can understand business challenges. The workshop should be held with a constant theme that involves the input of people who know the real nature of the threats in detail, and this knowledge is used to build a picture of challenges that are particular to the bank, one which *empathizes* with the bank in their battle to preserve the confidentiality, availability, and integrity of the bank's information assets and applications.

Of course, a three-day workshop is only the beginning. From this, more detailed discussions will come later in specific areas—and the influence of the Hacker ethic in the service provider to client relationship is allowed to grow by his or her manager as and when applicable. The Hacker can be used like a Swiss Army Knife, but should not be allowed to roam free.

The key word to come out of this example of a security service provider and the birth of security in a major bank is a verb: "empathize." It is not enough to be able to read a checklist if one does not know if the list items are applicable or not—under such a circumstance, a security analyst within an end user security department cannot empathize with the business and other IT departments, and a security analyst in a service provider cannot empathize with his or her client in helping to meet their security challenges in a cost-effective way.

Standards like ISO 27001 and the Payment Card Industry Data Security Standard (PCI-DSS) are perfectly applicable as a basis from which to start thinking about a security strategy, but they are not the oracle of all security. Some parts will not be applicable, and of those parts that are applicable, there is insufficient detail in the standard to facilitate a cost-effective solution for all operational security problems. A great deal will be needed more in the way of skilled security analysis on top of the higher-level management standards.

There are no definitive answers in security. Even firms in the same industry sector face radically different challenges from each other. Many organizations' security standards will prescribe use of centralized logging and correlation of security events. (Servers and other devices are configured, usually by default, to generate text log messages as security events and other informational or diagnostic events.

When networked devices are configured to send log messages to a central log server, this is usually referred to as centralized logging.)

Insurance company A may invest heavily in a SIEM project that allows them, supposedly, to not only capture log messages centrally but also correlate events across different operating systems and subnets. For insurance company B, there is insufficient complexity in their network or volume of log messages to warrant investment in a complex product integration project, and insurance company C has a deep-rooted IT culture of separate "silos" in Unix, Windows, and Cisco management. Each silo has aggregated logging, but to try to integrate them would cost the firm more in time and resources than the perceived benefit returned by network-wide event logging and correlation.

The insurance firm example gives a feel for how much analysis is needed on top of the checklist requirement that advocates centralized and correlated security logging. The checklist serves to eliminate thinking from security and treats all organizations in the same way, but if the analysis is AWOL, all three of the insurance firms may be at serious risk regardless of how much they are spending.

To once again quote Bruce Schneier, "Security is complex"—it cannot be reduced down to a series of checklists to be used by completely uninitiated staff in solving all of an organization's security problems.

Incident Response and Management—According to Best Practices

The two words "best" and "practice" seemed to find their way into a lot of CASE sentences after 2001—usually associated with, yes, you guessed it right, a checklist.

The level of awareness of this issue in security is increasing—as with *CIO Magazine's* March 2011 story titled "Secure Best Practices No Proof Against Stuxnet" where a firm had followed so-called best practices but still became a victim of the Stuxnet worm.

For example, in an incident management project, a client may ask "what roles and responsibilities should be deployed in composing a computer incident response team?" When you hear this type of question, nine times out of ten you will hear a response that begins with "best practices dictate that. . . ." So rather than digging out more information from the business to find a solution that fits the needs of the business, the analyst gives an answer under the pretense that there is this central deity in information security that sits there managing lists (there is that word again) of best practices that are universally accepted, subject to peer review, and carved in stone.

Take incident response as an example here. Many would argue that the overall corporate philosophy of "protect and proceed" versus "pursue and prosecute" needs to be decided by a senior figure first (and this decision will have a lot to do with legal factors and others in that country) before a computer incident response team can be formed, but there is nothing fixed in stone. Organizations' needs vary radically from one to the next.

Just as with checklists, best practices remove the need for any analysis, and this phrase is heavily used by CASEs in the industry. "Best practices" gives the professional's advice a foundation of authority where there is no authority, and as long as the CASEs remain straight-faced when they deliver this statement, there are very few who will question the so-called "best practice" that is being advocated, which often involves massive investment in security products with no return on investment.

In the incident response example, the phrase "best practice" will be used by a vendor/reseller/consultancy to sell a hugely expensive SIEM solution (read: hugely complex software, with a requirement for hardware and hundreds of hours of consulting from the vendor) because "best practices dictate a central log management and event correlation solution" as an essential basis of "every incident response strategy." The reality is, though, if actual technical security analysis is deployed (i.e., some of the potential of the human mind is realized), there are very few firms who can justify investment in this area.

There is no international central authority in security that rubber-stamps terms, phrases, job titles, or practices in the industry.

Overall strategies that are formed just from "best practices" will not be formed based on the reality of how the organization's information is stored, processed, and managed on nasty computers in freezing machine rooms with blinking light boxes called switches and routers that link everything together. Because "best practices" are used to form a high-level policy, there is no longer any need for any further analysis of what the strategy may mean at the ground level, or "at the coal face"—more essentially, what it may mean for other IT departments and the business in general. According to those who tout them, best practices are exactly that—they are the best practices known to mankind, the ultimate authority.

Like so many other facets of post-2000 security, the use of the phrase "best practices" gained momentum because, just as use of automated vulnerability scanners could be used to substitute the Hacker's wisdom in vulnerability testing, "best practices" could be used to negate the need for any further or deeper analysis in most other areas of security. The skill sets required to go deeper and really assess the pros and cons of whatever practice is being prescribed (at a practical IT level, with boring, nonchatty Unix consoles and MS-DOS prompts) were no longer necessary because the *best* practice was already being dictated.

The best practice tenet is often one that ends up being the final blow that severs links between security and IT operations departments. One example I can remember is as follows: "Best practice is to configure a remote console password, 12 characters with at least 2 upper case, 2 numbers, and 2 punctuation characters and each server must have a different password." IT operations responded, "you realize how many servers we have and how often we need to access consoles remotely? With 600 complex passwords to remember it's inevitable that we'll keep forgetting them, and then we have to physically go to the machine room," "uh . . . ok, so what is the problem?" "Well, what isn't the problem? We often need remote console access to solve critical problems fast, as in problems that are *critical to the business*," "well it is best practice to do this, and there is a risk here," "can you explain the risk to me—I mean how easy would it be for a person physically located in the data center [this was the only location with remote console access—a small office space of 20 seats] to access a remote console?" Very often the response from security in this case will be just silence or at best "What part of *best practice* don't you understand?"

As I have mentioned in a previous chapter, the situation where security and other IT departments do not "synergize" is a very common scenario. At best, the other IT departments will give the relationship lip service, but in many cases, there is no contact at all unless absolutely necessary—and if all the security team ever does is dictate best practices, checklists, and mandatory security standards, then there really are very few cases where any value can be found in consultation with the security team.

I talk about best practices in relation to incident response in this book because it is in this area that the phrase is used most often. Lists of best practices in first response to a suspected incident do exist, and they do serve to at least make IT operations staff more aware of how to respond (i.e., they are better than nothing), but what happens when a security incident response strategy is being formulated is nearly always that the best practices strategy is drawn up first and then handed out to the other IT departments. The IT departments were never involved in the initial discussions to formulate best practices, so the list is invariably one that ends up gathering dust on a shelf—it is never used to formulate an actual response plan that could be useful to IT departments.

The Hackers' (I use the term Hacker here as it was defined in Chapter 2) contribution is critical in formulating an incident response strategy. Why? The Hacker has detailed knowledge of what can happen at a machine, bits-n-bytes, "packet sniffer" level in an incident. The Hacker has familiarity with most, if not all, of the eventualities that can unfold in an incident. In general, there are none better qualified to formulate a strategy than a Hacker . . . mostly because one needs to think like a Hacker to be effective in such circumstances. Hackers know tools like Snort (a famous open-source tool that was originally designed for intrusion detection), for example, and mostly they are aware of actual system-level (as opposed to bird's-eye level) events in an incident. If a Hacker knows that he or she has to gather evidence of an intrusion, and the requirements therein, then he or she can give a practical appraisal of the possibilities of doing this in a real, machine room situation. Other IT departments need to be educated in detecting signs of an incident in order to be able to respond to an incident (these can be signs other than information in device logs)— and in order to help with such an initiative, best practices may or may not be applicable. In this case, it is better to let the Hackers draw up their own list particular to the actual environment and use it to raise awareness in other teams.

An incident response strategy can be formulated by having slightly more senior members of staff formulate a set of requirements such as "we need to gather evidence to build a legal case in an intrusion," "we need to increase levels of awareness with users and IT staff such that they can read signs of an incident—and know how to respond," "we need to set up effective time synchronization across the network," or "we need to aggregate device log messages across the whole network and correlate events." These requirements can be posed to individuals with a Hacker-like skill set, and of course, there will be more questions coming back in order to further refine, change, or even completely drop some requirements—but if the situation is managed properly, what will distill out of this is an efficient and effective incident response strategy that is tailored to the actual IT environment. Higher level and lower detailed tenets of the strategy will govern overall concerns that apply into the future, but when there are major structural changes in IT (such as with the introduction of cloud-based services), the base level strategies need to be reviewed by the Hackers and other IT departments.

Best practices here are more useful in terms of formulating future-proof strategies, but not so useful in telling us what we should be doing here and now.

Basically with this incident response case and Hacker engagement, this is about having a security manager engage with his or her team of Hackers in the way "the business wants to achieve this, can we (the organization as a whole) do it and if yes, how are we going to do it—let's draw up strategies and processes, including an incident response plan (IRP)." There will be parts of this that will be "how useful would a SIEM solution be here . . . is it worth the investment?" All this sounds simple? If the right skills are deployed under an effective security manager, it is a lot simpler than can be imagined—certainly a lot simpler than most strategy formulation attempts at the time of writing. The incident response strategy will be easier to understand for all who need to use it, and smaller in size—a lot of the items that find their way into an incident response strategy from *best practices* will not actually be applicable to an effective strategy; they will have been stripped out after consulting the Hackers.

Most IRPs these days are not living processes because too few people with any practical involvement in IT were involved in the creation of the process—it was only a CASE security team initiative, and the IRP is for all intents and purposes broken. Because of the increased frequency of *reported* incidents these days, IRPs have been brought back from the dead, but I have no reason to suspect that the second crack at an effective IRP will be any more successful than the first.

Of course, many organizations have only just got serious about an IRP in the last three years or so because of the perceived rise in incident numbers. If we are talking pre-2008, there was a "chicken and egg" situation with incident response strategies whereby companies would not devote resources to an incident response/management strategy because, for whatever reason, they did not see the need for one—but if they suddenly configured and turned on a SIEM system (prior to which many of their systems were not configured to generate logs at all), it could reveal signs of past or ongoing skullduggery on their network. There were several of these cases that I came across in my time with TSAP where companies had no IRP, but during onsite testing, my colleagues and I found clear signs of intrusion. One of our clients in Seoul thought they did not need an IRP. During a penetration test of their network, we discovered that a German Hacker team was using their servers for Internet Relay Chat (IRC), anonymous FTP, and we had reason to believe they were staging other attacks from our client's servers.

"Best Practices" in Security Service Provision

The "best practices" phrase finds its way into so many areas of security these days. With service providers, "best practices" is probably the most oft used word pairing—and it spreads like a virus to end users and then it reaches CISO level, and once it gets there, you have a situation that is hard to reverse.

The "best practices" issue is one that can affect a security service provider in a very damaging way. Many of the service providers will advocate best practices for their clients. The problem is these best practices, as we have said, are generic. Can they be applied to any organization in any situation? No, because organizations' information risk management needs are too complex to be addressed with rigid best practices.

Probably the most severe side of the best practices code, however, is just the fact that best practices in security can be found by doing a Google search. Any security analyst can find a checklist of best practices within a few minutes on a popular search engine.

In London in 2008, I met the regional manager of a large telco's security service provision unit. I asked him what the firm's current direction was, and he replied, "I have two dozen extremely skilled consultants out there preaching best practices to CISOs." OK, so then I asked what he thought his competitive advantage was, to which the reply was, "we have underground intelligence from all over the world. Because we're a telco we can tap into Internet backbones and forewarn our clients of upcoming trouble." I later discovered that "underground intelligence" was merely a database of vulnerabilities with various different products, a very good version of which is available completely free of charge as in the Open Source Vulnerability Database (http://www.osvdb.com). So really what was the firm's competitive advantage?

At the time of writing, successful security service providers are those who are able to use social means to wean over CISOs. The meetings and trust-building are essential of course, but there has to be something backing up the promises from the service provider. If there is no actual real competitive advantage, then obviously the client relationship is going to be somewhat flimsy. The CISO moves on to another position, and the security service provider loses a client in most cases.

There is a lot of talk about best practices from the service provider, but internal security departments already know the best practices— and if they do not, they can "Google it."

What service providers need to be able to do in order to distinguish themselves and take a lead in their field is to be able to tell clients something they do not already know. The competitive advantage in this game comes from one place: human intellectual capital, and as I have explained in several parts of this book, that element, the Hacker element, was literally phased out of security almost a decade ago.

The Hacker is a practically bottomless well from which service provider clients can draw knowledge. The only part missing in the pre-2002 picture was an IT-centric manager who could tailor the Hacker offerings to the needs of their clients (I will talk more about this topic of Hacker Management later in Section 4).

Tip of the Iceberg—Audit-Driven Security Strategy

I mentioned briefly about audits being the main driving factor for security spending in Chapter 1, and also about "keeping up with the

Joneses" where firms will reach a certain level in their audit compliance that is similar to their competitors in the same industry sector.

Many countries have a central banking authority, which dictates that in order to carry out financially oriented business, the firm must have passed an audit program laid down by the central monetary authority.

Passing the audit is one thing, but making your entire information risk management strategy as minimal as possible to merely pass the audit—that is quite another—but unfortunately, this *is* the strategy used by more than 90% of firms these days.

I will first outline roughly what happens in an external audit and cover some problems with the typical approach, and then I will cover how the whole bare bones, audit-passing strategy came about in information risk management.

Taking an external audit from a Big Four consultancy as an example, what unfolds is basically that a team of auditors, usually fairly junior staff, will physically visit their client's office(s) with a list of metrics (criteria to be assessed in the audit—depending on the program, this can be an IT-only show or it can be all-encompassing audit a la ISO 27001).

With the IT-related tests, the devices to be audited are decided beforehand, and then some tests will be performed. Not all of the auditors' metrics will be actually tested firsthand by the auditors. Some information will be gathered just from meetings (and I am talking *a lot* of meetings—with staff of nearly all levels of seniority). Generally, these external audits are performed annually or bi-annually, and they cause a lot of disruption for security and operational managers. My line managers both in HELL and Q were well prepared to pass their audits (they were fairly trivial requirements to meet in both cases), but nonetheless dreaded the auditors' site visits because of the huge resource requirements involved.

In my previous description of audit activities, I mentioned "a team of auditors, usually fairly junior staff, will physically visit." OK, so what about the auditors themselves? How well qualified were they for the task at hand? Big Four firms occupy by far the hugest chunk of the audit landscape. Generally the only pieces of the pie left for others are those that the Big Fours could not eat because internal risk management regulations blocked them from partaking in audit engagements with clients with whom they had previously taken on audits (i.e., they want to avoid conflict-of-interest situations whereby something in the more recent audit might conflict with a finding in the older audit).

Some of the Big Fours' hiring policies are to hire on an army of junior staff (the internal position is titled "consultant") to do audits while the market is good, but then quickly make them redundant when the demand subsides. In the assessment of consultants' suitability for hiring, their experience is not as important as their level of gullibility and/or vanity at wanting to be associated with a big consulting firm with office spaces that resemble the Tate Gallery.

The Big Fours charge out a consultant to clients at a daily rate that is between 1.5 to two times the consultant's monthly salary, and send them to clients with no training, armed only with a checklist–and the source of the checklist is completely arbitrary (the consultants may have percolated something themselves). In my time at a Big Four, I was aware of an internal intranet site that hosted server configuration checklists that were surprisingly detailed and well maintained, but I was lucky to have become aware of this. There is no new starter guide for new-hire consultants.

At HELL, there was an incident whereby I was asked to cooperate with a Big Four auditor who was supposed to be checking Linux security. What actually happened was that my line manager passed me the shell script they used for testing, asked me to run the script, and passed the results back to the auditor. When I checked the script, I was shocked first at how minimal it was (the script only tested for six aspects of platform security—patch tests and all of the most common local privilege escalation vulnerability tests were missing), and second there was evidence of what were either just plain old mistakes or worse, a total misunderstanding of some aspects of Unix security. For example, one part of the script tested for File Transfer Protocol (FTP) security in the way of user access control with the *ftpusers* file, usually located under the /etc directory. The script generated a FAIL result only if the text string "root" was in the file—so the understanding of the script's author was that the file contained user names of users who were *permitted* to use FTP, but in fact, ftpusers has the opposite effect. /etc/ftpusers contains the names of users who are *blocked* from FTP login. With "root" being the highest privileged user account in

Unix flavors, it is a good idea under many circumstances to prevent a direct login by root—because FTP gives some access to the server's file system, leaving it open to direct access by root should be prevented wherever possible (although I did come across one case in 10 years where I could condone opening FTP to root once I understood the business case behind this).

So in the above-mentioned Linux testing case, not only was the auditor unaware of the script functions but also even the script designer showed some evidence of severe lack of experience in Unix security. Usually the auditors would interrogate clients as to why they were even using FTP as opposed to its encrypted form: Secure Shell or Secure Copy for file transfer, but in this case, there was also a misunderstanding of the security implications with the items in their shell script.

I have heard many stories such as this with Big Four auditors, but it goes without saying that it is not the case that all Big Fours have nothing of any value to offer. Certainly the consulting team in security at a Big Four in Thailand was the most competent I have come across in Web application security testing. Overall though, the technical value offered by the Big Four audit in actually measuring security controls was sorely lacking in many cases—and I have heard similar stories from across the globe. Internally the Big Fours do have good resources devoted to maintaining the quality of their audit programs, but the output of these efforts is hidden to many new consultants.

The testing targets are of course only a tiny sample of the whole—in fact, whereas the visible tip of an iceberg above the water is a small fraction of its whole, the sample of devices tested in most external audits is even less than this (in HELL, it was roughly 1%).

The audit targets will be decided usually on the first day of the audit in a meeting between IT heads and the auditors. The auditors will usually stipulate mission-critical, and "high risk/exposure" devices (although the auditors will not know themselves if the targets selected are really the most critical ones), but there is of course the opportunity here for IT bosses to be selective—they will have been "tipped off" by their staff as to which devices are more audit-ready than others—add to which, if the auditors' testing tools are as flimsy as the Linux script I mentioned above, then what you have is a circus act. You can picture a scene where an auditor's script is full of the epic holes I mentioned above, and the IT boss has selected a highly locked down, although relatively insignificant target, only for the auditor's script to declare the audit a total failure. We will just call this an urban myth for now: I am sure such a scenario never became reality.

The typical external audit scenario that I have just described is clearly some way short of being an effective security risk assessment strategy, but it is nonetheless exactly the bedrock of larger organizations' information risk management strategies. How did this come to be?

From my experiences at Q (I have not mentioned much about Q thus far, so here is a recap: in 2008, I was working with a multinational insurance firm based in London—this firm goes under the pseudonym Q here), and from what I have read/heard from others, the reduction of security practices down to barely compliant levels can come from below or it can come from above.

The case where this ill-advised strategy comes from above goes something like this: As I mentioned in Chapter 1, I do believe that C-level execs have shown real concern over security threats in the past, and more so in the past two or three years, but what sort of advice have they been subjected to since the first corporate infosec practices in the 1990s?

Advice on security strategies came first from Hackers who, as I mentioned in Chapter 2, were out of sync with economic realities. Things may have seemed better after this when Hackers were replaced by buzzword touting, aesthetically pleasing CASEs, but it has been clear for some time now that the CASE ethic is just as ineffective as the Hacker ethic. Even before the current wave of large-scale incidents, there was some doubt from the C-levels as to the effectiveness of the CASE ethic in security. When the top levels in a firm ask a CISO what is happening in information risk management in their company, they will get a lot of words like governance and synergy thrown into the answer—it sounds nice and it is professionally delivered. There may also be some nice graphs, green colors, and pie charts on display—autogenerated from an expensive vulnerability management suite. But how many CISOs really believe their security strategy is effective? In a 2011 survey conducted by Harvey Nash/PA Consulting Group of U.K. chief information officers, only 37% felt they were "very well positioned" to deal with a cyber attack. If I had to estimate, I would say the proportion would be considerably lower than 37%.

So many CASEs will tell you that checklists are fine, IT operations cover the technical risk management, and that security is really only about employee awareness—however, the reality is that most people involved with security are intuitively aware that their approach is not sufficiently analytical. This contradictory professional status held by CASEs leads to a lack of self-confidence that is transmitted up the chain to the CISO. The CISO may be proficient in the art of hiding his or her insecurity, but there are very few people in the world who are better at detecting fiction than a CEO. A CEO gets to be a CEO partly because of an ability to deal with politics—key ingredients of which are lies and duplicity.

First security was overanalytical, and later it was underanalytical. The end result of this is that the time-strapped top levels in firms just fell back to advocating the bare minimum necessary to keep functioning as a company (i.e., just being compliant with central authority regulations by passing the audit—and not necessarily with flying colors). The top levels of management have no evidence to the effect that anyone in their security practice actually has any idea what they are talking about. Under these circumstances, the easiest thing to do is just to ensure compliance without blocking anything that generates revenue, while taking shortcuts whenever possible—and if the organization's domain name appears in other organizations' spam blacklists, it can be brushed under the carpet for now.

My role at Q was to assist in the development of a security practice. The company had gone through several mergers. Q's U.K. operation up until a few years before had been tiny, but then it went on an aggressive acquisition streak and became a medium-to-large sized operation in a relatively short period of time. Q had a baseline security policy still in review and development, and I was working on security standards for Cisco, Web applications, IBM AIX, Windows, Microsoft SQL Server, and Oracle.

Q had been duped into purchasing an expensive vulnerability management suite, and this was to be the basis of their vulnerability management strategy—generally an inefficient and ineffective strategy. A common scenario with company mergers is that for several months to a few years after merger, both companies' Internet "choke points" still exist because the different firms' networks have not been merged (the integration will go as far as a border router and routes in each network to divert traffic between networks). In Q we knew nothing of the security posture of the other connected corporate networks (OK, well Q had asked a service provider to do penetration tests of the other firms' networks—but personally I was not going to rely on the output of these tests), and with this in mind, the vulnerability management side of things in Q had to be improved. So with management support, I had a mandate to lead the new vulnerability management approach that would involve a combination of remote and local/scripted tests—with the depth of analysis dependent on the criticality/exposure of the hosting device.

The proper way to carry out a vulnerability assessment program is with a platform of signed-off security policies behind you, even if the authority of the standards is not necessary (as was the case in my time at HELL, the standards were not necessary because I was able to co-opt with other IT teams in a way that resulted in a mutual understanding of risk).

As is so often the case, the standards and policies that underpin the information risk management strategy can take eons to be reviewed by other teams and finally get signed off by management.

Along with the slow development of security policies, and with the impact of various other security initiatives being loaded onto an already-stretched security team, the progress of the planned vulnerability management scheme was severely impacted. Unfortunately for Q though, the successful completion of this project was a security management key performance indicator (KPI). KPIs are used to assess employee performance and are linked to the amount of bonuses paid out, and there was a tight deadline on this KPI.

With tight deadlines on management KPIs, security initiatives that would actually result in efficient and effective risk management processes are shelved, and the quickest ways of doing the bare minimum are adopted, that is, how can we pass the audit with as little fuss and analysis as possible? This usually entails spending on ineffective but highly expensive products that give an illusion of security and a short cut to regulatory compliance.

With the KPI-driven bottom-up regression to an audit-driven infosec strategy, it is as Upton Sinclair once said: "It's difficult to get a man to understand something if his salary depends upon his *not* understanding it."

Summary

In this chapter, I have covered some of the most detrimental developments in security since the Hackers were largely phased out of the industry around the early 2000s.

In some way or another, all of these developments share a similar theme—that of the intentional or unintentional creation of an illusion that technical analysis skills in security are not necessary, and that everything the Hackers had to offer in security could be summed up in an easy-to-understand list of checks or "best practices."

One of the bigger changes in security since the early 2000s was the migration of analysis functions in security to other IT departments such as IT and network operations.

IT operations skills are something of a subset of the ideal security Hacker-like skills. Typical skills in IT operations will relate to some particular operating system or another. For example, a Unix administrator will know something about Unix security in terms of file permissions and other such areas, but this is some way short of being able to assist an information risk management program in the way of cost-effective safeguards. Security analysts need to know attack vectors and threats; in short, they need to know how APT and full manual attack threats are staged in order to be able to make recommendations to safeguard against such threats.

In the case of the aforementioned island in the corporate information management scene that is Unix, the security analyst needs to know how a Unix system can be compromised. The analyst has to know at least the main threats. For example, how is local privilege escalation actually achieved? This is a question that analysts need to be able to answer. Essentially the analyst needs to be flexible and to be able to think like a hacker.

In many cases, security initiatives such as vulnerability management, SIEM configuration and operation, firewall configuration, identity management, risk assessments, and other areas are handled entirely by operations teams, with no direction from security at all.

Security is a multitude of technical challenges that should be knitted together by a security manager who can relate the problems to the overall network architecture and business challenges to create a picture of risk. That is security. IT operations is administration and support of IT systems—it is some way short of security, but most organizations leave everything except provisioning of audits, security standards, and checklists to IT and network operations.

If you sign up for a career in security (I will cover careers in security in more detail in Chapter 6) in some operations team and you have an interest in computing, be prepared for a disappointment. Most likely your role will involve covering tasks such as installing patches, monitoring IDS, running autoscanners and sending the reports with either extensive or minimal false positives checking (either way, it is bad!), monitoring SIEM logs, or performing user account provisioning and decommissioning. This is not security!

Then there is the use of checklists as a substitute for thought and analysis in security. Checklists in security are used in so many ways now. An automated vulnerability scanner is a tool that runs a checklist of vulnerability tests against a target, and if the vast majority of security pros are to be believed, such a tool can be used in place of a more expensive manual penetration test.

Operating system security controls are critical, and the way the security industry handles this area serves as an illustration of the frailty of the checklist approach to security. Operating system (OS) controls are central to the way we should be managing vulnerability, but this area is rarely given any attention. If the proper amount of analysis is deployed in the area of OS security controls, we can maximize our security benefits while reducing our spending on ineffective products.

The checklist ethic implies that a Solaris Unix server hosting a critical database can be assessed by an analyst with no Solaris experience, either by some automated means, by running a script, or by reference to a checklist of Unix shell commands.

In reality, many firms do not actually check OS security at all (in many cases, they *think* they are checking OS security, but in reality, all they are doing is running an autoscanner against the targets—this is very far from checking OS security).

The problem with the checklist approach here is twofold: firstly, if CASEs with no Unix/security experience run tests and find problems, how are they going to be able to convince IT operations to address the problem if they cannot explain anything about it (certainly they will not understand the inherent risks)? The fix may after all end up costing severely.

The second problem is that personally in 10 years I have never seen a Unix checklist that comes close to the mark in terms of a decent checklist, as in a checklist that does actually cover the bases that need to be covered in a critical server (perhaps a server that hosts "crown jewels") type of situation. There are some of the more obvious concerns with Unix security, but then there are privilege escalation vectors that are used frequently by Hackers but are not covered in the checklist.

In these types of situations where critical devices need to be meticulously checked, the Hacker skill set is sorely needed. Hackers understand the threats and attack vectors. They know how they would first break in remotely and (if needed) escalate privileges locally. With the CASE situation and checklists, there is one problem in that the checklists miss critical checks, and then there is the aspect that the CASE is unlikely to understand the implications of vulnerability detected by his or her script or whatever automated methodology that is deployed. The only justification he or she can use to make a security fix is that it is "best practice" to do so, or there is a security policy that mandates the fix. In the latter case, the security department will just grant a policy exemption in the event an objection is raised against the fix implementation.

Even organizations in the same industry sector face radically different security challenges—*security is complex*. The checklists and best practices method is one where there is the explicit implication that the same checklists and best practices are applicable to all organizations. No further analysis or justifications for risk mitigation measures are needed. Best practices are exactly that—they are the best. Enough said, right? Of course not!

A security guy says, "It is best practice to use SCP (Secure Copy—an encrypted 'tunnel' method of data transfer) to copy data," with the response "OK but that will slow down my application batch data transfer by four hours—we tried SCP before and it hurt us pretty badly . . . this is an application that is used by paying clients"; "did you not hear the *best* in best practice?" "You are aware that the data transfer is across neighboring internal VLANs off the same switch?" The aforementioned scenario illustrates how it is possible that CASE security departments can become so unpopular in organizations. Where there is a lack of actual practical IT security knowledge that can be used to assess the risks, it will be replaced by a belligerent use of the best practice phrase and/or the company's information security policy (i.e., a checklist), or as I explained in Chapter 2, there often will not be any response at all—just a deathly, defiant silence.

The third post-2000 development that was covered in this chapter was the rise of the audit-driven security strategy where an organization will gear its security strategy in as minimal a way as possible just to meet regulatory compliance requirements.

With the audit-driven strategy, there is first the problem that the audit itself only covers a small percentage of IT resources, and the targets will most likely not be the most critical targets. The audit is really only a sampling exercise, and the targets in the sample can be doctored to be those that are known to be compliant.

Second, although more subjective, is the problem that most auditors are junior, and what actually qualifies them to do security assessments? I have been witness to numerous first- and second-hand reports to the effect that OS security audits were carried out by auditors with no experience at all—they were using shell scripts prepared for them by others in the company, and the scripts were full of holes (the vulnerability tests performed showed a lack of understanding of the vulnerability, and there were far too few checks performed by the script; in the example I gave in this chapter, there were only six tests performed for Linux, and one of the tests demonstrated a misunderstanding of FTP user access controls).

Clearly the minimalist approach to security is not going to prevent bad things happening with business-critical information assets and applications, but this strategy is exactly the one used by most large organizations globally: how did this come about?

Organizations can adopt a pass-the-audit strategy as a result of either upward or downward pressure. The downward pressure case came about as a result of C-level execs losing patience and trust with their security team. First there was the Hacker ethic in security that, while showing confidence, failed in its appreciation of business and corporate cultural goals. Then there was the CASE ethic that was so far off the mark in its analytical offering that C-levels felt blind to the risks in their organizations. The result of all this was to give up trying to understand the real challenges in security and revert back to the simplest and most minimal solution—an information risk strategy geared up to just about meet compliance goals.

The upward pressure to adopt a pass-the-audit approach is the more common scenario; it arises out of a lack of the technical security skills necessary to combat risks, and sometimes also there is a pressure on managers to meet KPI target deadlines (or they will not get their bonus or promotion opportunities). Trying to be too analytical in security is seen as merely slowing things down, and even if the skills exist in the security team, analysis is seen as a bad thing when there are KPI targets involved. KPI targets are often geared around audit milestones because the audit is practically the only measurable activity performed by the security team.

An example of the upward pressure situation is where it is known that a vulnerability management strategy based on the use of expensive automated tools does not work in terms of an actual risk mitigation approach—but this approach is adopted nonetheless because it is faster and easier to implement. The vulnerability management tool supposedly measures items of OS/application security that are applicable to the audit requirements. The reality is though that such tools can only make "guesses" in vulnerability testing, and the most critical and obvious security problems will be missed.

The real folly of all this checklist/best practices/audit-driven approach to security is that one of the bonuses that came with this minimization, to put it crudely, was that security could be delivered with cheaper staff who did not necessarily have any analytical skills at all. But having said that, graduates, MBAs, and even master's degree holders are employed in infosec. If the role of the modern security pro is merely to get firms through their checklists of compliance requirements, then why would management even bother hiring graduates—doesn't this sound a bit expensive? Isn't it the case that all you really need is a person with a pulse who at least looks neat and respectable?

If decision makers in security can actually swear that they do not have a problem with their information risk management practices in their respective organizations, then clearly they are spending too much on security staff. Why even use fresh graduates? Big business can go even cheaper than fresh graduates, or even undergraduates for that matter! But on this point, I will leave the details up to the reader.

5

AUTOMATED VULNERABILITY
SCANNERS

This chapter is quite technical in some areas. If your security strategy is geared purely toward compliance and passing the audit with minimum analysis, and you are happy with that picture, you may skip this chapter and pretend it never existed. You may continue to rely on near-full automation in your vulnerability management strategy, but I do need to give a warning: I would be more than happy to make a huge wager to the effect that *more than 90%* of the victims of recent unauthorized activities based their vulnerability management purely on the use of automated assessment tools.

Automated vulnerability scanners are tools such as Nessus and GFI LANguard, which supposedly can be used to replace the Hacker in remote vulnerability assessment—at least this was the premise widely touted in the industry for the past 10 years or so. Instead of getting a Hacker team of four to assess your perimeter security for two weeks at a cost of US$40,000, you can instead use open-source software, in which you can punch in a few target IP addresses, hit the enter button, and as if by magic a few hours later (or less—depending on numerous factors), you have a nicely formatted report. No IT experience is needed to perform this automated analysis function, and any security analyst, regardless of his or her level of experience or knowledge, can appear to be a Hacker. Sounds great? Please read on.

Just to put some perspective/prequalification on this chapter—I am not of the opinion that automated vulnerability scanning techniques are useless and that manual penetration testing is the answer to all our prayers in security. In fact, after a few years in security, I could see that remote penetration testing, even when performed under optimum conditions, in most cases does not deliver the kind of value that many expect it to deliver (more on that in Chapter 7). In this chapter, I am only covering the nuances of autoscanners, and in some parts, I compare autoscanning with manual penetration testing from a required-skills point of view and also from the point of view of "return on investment" in time and other resources.

In Chapter 4, I commented on the "rise of the automated vulnerability scanner" and covered the story behind the industry-wide, global adoption of this genre of tools since the early 2000s.

With automated vulnerability scanners (I will call them "autoscanners" for the sake of brevity in this chapter), there are some embryonic signs of awareness starting to creep into infosec as to the disadvantages of a fully automated approach to vulnerability assessment—but the extent of the problems does not appear to be well known. The main reason why this is the case is because the people in the industry with the skills or enthusiasm required to know what happens "under the hood" with autoscanners were either laid off or fired before 2002, or they were branded luddites (when they gave negative reports on autoscanners, they were accused of merely trying to protect their jobs as manual penetration testers).

For service providers such as TSAP, there was a real danger of giving clients overinflated expectations with autoscanner-based services. For three years or more, the message given to clients by regional folk was that TSAP's automated vulnerability scanning service delivered the same quality as a manual penetration test, but the cost was 97.5% less! So in 2004 I decided to take on an impossible task and go against the security industry tide. I called a regional webinar in order to help analysts and sales people bring client expectations more in line with reality.

In the webinar, I had two major factors working in my favor: one was that the firm had recently phased out its manual penetration testing service (if we no longer delivered manual testing, I could not be accused of merely trying to protect my job by speaking out against full automation), and the other was that I enjoyed good relations with regional analysts. However, despite these factors, I was shocked at the reaction of the crowd to my webinar content. I was practically booed off stage!

There was palpable discontent on display when I showed a chart that put the value returned by autoscanners at slightly more than that returned by use of a simple port scanner (like nmap for example). Angry murmurs and mutterings were heard. Angry? Well, this also surprised me. Anger was quite a strong emotional response, I thought. I did not realize it at the time, but there was a strong emotional attachment to autoscanners. I did not consider the fact that autoscanners had been making buffoons look like Einstein for several years, and the sales people (and therefore the managers) loved the fact that they could sell cheaper services. If something is expensive, it takes a lot more brainwork to sell that thing, as compared to something that is 97.5% cheaper.

Later in the slide show, I suspended the talk in order to try to rationalize responses and get some actual solid feedback other than primordial groans and chest beating. Was it possible I overlooked something in my webinar? Maybe there were gems in the use of autoscanners that I was not aware of space to clear? After all, I had made mistakes before. If my audience could give me a logical point (based on reason) as to why my content was erroneous, or perhaps I had overlooked something, then I would happily stand corrected. If there was no such logic in the discussion, history told me that the motivations for the malcontent were based on emotion or politics or both. As it turned there were no technical or logical explanations produced to refute my presentation content.

There was one analyst who compared the autoscanner functionality with a "script kiddy" type of testing, thereby showing either a misunderstanding of the term "script kiddy" or a belief that autoscanners are more functional than they really are. Autoscanners do not attempt to exploit vulnerability they detect. The term "script kiddy" was coined from the Hacker era of the 1990s, and it describes a security enthusiast who scans for potential vulnerability then "Googles" for public-released exploit code. So the hacking methodology of the script kiddy is merely to use other people's work and show no creativity or "genius" (according to the Hacker fraternity). Autoscanners never had anything close to this type of functionality. These tools made bad guesses at vulnerability, and that was that. There was no further testing or probing.

The autoscanner was, and still is, seen widely across the industry in general as being a replacement for technical know-how in security. There is a strong emotional connection with many analysts and these tools. The U.S. side of the TSAP operation was even rolling out an "early warning system" that was based on using autoscanner "nodes" in client subnets that would theoretically alert the client of a new vulnerability in their network—"within minutes" of the zero-day going public. The new vulnerability details (in the way of a Nessus plug-in, if one existed) were fed into the network central management server from an all-seeing, all-knowing source of "zero-days" and "underground activity" (but was in fact a publicly available resource of vulnerability data similar to that of the Open Source Vulnerability Database). The management at TSAP was firmly behind this project and saw dollar signs in its deployment.

The belief that the autoscanner is an effective weapon to use in vulnerability management is deeply ingrained in security and has been for a very long time. In some quarters, usually the lower levels of security line-management and up, there is real belief in the quality of autoscanners. In other areas, there is some awareness of the weakness of these tools, but also hypothetically they can be used to compensate for a lack of technical skills while cutting labor costs. "Cutting labor costs" you hear? In the capitalist world, this is the all-powerful opiate that can lead to the kind of emotional attachment I described earlier in this chapter—plus as I mentioned, the tools can make a CASE appear to be a Hacker to the uninitiated.

Did information security stumble into this autoscanner trap, or enter it knowingly? In reality, it is a combination of both.

Internally for end users such as retail and investment banks, the autoscanner paradigm supposedly enabled massive cost cutting in that there was no longer a need to outsource the security assessment or employ dedicated internal staff with the necessary manual skills. For security service providers, so the thinking went, they no longer needed to hire highly skilled (and therefore expensive) experts; the autoscanner software revolution saved the day.

The autoscanner finds its way into corporate information security practices either directly or as an "engine" for expensive vulnerability management software suites, and it does play a major part in security these days. When there is a need to assess the vulnerability of an application or network/server, 99 times out of 100 there will be a recommendation from a security analyst to "run a scanner against it," meaning a tool such as Nessus, for example. You will see this recommendation time and time again in forums, blogs, and so on. If the scanner gives a green light, then supposedly all is OK, and everyone can sleep at night.

There are autoscanners that scan target IP address ranges for listening services bound to open ports, then try to guess the software (and version) bound to the port, and then attempt to guess at vulnerability with those services. Then there are automated vulnerability assessment tools that were designed to autotragically assess the vulnerability of Web-based applications.

Around about 2003, organizations celebrated in their belief that they had finally cracked firewall configurations—and to be honest, it was rare to find open ports in corporate perimeters that were obviously not required to be open to the whole Internet (before 2003, it was quite common to remotely find wide-open services such as Windows SMB and Cisco device HTTP and telnet services). But then the realization dawned that there were custom-built Web applications listening on ports 80 and 443 that by business logic had to be "open" to the whole Internet. The network access control (NAC) offered by firewall technology could not protect an application that, by business requirements, had to be open to whichever client requests a connection. "What about the security of these applications? We can't protect them with our firewall so what are we going to do?"

Automated Web application vulnerability scanners (in this chapter, I will refer to them as "Web app autoscanners") do exist as commercial and open-source offerings, but 100% automation in Web application security testing is also an inadvisable strategy; I will cover these points in Automation and Web Application Vulnerability Assessment.

In this chapter, I will give some coverage to the autoscanner and Web app autoscanner dilemma from the technical side, as in what do the tools actually do?

Law of Diminishing Enthusiasm

Through this and later chapters, I talk extensively about service quality in security and I often use TSAP as an example firm, so it is worth trying to give an indicator of the levels of experience in the TSAP Asia–Pacific (APAC) region. TSAP was made up of six regional staff based in the Hacker lab in Thailand (with the skill levels as was depicted in Chapter 2) and one or more security analysts in each of the APAC countries—South Korea, Hong Kong, Taiwan, Singapore, Indonesia, Australia, and Malaysia.

I could best illustrate the levels of experience with the TSAP regional analysts as follows: the most experienced analyst in the region (outside of the Bangkok "Hacker lab") was supposedly a Unix guru because "she knew the vi editor." Vi is a standard Unix text editor with some very useful text manipulation commands, but it can be difficult to use at first. Some time is needed to learn the commands—it is certainly not as intuitive as learning Microsoft Word. But on the other hand, it is normally expected of Unix administrators that they learn the vi editor in the first month of their career. Let us just say that if one were of the disposition to brag about something, knowledge of vi would not be up there near the top of the list of proud achievements—it is not something you would tell your grandchildren about. But by the frame of reference of regional TSAP security analysts, someone with vi experience was seen as the god of Unix.

When I joined TSAP, I arrived with good references from IBM—but most importantly, I loved IT to the extent that I was coding (mostly in Perl) and researching in my spare time. However, I did not have the almost psychotic devotion to IT held by my Hacker colleagues, and so my experience in areas such as hacking techniques and so on was limited. So my own level of experience was somewhere between the Hackers and the regional analysts, and it is for this reason that I was the "chosen one" who was tasked with autoscanning for the APAC region. The autoscanner role was beneath the Hackers, but also it was seen as too challenging for regional analysts.

I doubt there are too many security pros around who know autoscanners as well as I do—and there is no narcissism in this assertion whatsoever. I happened to be in a somewhat unfortunate position of being in an ever so Dickensian Victorian workshop type of situation whereby I was levered into a role that required me to conduct many scores of perimeter security scans in my first two years in TSAP. Believe me, I would not wish such a fate on anyone.

My personal dealings with autoscanners go back to the very start of my career in information security with TSAP in 1999. TSAP was engaged in selling its own security certification program, the more expensive version of which ("enterprise certification") would get clients forking out US$100,000 per annum (I say "per annum," but not so many of them renewed their program after the first year).

Perimeter security assessments for TSAP certification clients were carried out using a now-extinct autoscanner from NAI called Cybercop Scanner—not a cheap piece of software (after all, the tool would generate a 3D rotating network map, only if the targets were on your physical VLAN/subnet—a brilliant but completely useless feature). Clients were under a mandate to mitigate or work around vulnerability discovered by the tool if they wanted to be certified, unless they had valid business reasons not to do so.

I have to say that initially, in my early career naivety, I was quite enthusiastic about the scanning task. The buzz in TSAP and the industry in general was all about autoscanners at the time. The thought of a software tool that would automatically do what my Hacker colleagues could do (I had worked with them on penetration testing engagements, and I was very impressed by their assessment acrobatics) was somehow compelling.

To illustrate the negatives of autoscanners, some of my experiences in actual live autoscans are covered in the next section, but just for now, I want to explain how my attitude toward autoscanners changed from one of enthusiasm to one of doing everything I possibly could to avoid the autoscanning task.

My first scan was for a Korean client and approximately 30 items were returned as potential vulnerability by Cybercop Scanner. Of these, after some lengthy testing that went well into the wee hours of the morning, there was nothing useful to report to the client apart from the port scanning results [a list of "open ports" or listening network services against the IP address of the target(s)]. With all of my testing, I also used Nessus as a "backup" in order to hopefully validate or even extend my results.

My second scan was for a Malaysian bank, and the tool returned a similar result, except there was a somewhat negligible vulnerability reported that was actually valid but also one that the client was probably aware of. Again the only real value in the results (after a whole day of false positive testing) was the port scan result, which could be attained by use of an open-source port scanner like nmap, with considerably less diligence.

There was a pattern developing here. In my first 10 client scans, the handful or so of reported vulnerabilities that were real, bona fide vulnerabilities were barely even worth reporting to the clients. These were vulnerabilities in the "intelligence vulnerability" classification that was basically information from the target that could be used by Hackers to expedite their attack—for example, the scanner could report that a Webserver was listening on port 80 of a target and the product was Microsoft Internet Information Server (IIS) version 4.0.

The version information (also known as "banner") is detectable by a Hacker, and given the product and version, he or she can better direct her attack—maybe she has exploit code available for vulnerability with this service. If this information is not available, it can take him or her longer to deduce the product and version listening on port 80.

The level of effectiveness of a security safeguard is not a quantitative measure in that numbers can be put to it. If we are talking about something like an intrusion attempt from an unauthorized party from somewhere outside your private network, then the measure of effectiveness of a safeguard can be roughly imagined by how much additional time is required to mount a successful attack as a result of your safeguard implementation.

All attack attempts will be successful eventually. Improving your defenses only increases the time required for a successful attack—it does not completely mitigate your vulnerability forever. Hopefully attackers have insufficient resources in time, materials, and/or motivation, and they give up their attack effort.

With the IIS banner issue, there is no straightforward fix other than using a third-party product such as a proxy to filter the banner information from the response. But anyway how much benefit is there in hiding the banner? Attackers will generally be able to fairly quickly deduce the product, and even automated attack designs include trying a whole range of vulnerability probes regardless of any banner information returned. So in this case, is there any justification in installing a third-party proxy product in a stable production environment—a potentially disruptive change requiring testing, rollback plans, and significant resources (i.e., the cost is not negligible)?

Microsoft release patch fixes for security vulnerabilities, but they never chose to give administrators an easy way out for this IIS banner intelligence vulnerability. There is no real benefit in even reporting this banner issue for clients. Even if a ready-made fix exists (other products such as Apache Webserver and Sendmail give administrators a configuration file directive for hiding or deliberately misreporting product identification banners), implementation of the fix would not make an attacker's goal significantly more challenging to attain.

From my first 10 scans, I had zero vulnerabilities to report (for which I thought there might be some value in fixing the issues discovered) to clients. The banner issues were reported as "informational," but I did not attach a relative/qualitative risk rating (such as high, medium, or low) because quite frankly these vulnerabilities were off the lower end of the scale.

There were some vulnerabilities reported in a handful of later scans to do with File Transfer Protocol (FTP) problems and some problems with mail relay and simple Network Management Protocol (SNMP), but these were issues that clients were already aware of.

After my first three months or so of scanning, I was asked for a feedback report by management, and I had to give an honest report that said I had not seen *enough* to suggest the scans were ineffective or lacking in value, but at the same time, I also had not seen any value in them after a short period. I had been using these tools for a period of only three months, but the picture was emerging of their effectiveness—and it was not a pretty picture.

In client tests, there were often 50 to 500 vulnerabilities reported for 20 to 30 "visible" target IP addresses. I was spending hours testing for false positives (I will give more details in the next section as to my methodology); quite often there was a deadline of five business days for the report delivery, and I was juggling the false positive testing with other professional services tasks.

The expectation could be that the time taken to perform false positive testing would fall over time as one became more experienced with the tools and their nuances, but this is not really the case. There was a slight drop-off in testing times over six months, but the tool did very often loudly declare highly critical vulnerability with a real, existing service name that did at least match the reported vulnerable service name. The vulnerability could not so obviously be dismissed, even if one had found the same reported vulnerability to be a false positive in previous tests occurrences.

The majority of the vulnerabilities that are not at first clear false positive candidates do not become more clearly false positive candidates with time. They always have to be assessed "manually." The obvious false positives (what should be quite an alarming issue for the autoscanner developers was that quite often the tools would report an issue such as an Apache "buffer overflow" problem when the application was clearly Microsoft IIS!) stay obvious—they were obvious from the beginning and that never changed!

Six months down the road, I was already advocating that autoscanners should be banned, just as the 1997 Ottawa Treaty placed a ban on the usage of land mines. Automated vulnerability scanners had a similar effect on the information security postures of our paying clients. The autoscanner would give a green smiley face (i.e., no vulnerability) with a client's network perimeter, whereas a security analyst with even an inkling of knowledge in their field is aware (from knowledge of public-disclosed product vulnerability) that there are very likely to be issues that the autoscanner failed to detect. In one case, there was a Secure Shell (SSH) port open with a root password of "root123," and from a root shell, it was clear there were many other severe directly exploitable problems with this server—none of them reported by the autoscanner.

How did the TSAP managers in APAC react to my feedback? Their reaction was the same as so many others in similar positions in security at the time. "Selective hearing" was deployed. Only the scant positive parts of my report after three months were retained as absolute, undeniable evidence as to the efficacy of autoscanner tools, and their undeniable quality led the management at TSAP to review the need for the Hacker lab, with the potential for cost savings in two main aspects: Hacker salaries and also their associated travel and hotel expenses (with use of autoscanners, allegedly, local in-country security analysts could deliver remote security assessments instead of having Hackers flying all over Asia).

The aforementioned TSAP management support for autoscanning was very much typical of the service provider scene at the time—much of this support coming from managers who in a few cases did actually believe the negative stories coming from their Hackers about autoscanners, but they lacked the will or means to do the right thing and at least discuss the issues with clients.

I am not aware of even one case from the 2000 to 2003 period where a service provider valued integrity (and the well-being of their devoted employees) over client demands. As a service provider, of course you have to listen to your clients, but if a client cuts your invoice amounts by 90%, when it is certainly not in their best interests to do so, and tells you to reduce your security service quality down from being a top regional player to the level of fast food, do you necessarily have to do as they ask? In fact, fast food is a bad analogy because it is possible to overcook or undercook a pre-prepared, thawed hamburger. It is even harder to do a bad job of an autoscan—although I did hear of a case where the wrong IP addresses were configured and the analyst wound up scanning the U.S. National Security Agency.

False Positive Testing Revelations

The methodology employed by a manual penetration testing expert and the operations performed by an autoscanner are similar in that, as a first step, they will perform a port scan of their target IP address range—but this is where the similarity ends.

When a Hacker carries out a penetration test, there are two phases to the test, and with the second phase, the methodology cannot be generalized. The first is "intelligence gathering" where as much information about the target hosts and organization is gathered as possible (this can include domain name service record harvesting, Google searching methods, and other methods as well as port scanning) so as to give some idea of what to do in the second phase, but as to what actually happens in the second phase, it is different every time (I will cover penetration testing in Chapter 7).

In an autoscan, the second phase methodology is the same for every scan, with some minor variations based on the scan configuration. So first there will be a port scan (this can be configured in different ways, for example, TCP or UDP or both, or all 65535 ports or a smaller subset of ports, or maybe just 1000 or so "well-known services"), and then, after a list of open/listening services are found, the autoscanner will consult its list of vulnerability test modules for the detected service(s). For example, if a sendmail mail server was found (usually listening on TCP port 25) and it was deduced from the service "banner" (I introduced the idea of banners in the previous section) that the version was 8.12.11, then the scanner will go ahead and perform a number of generic Simple Mail Transfer Protocol (SMTP) tests (such as testing for "open relay" and "mail sender forgery," among others), plus some that may be specific for Sendmail 8.12.11 and older.

I mentioned in the first section about my experiences in my earlier days with TSAP and autoscanning. Each and every scan would produce reams of vulnerabilities, most of which were false positives, plus there were usually a handful of "informational" vulnerabilities such as version banners. But there were also some findings that were not so obviously false positives and also not so obviously real vulnerability. In these cases, I first had to figure out what the scanner was actually doing in order to rationalize my findings. I had a Linux PC next to my desk, so I installed a packet sniffer (the packet sniffer was Ethereal, now known as Wireshark) on the machine and then directed the autoscanner at the Linux box. Analysis of the packet data captured in some cases (in particular, with plain text, unencrypted application layer protocols such as FTP, SMTP, Post Office Protocol, Trivial File Transfer Protocol, and HTTP) could help me deduce exactly what the scanner was doing in its vulnerability testing.

In one case, there was an assortment of vulnerabilities reported with FTP for a Korean client. As a brief side point relating to FTP in general and "best practices": the standard line from security analysts is usually that FTP is a plain text protocol and therefore vulnerable to eavesdropping—if possible, it should be disabled and replaced by something like encrypted secure shell file transfer as a matter of best practices. This is a valid point except the last part about best practices. Implementing secure shell access is only best practice if *there is a business case for secure shell given the risks involved*. In many cases, FTP will be just fine.

The scan results for the Korean client included a note that anonymous FTP was enabled (i.e., it was possible to log in to the client's FTP server without having valid authentication credentials), which in itself is not necessarily a problem—it depends how the server FTP directory permissions are configured. However, when I tested the server manually myself using a command-line FTP client, it was clear that anonymous FTP access was not available. So what was happening? Different FTP packages (some of the more common are Microsoft's version, Very Secure FTPD and ProFTPD) give a different error message in response to a failed login. The autoscanner did not actually read the FTP version banner and base its test on the actual FTP version found. Instead it just performed a generic login attempt and then tested for a very specific error response from the FTP service. If that particular error message was not found in the server response, it was deemed that anonymous FTP access was enabled. The only good thing to say about this is that it could be worse (we are supposed to always see a "glass half full" right?). At least in the case where the autoscanner makes a mistake or is not sure, it falls back to reporting vulnerability rather than not reporting anything. As it turned out, the autoscanner reported correct results only in the case of WU-FTPD. Our client was running the IBM AIX 4.2 (first released in 1996—the time of my test was late 2001!) FTP implementation.

In a similar issue with another client, a vulnerability was reported where it was alleged that it was possible for a user to "chmod" under the FTP service (chmod is a Unix shell command used for changing file permissions—FTP servers may be configured with a "chmod" command for changing file permissions with the FTP interface).

There are two aspects here, first of which is the testing methodology used. From my protocol analysis, I discovered that with the reported FTP chmod vulnerability, the autoscanner performed a chmod test and based its verdict on whether or not a specific error code response of "502" was at the very start of the response string. The autoscanner performed its CHMOD test and if the 502 code was not returned (in a specific location in the text string response), the FTP server was flagged as *highly critical* as in Armageddon, the end of all things. However, not all FTP servers will actually return specifically a 502 code, and even if they do, it may not be at the start of the resulting response string. The text string E-R-R-O-R or I-N-V-A-L-I-D could be in the response from the FTP server somewhere, but if the "502" string is not at the start of the response to the chmod command attempt, then the server is flagged vulnerable.

The second point to note is about the validity of the test itself. What were the designers thinking when they implemented this test? What were they hoping to achieve? CHMOD was implemented in FTP so as to allow users to change permissions on their own files, and this is standard FTP functionality. Whether or not it constitutes vulnerability depends on the permissions on the home directory and other permissions on the target. If users can add "world/other" permissions (for unauthenticated users), there could be an issue, but it is subjective.

This will usually only be a problem if the user's home directory is traversable by other lower privileged users.

Should the CHMOD test be to change permissions on other user's files or the user's home directory? If users are able to change permissions on files and directories outside of the user's home directory, then this could result in a security issue, but again, it is subjective. The text in the automatically generated report was only something to the effect "CHMOD enabled on the server" and it was flagged as a critical issue.

Suffice it to say it takes an analyst who knows Unix, hacking, and FTP to make a call on the technical aspect of the vulnerability and the inherent risk. Pure usage of automated tools achieves little in terms of risk assessment and lots in terms of resource wastage.

Putting yourself in the shoes of a client who is paying for your automated vulnerability scanning service and they receive a report with red colors against the aforementioned FTP "vulnerabilities" I have just described, just how confused do you think your client would be? Also if you are a CASE security analyst (see Chapter 3) in an internal security department of a Fortune 500 company and you send this same report to your IT operations team, how much interdepartmental "synergy" will there be after this false positive incident? (I mentioned in both Chapters 3 and 4 about how automation and checklists have served to drive a wedge between security and IT departments in large organizations). In either the end-user or the service provider scenario, how much time would it take them to resolve this, and at the end of it all, how much value have they drawn from the experience? And in order to resolve this conundrum, is it really the case that analysts with no related skills (in this case, Unix, FTP, and penetration testing—specifically knowledge of vulnerability and threats) can be deployed in false positive testing? I think the answers are clear.

As a further example of erroneous vulnerability checking by autoscanners, a few years later, in 2003, there was a Microsoft announcement of a vulnerability in the webdav component of IIS (Microsoft Security Bulletin MS03-007). There are two things to note here: it was a week or two before a patch was made available, and also that the webdav buffer overflow issue was not specific to webdav functionality; it was a wider problem to do with a bug in a Windows Dynamic Linked Library—the file nt.dll. nt.dll (take a hint from the file name) is a core part of the operating system, and it was used by various other software packages.

Exploits were available for the webdav problem within a few days of its announcement. The problem could be exploited through webdav or local exploit of the nt.dll buffer overflow.

I have to say that as with many other plugins, the Nessus plugin for the webdav vulnerability test was released very quickly. But what did the plugin actually do as a vulnerability test? Packet sniffing revealed that the autoscanner was only sending an HTTP METHOD string ("OPTIONS * HTTP/1.0") and then searching for the string "DAV" in the output. If "DAV" was found, the vulnerability was flagged red, critical, doomsday.

Several points arise here. Just for brevity, I will cover two of them. First was that the issue was wider than just an issue with the webdav functionality of IIS. So even if clients had followed the Microsoft workaround instructions and disabled webdav, the vulnerability could in all likelihood be locally exploited—slightly less risky perhaps (although in most cases, not significantly so), but vulnerability still exists nonetheless. If clients disabled webdav, the string "DAV" no longer appears in the output of the OPTIONS method request, and there is no vulnerability flagged. This clearly smells nastily like a false-negative situation. The likelihood of remote compromise is reduced, but the local threat remains—and in all but a few cases, it cannot be ignored.

Second was that even after the patch was released, many organizations went right ahead and immediately installed the patch (although this was not usually as a result of a recommendation from security; it was usually an IT operations initiative). So what happens after the patch is installed? Well, in all likelihood, the system is no longer vulnerable to this unchecked buffer problem, but the string "DAV" still appears in the response to "OPTIONS * HTTP/1.0". So even if the Microsoft patch had been installed, the system is still flagged as vulnerable and at *high risk* by the autoscanner.

The Great Autoscanning Lottery

Overall then, how can we best summarize the technical methodology that was programmed into autoscanners?

When I first came across Nessus, there were approximately about 1200 or so vulnerability "patterns" or tests included in the scanning engine database. Now there are more than 40,000 to cater for new product releases, older versions of software, and also since I first used Nessus in anger, there have been a number of tests added for operating system tests under an authenticated login session (there are tests for Microsoft Windows platforms, and the option is given to provide secure shell access credentials for testing; mostly these operating system plugins test for the existence of security patches, and in the case of Windows, there are some tests made on user accounts configurations—issues such as empty or unchanged passwords and so on).

There are more test patterns available for use with autoscanners now, but the testing modus operandi has not changed, and neither would I expect it to change.

There are different classes of vulnerabilities, such as intelligence vulnerability, for example. Autoscanners report on these as low risk issues, really just informational points. Then there are other vulnerabilities such as buffer overflow issues and known (publicly declared) vulnerabilities with services such as IIS, Apache, and Berkeley Internet Name Daemon Domain Name Server (BIND DNS). These are vulnerabilities for which an exploit may or may not be available "in the wild." If an attacker has access to an exploit, he or she can use it against the server, and from there, several different outcomes can occur, depending on the nature of the vulnerability and/or the exploit. Perhaps the server or service could crash or the exploit could result in the execution of shellcode that results in a shell opening for the attacker on a higher port. The shell gives the attacker the potential to enter operating system shell commands under the privilege level of the service that was exploited. So if an Apache Webserver was running under the process ownership of user "www," then the attacker gains the privileges of "www."

What does the autoscanner do in order to test for buffer overflow/ programming error type security bugs? *The answer is that it does not actually do anything.* If we take a case of an Apache buffer overflow problem with versions 2.0.36 and higher, the autoscanner finds port 80 in its initial port scan. It knows that port 80 is typically bound to by an HTTP Webserver process, so then it passes a query such as "GET/HTTP/1.1" plus some returns. If the service is some kind of Webserver, it will respond with a bunch of text, perhaps an error message, but in there, somewhere, will very likely be a string that identifies the product and version of the Webserver. In this case, the autoscanner finds that the Webserver is a variant of Apache, and its version is 2.0.36. What is next? It looks up in its database of publicly disclosed vulnerability with this version, finds some buffer overflow issues, and reports (usually) highly critical vulnerability with the service bound to port 80.

With this class of potentially exploitable software bug vulnerability, the scenario will in nearly all cases be the same. No actual testing is done. The presence of a certain version of software is known (from the banner), and the autoscanner pulls out all the vulnerability it knows for this version and flags highly critical vulnerability—based purely on guesswork.

What is the problem with this you may ask? Granted, there is a chance that the vulnerability is present on the server under testing, but in the real world, there can be many factors that would prevent an exploit; in fact, more often than not, a direct successful exploit whereby an attacker can connect remotely to a shell will not be possible because the standard-issue, script-kiddy exploit (found from a Google search) binds a shell to a higher port that is filtered by a firewall (the shellcode execution results in a port opening, but access to the port is denied by the firewall). And then, even if attackers can attain a shell, they then (although not in all cases) need to raise their privileges before wreaking havoc on the network in general. Depending on the situation, there are several steps involved before financial damages can be inflicted. Just because a perimeter device exploit is successful, in many cases, that particular exploit will not directly result in financial damages for the hosting organization.

You know it really does not matter how hard you try; you can never reduce network security down to the level of simplicity where you see a down-level version of software (or you *think* you see; in many cases, banners can be made to display whatever the system administrator wishes), look up publicly disclosed vulnerabilities with that service, and flag them as highly critical risk conditions without any further brainwork. IT operations staff responsible for fixing this "vulnerability" will have a lot of questions about this issue because nine times out of 10, even something as apparently simple as installing a patch involves a lot of work in terms of raising change records and the impact studies required therein. Security analysts issuing autoscanner reports that flag highly critical vulnerability based on guesswork had better be ready to explain their findings in terms of how easy it would be to exploit the vulnerability; and then once the exploit is successful, what does it mean for the overall security posture? Are today's CASE-oriented skill sets geared up for this kind of interaction with other departments? The answer is unequivocally "no" in most cases. The security department loses out in these situations. What happens next time an automated vulnerability scan report is sent to operations? The email will be deleted or given a cursory glance-over at best.

I have conducted some of my own testing recently of autoscanners because between 2003 and 2010 I rarely used these tools mostly because of the lack of value returned from the time invested. My opinions today are unchanged from 2003, although I cannot state for sure whether the buggy vulnerability tests (such as those described above with the webdav issue) still exist.

A test on my own Ubuntu Linux test Virtual Private Server (VPS), with out-of-date software, open FTP, MySQL open on the default port, and no firewall, revealed exactly what I suspected—the autoscanner tools are the same as the good old days in terms of value returned.

The report generated from my VPS scan was 120 (!) pages long (if I was going to print it out, which I did not). Forty percent of the report content was related to banner information and other intelligence vulnerability. Another 30% was related to SSL certificate problems such as "weak cyphers deployed" and various bits n bobs to do with the certificate information not matching real information. The remainder of the report informed me that I have several *critical* risk issues with my Apache Webserver—but as I described above, this can be translated roughly as "I, your loyal autoscanner, have deduced from your banner on port 80 TCP that you run Apache Webserver, and according to public sources of vulnerability information, there are several highly critical vulnerability conditions with your version of Apache Webserver. I have not actually run any vulnerability tests, I am merely guessing, but anyway for your own safety I feel obliged to inform you of this."

The most disappointing aspect of my test scan was that the autoscanner is supposed to be able to do application layer tests in order to identify a product version. I have ProFTPD bound to port

1980 TCP (not its default command port 21), proudly displaying the default product banner. However, the autoscanner did not recognize the service bound to port 1980 as FTP. So in this case, just configuring a service to listen on a nondefault port defeated the autoscanner. Even a simple port scanner, such as nmap, can be configured to run (with the -sV option) to identify services bound to a port, and it usually does a decent job of this.

Of the 40,000 or so vulnerability tests in the autoscanner database, what proportion are actually reliable tests? Back in 2003, it was less than 5%. More recently, some tests have been added for administrators such that they can add some authentication credentials and ask the autoscanner to perform some tests on Operating System configuration. But even with tests performed under an authenticated session, the number is still less than 10%. The vast majority are really not tests at all; they are only there to inform system administrators that their software is not the latest stable release—something that in nearly all cases, they are aware of anyway.

Of the authenticated session tests, in the case of Windows, some aspects of user account configuration are tested, but with both Unix and Windows, the vast majority of tests are for patch levels. The autoscanner will theoretically inform administrators of missing patches. In terms of security, what would be a good idea here is to include some classic privilege escalation vector tests. For example, under Unix, it could be useful to check the ownership and permission of root cron jobs (scheduled tasks run under the top level admin's account—if any of these are owned by a lower-privileged user, and the script can be edited by a local attacker, when the script runs, it will run under root privileges).

Judgment Day

In this final section on autoscanners, I will attempt to give an overall verdict on the autoscanner phenomena that swept information security since 2000 and one that majorly contributed to the dramatic shift in skills deployment in security.

In most cases, especially when an autoscanner is used for vulnerability assessment of a network from "the outside" (i.e., a network is scanned from the public Internet or some other untrusted network), the value returned by the autoscanner is really only the port scan results. But the report generated will be huge in all cases, even with only one target IP address.

The time taken for system owners to sift through the report for false positives, compared with the minimal value returned, which is usually only the port scan results, represents a fairly dire waste of corporate resources.

What about the case where an organization wishes to scan a critical internal subnet without any firewall/NAC hindrance? Because the autoscanner will find more open ports, it will run more tests and generate even more report pages. The volume of information produced is quite staggering in this case, but what of the quality/value of the information? The internal case is considerably more damaging because the report findings take longer to validate, and again, the value returned may at best be only marginally better than the external case (internal scans can reveal issues such as NULL sessions for Windows SMB services and default "community strings" for SNMP).

I mentioned the ability of autoscanners to detect issues related to open SMB and SNMP default community strings. In practice, when you raise these issues, the internal operations staff responsible for Windows and network operations/Cisco, respectively, will be aware of them. These days, most network operations teams are aware that default community strings are a problem—having said that, it could be surprising how often you will see the default community strings in use. (But not surprising at all when you consider that changing community strings is in most cases highly disruptive, and therefore carrying a high initial cost. Do the necessary skills exist in security to build an argument in favor of technical risk mitigation in this area? Not in most cases.)

If the SNMP strings have been changed from their default value in a corporate-wide change, then in theory, you can use the autoscanner to regularly scan for "rogue" default SNMP strings on the network. The same can be said for the other few vulnerability items that the autoscanner detects reliably. You can disable the "guesswork" buffer overflow-type tests and just stick to things that you know your autoscanner can do well.

One more point to note with autoscanners is that if you are deploying an internal scan, you will need to coordinate with other departments. The usual expectation with CASE teams is that your automated scanner is nondisruptive—you can set it off merrily scanning the entire internal network with no side effects. I am personally aware of seemingly random Cisco devices crashing just with default TCP port scanning. These were devices with plenty of memory, and the problem cannot be narrowed down to specific devices and models. Also, if there are servers that are especially old, with legacy software, they may well be susceptible to crashes when subject to autoscanning. Around 2006, an analyst in Malaysia kicked off an internal scan in HELL's Prague data center without any warning. The estimated damage of the unintentional denial of service attack was put at around 200,000 euros.

Really then, if we look at the big picture with autoscanners, where the problem really lies in their corporate deployment is in the level of expectation. The value returned with autoscans in most cases is minimal, while they can be disruptive, and the report processing consumes immense corporate resources in the way of internal communication, printouts, and false positive analysis. The vast majority of scans deliver only port scan results as a point of any value.

Autoscanners absolutely should not be used as a replacement for skilled penetration testers and analysts in general. Challenges in security are too complex for full automation. Certainly it is critical to avoid a situation where you are purely using autoscanners to deduce the levels of vulnerability for critical infrastructure.

There can possibly be a vague benefit in use of a free or very cheap autoscanner in the capacity I mentioned above, that is, only scan for security problems that the autoscanner can detect with an acceptable level of reliability. I cannot imagine a situation where any amount of investment in autoscanner tools can be justified—and some of them are very expensive. Even in the case where the autoscanner is a free open-source tool, remember that human resource is required to configure, run, and coordinate with other IT departments in these activities and in results analysis.

What the autoscanner effectively does is give a list of public disclosed vulnerability with some of your services (as long as they are well known and bound to their default ports), but you can get this with a lot less pain just by applying filters on Websites that display information of products and associated vulnerability (this should not be a stretch: security teams need to be monitoring for new vulnerability announcements anyway). Likewise, for port scan results, use of a free, open-source tool such as nmap gives you the required information in one or two concise, well-presented pages (optionally with product names and versions identified), as opposed to a 150-page report from an autoscanner full of false positives.

Automation and Web Application Vulnerability Assessment

Around 2002, moving into 2003, network operations staff had in most cases configured external firewalls such that where access to ports was not needed, such access attempts were blocked. For example, outside (public Internet) access to a Web-based administration utility bound to port 10000 TCP is usually not needed. By 2003, in most cases, access to this port from the public Internet would be blocked.

Investment in firewalls is to this day still the most effective use of safeguards funds, but what about the case where there is a business driver to make available a Web-based service to whoever may wish to use the service, regardless of their source IP address?

Around 2002, the realization dawned that Web-based applications that were required to be open to the world could not be protected with network-layer firewalls alone, and consequently, there was an explosion in low-quality Web application testing services, performed entirely with use of automated tools. Buzzwords began to emerge in the industry, such as cross-site scripting and Structured Query Language (SQL) injection, and these buzzwords did represent real, genuine concerns.

If an organization develops in-house or outsources development of a custom application, such an application will not have been put to the sword of the security hobbyist community in the same way as a product such as Microsoft Windows XP, for example. Applications in wide, popular circulation such as Microsoft's OS products have been subject to years of intense scrutiny by the hacker community. Much vulnerability with these products will already have been discovered and made public by "researchers," with the subsequent release of security patches from Microsoft that (in most cases) mitigate the problems.

There are allegedly databases full of undisclosed vulnerabilities with Microsoft products that have never been made public, and it goes without saying that because of the complexity of code, and other factors to do with programmers' lack of security awareness, it is inevitable that there will be plenty of security bugs in these products. But at least many of the vulnerabilities have already been discovered.

If you take a complex, custom Web app with many HTTP form input fields, a backend database, an administrative interface, as well as a client interface, such an application will most likely never have been subject to security assessment, and the developers, for several possible reasons, will not even have been aware of secure coding guidelines.

Most vulnerability with Web applications revolves around a failure to properly validate user input, such that you can have cross-site scripting situations. There can be problems occurring when an application that allows user input also fails to remove HTML or JavaScript syntax from the input. The input text string is regenerated in other parts of the application (perhaps a forum feed or generated email for example), where the user's browser interprets the nasty text as JavaScript (that perhaps can result in a session cookie for a banking application being stolen) or some sort of malicious Uniform Resource Locator (URL) link.

One of the more famous hacks of 2011 involved the U.S. security consulting firm HBgary (the case is documented here: http://arstech nica.com/tech-policy/news/2011/02/anonymous-speaks-the-inside-story-of-the-hbgary-hack.ars).

In the "Anonymous" group attack on HBgary, the first stage was an SQL injection attack of their content management system (CMS). The URL used in the first stage of the attack was http://www.hbgary federal.com/pages.php?pageNav=2&page=27. The parameters entered by the user were cobbled together to form an SQL SELECT statement by the application, the results of which were regurgitated back to the visitor's browser. Unfortunately though, the parameters were not properly validated before being processed. The attackers exploited this condition to formulate an SQL query that resulted in user names and passwords for the CMS being leaked. Although the passwords were MD5 hashed, they were brute-forced in a short time frame. The same authentication details were successfully used elsewhere in HBgary, and several stages later, the attackers had achieved their goal.

SQL injection and cross-site scripting problems are only two classes of vulnerability with Web-based applications; there are more than a handful of others.

There are several commercial (some of them costing more than US$10,000 to license) and open-source Web autoscanners on the market, and just as with autoscanners (as I discussed previously in this chapter, these are tools such as Nessus), the overriding perception among security professionals is that these tools are a means to an end of Web application vulnerability. I have come across three different forums where opinions were sought on automated Web application scanning technology. More than 90% of the 500 or so responses spoke in favor of some product or another, although more than 50% of those were from nonindependent sources (e.g., IBM employees advocating Appscan—an IBM licensed product).

Again, just as with autoscanners, there is a growing awareness in security as to the ineffectiveness of Web autoscanners—but the full picture is not at all visible in security circles. Take the example of the HBgary SQL injection case described above. Is there an automated tool that would have detected this problem? Not likely, because of the complexity of the issue. If you were going to design a tool capable of detecting these problems, how on earth would you go about it? There are so many permutations of input combinations even with one field or URL of an application. Most applications in use by organizations are highly complex. The server code can be hundreds of thousands of lines long in total.

Hackers usually pick up on an SQL injection problem by probing different areas of an application. They will do things like adding a single quote in fields or at the end of URLs, hoping to see signs such as a raw database-generated error message that would indicate the potential for SQL injection. After picking up on the signs of an SQL injection condition, the story is far from over; many times it will be necessary to exhaustively try different combinations of punctuation and SQL syntax in order to get a result. Given that the error messages vary radically from one application to the next (and many times, as a security measures, the error returned will be completely nonspecific and contain no details that could be helpful for an attacker), it will be very tricky indeed to program a computer to analyze error responses.

There are freeware tools that can be used to help find SQL injection problems *in very specific situations*. Such tools can be used to increase testing efficiency in specific situations—but they do not replace the need for real expertise in Web application security assessment.

Attackers who have themselves developed database-driven Web applications are in many cases adept at "sniffing out" areas of an application where there might be an SQL-related security issue. Is it going to be possible to program a computer to do this automatically? Theoretically perhaps it is possible, but in practice, it is nearly impossible given the development budgets involved (also, developers rarely have any security expertise, and to be able to detect security issues in complex applications, detailed knowledge of the attack methodology is mandatory).

Many Web autoscanners allow the user to "teach" the testing program how the application is navigated by the user. In theory, this should reduce the guesswork of testing, but in practice, it does not seem to help much—many glaring critical vulnerabilities will be missed regardless.

If we were to compare Web autoscanners with autoscanners, we find a similar trend in terms of useless information being reported (false positives and basic informational items), but the situation with false negatives is considerably worse, mainly due to the application complexity reasons I mentioned above.

Again, when you see reviews of Web autoscanners in magazines and other media, tests will be conducted on a system with known vulnerability, and the magic 50% accuracy rating pops up again. I can assure the reader that this number is vastly inflated in the case of a typical custom-developed Web application that is in actual live production usage in a large organization.

Some of the scanners will miss some fairly basic business logic security problems such as tampering with parameters to gain access to other users' information. Other stars of the false-negative show include failing to detect session-related issues, such as when the application fails to maintain a user-authenticated session through the cycle of the user's transaction—thereby making possible the final stages of the transaction completely unauthenticated.

Where automation can be useful is in "crawling" a site (i.e., building a site map of the application), but then, errors returned by the application can throw the crawler off. It can be troublesome to configure the crawling functionality of an autoscanner.

Earlier Web autoscanners were completely hopeless in terms of detecting cross-site scripting problems. More recent versions of tools are better, but not to the extent that an inexperienced analyst can be trusted to handle the assessment, and false positives will be produced that will need later analysis by a technical expert.

Some tools can detect a blatant cross-site scripting problem where the submitted marked up attack string is returned in the "next page" generated by the application, but the malevolent user input can be "stored" in many places in the application output, such as in logs or alert messages, or emails sent out by the application.

Generally speaking, there is slightly more advantage to be gained in usage of Web autoscanners as compared with autoscanners, but in terms of business-critical Web applications, it comes nowhere near the level sufficient for organizations to be able to avoid usage of Hacker skill sets and manual testing.

The main tool of choice in Web applications testing is a simple, freely available tool—it is merely a proxy, such as Paros (http://www.parosproxy.org) that can be used for manipulating/intercepting parameters in Webserver GET and PUT transactions.

Also some of the Burp Suite tools are purportedly useful and appreciated by expert testers—the proxy tool is popular and the scanner can be directed to increase the efficiency of testing. The user can highlight areas of the scanner's history file and direct the scanner to scan URLs identified therein. Of course, it takes an expert to know to what parts of the application the scanner should be directed, and also for interpretation of the scanner output (if any).

Web Application Security Source Code Testing

An alternative to "black box" security testing of Web applications (where the testing team has little or no prior knowledge of the Web application details) is the white box approach where the testing team has access to the source code of the application.

Again there are plenty of commercial offerings in source code testing, many of them hugely expensive.

Automated tools in white box testing are certainly more effective than the Web autoscanner tools used in black box testing. Clearly with access to source code, there is at least the potential for a tool developer (who also has a Hacker-like skill set) to be able to code something that works. With black box tools, with the "blind" approach, the job of the Web autoscanner coder is much more difficult.

White box tools are more effective at finding issues with cross-site scripting and SQL injection, and they are useful for mapping data flows in an application; but again it takes an expert to analyze false positives and then "walk" the application designers (or the customer of the service provider) through the vulnerabilities uncovered. Many of the application designers, in fact nearly all of them, will have no awareness of secure coding practices—and anyway a checklist of best practices in secure code design does not actually help a nonsecurity expert very much. In fact, many of the problems with source code analyzer tools arise because even the Web autoscanner developers were not themselves aware of the real nature of Web application vulnerabilities or how they may be exploited.

Programmers with no experience in Web application security can familiarize themselves with the concepts of Web application vulnerability from a site such as the Open Web Application Security Project (http://www.owasp.org) and their Webgoat project. But the principles explained there do not prepare one for actual testing with a live application. The vulnerabilities such as SQL injection can manifest themselves in so many different ways. Should a nonsecurity expert be developing source code analysis tools with no guidance? The answer is no, but even so, in reality, these white box source code testing tools are in some cases more effective than the Web autoscanner black box tools.

Summary

In this chapter, I have covered automated vulnerability scanning tools (referred to as "autoscanners"), Web autoscanners, and white box source code analysis tools from my own experiences and those of others.

Autoscanners and related Web application testing products take a very high-profile role in security. The tools take center stage in most large organizations' vulnerability management strategies.

The security industry is slowly becoming more aware of the problems of a fully automated approach to vulnerability assessment, but the full extent of the problems does not seem to be at all well known. Both with autoscanners and Web autoscanners, whenever there is a risk-related query against some aspect of infrastructure security, 99 times out of 100 the CASE analyst response will be something along the lines "run a scanner against it." If the tool reports no critical vulnerability, then allegedly all is fine with the world.

The autoscanner modus operandi is to find products and services on a target IP address by grabbing banner information, and then correlate the discovered service names against an internal database of vulnerability testing modules against those services. Most of these "tests" are not actually tests as such in that no vulnerability probing/testing is performed. They are merely guesses at vulnerability. Other tests are for negligible/informational issues such as intelligence vulnerability and a few others that actually test in the verb sense, in that configuration aspects of the target are interrogated.

The actual tests that do involve some application layer interrogation and come with a decent level of reliability are by far the minority— roughly less than 5% of the overall library of what may be more than 30,000 test modules.

With the vast majority of autoscans, reams of false positives will be output. If a tester is conscientious and lacking industry experience, it will take the analyst hours to process the report for false positives. In most actual tests, especially those from "outside" of corporate firewalls, there will be no vulnerability reported of any note. The only section of the report that has any value will be the port scan results.

Where a target network owner has down-level/old services, and there are publicly disclosed vulnerabilities with these services, the autoscanner effectively informs to the effect "you have old vulnerable software, and here is a list of publicly disclosed vulnerability with your software." Whether or not these issues constitute real exploitable vulnerability is another matter. Many factors can work against a successful exploit, and this is a complex area that cannot be made simple with use of autoscanners.

The false-negative (i.e., the failure to detect real vulnerability) situation with autoscanners is another story. Ratings given in magazines and other media for the accuracy of autoscanners put them at around 50%. It is always 50%! The real figure is way below 50%—not that I doubt the integrity of the reviewers.

There are some autoscanners that were designed to take the testing a step further and actually attempt an exploit of software bugs (e.g., buffer overflows)—and this scenario obviously does give more bang for your buck, but for reasons that will become clearer in Chapter 7, the high price for these tools is still very hard to justify. Attempting the exploit takes the tool slightly past the point of mere guesswork, but it is still several steps short of effective or advisable automation.

With Web autoscanners, over the years since 2002/2003, when these tools were first actively used for business purposes, they have become more effective, but because of the complexity of Web applications and lapse secure coding practices (the reasons behind this are many), the situation with false negatives is severely negative. There is no "cup half full" here. It is what it is—a problem that should never be swept under the rug.

One of the more modern CASE assertions (especially with the onset of frequent large-scale corporate incidents) is that you will never fix all the problems, or as I used to hear almost everyday in my TSAP days, "there is no silver bullet." This is true, but then there are the severe security problems (that lead to severe financial risk) that stare a Hacker in the face within two minutes of root access from a command shell that were missed by the autoscanner.

You would hope that the autoscanner or Web autoscanner could find at least some of the critical vulnerabilities and return some value for the resources invested (which may include a huge license fee)—but such a result is impossible with automated tools because they were not designed to do this. It is not the case that the tools are badly coded—it is just that they were not designed to intelligently probe a target in-depth, in the same way as a Hacker would do in a manual penetration test. Moreover, it is really impractical to attempt to develop such a tool—even if it is possible, the license fee would cost more than the skilled human resource.

Autoscanners do have some "buggy," invalid testing modules (I highlighted some of these in this chapter) where it would appear that the developer was not at all familiar with the security problem under assessment (I will spare you from the details of another story where I once tried unsuccessfully to explain to a developer why having a dot character in a Unix PATH variable setting can be a bad idea). But even if the tools were well conceived, as I am sure some of them are these days, there is the faulty principle of investing considerable resources into a tool that, for all intents and purposes, gives you a port scan result and warns you of *critical* vulnerability—whereas really all the report is telling you is that your software is out of date.

There is a level of expectation with use of automated tools that is vastly overinflated. For so many years now, there has been an expectation with many end users and service providers that the tools do really give a good picture of vulnerability, and that the Hacker skill set is obsolete in security. This level of expectation is light years away from what is actually deliverable with autoscanner usage.

In terms of how we ended up in this autoscanner mess, the closest I can get to a "glass half full" scenario is that the industry decision makers were not sure if autoscanners could deliver, but given the cost savings, they thought they would at least give it a shot. After all, the only people who were in a position to explain the disadvantages of a fully automated approach were the very people whose jobs were on the line—the Hackers. Why should they be believed?

I apologize for belaboring the point about the disadvantages of full automation, but the amount of the labor is proportional to the depth of the problem. A fully automated approach to vulnerability assessment is a very bad idea in highly sensitive situations such as the database server hosting intellectual property or credit card numbers. I would extend this further though and say that the fully automated approach should be avoided at all costs. However, full automation is exactly the strategy deployed by many of the Fortune 500s and multinationals.

Robots on a car assembly line deliver. They put things in the right places. They screw in bolts and punch pop rivets faster than a human can. This works. It is accurate enough. Some aspects of the auto manufacturing industry could be automated. In security, there are some things that autoscanners can do reasonably accurately and faster than by manual means, but not many.

Machines gradually infiltrated factory floors, and in general, the production process got less human/manual and more automated. While the auto industry is considerably older than information security, even today, there are still humans in car factories—not everything can be automated. The process of getting machines to do human tasks took years of evolution, and as the machines got faster and more accurate, more jobs were lost. In security, someone came along with an idea that a piece of software costing nothing could replace a team of four Hackers. The industry jumped on the idea, and this was when corporate security practices were barely five years old. Security is not ready for this level of automation.

The difference lies in the measurement of failure. If robots in car assembly screw up, people end up in the hospital or die. For a year or two at the start of the 2000s, Hackers tried to tell the world that full automation in vulnerability management was a bad idea, but who was listening? That was so long ago that anyone who was listening to the Hackers will have forgotten their message. Now we are in a position where we see almost daily headlines in nontech publications telling us about corporate espionage, malware, APT, privacy violations, identity theft, and so on.

The robots in security are not yet smart enough, and perhaps never will be.

This same Luddite story has been repeated under different guises time and again in the course of the industrial revolution. The Hackers, however, are not automaker assembly line workers, and in most cases, they could not care less if they were so ungraciously phased out by the corporate world. Such multitalented individuals will always find means to make ends meet, by fair means or foul.

6

THE ETERNAL YAWN: CAREERS IN INFORMATION SECURITY

Thus far, I have spoken of the old and new skill sets in security. The Hacker was the typical security analyst of the late 1990s era, as described in Chapter 2. In Chapter 3, I introduced the checklists and standards evangelist (CASE) paradigm—and it was this phenomenon that replaced the Hacker ethic in security service provision and end-user information risk management. The CASE is a skill set as deployed in security today. It can be technically oriented in that they do have IT skills, but the actual practices of modern-day security departments are mostly nontechnical in nature.

In this chapter, I analyze some of the motivations people have for getting into security. Much of the content of this book so far will have given the reader a few tastes of what it is like to be a security professional. In this chapter, I try to paint a more comprehensive picture than I have given so far—a picture you are unlikely to get if you just ask a random security pro. People have different ideas of what it is like to be a security pro, and I will try to put each of the more common ideas in perspective. One expects to get something out of a career in information security; I hope to be able to give a clear picture of whether or not a budding security pro is likely to find what they are looking for in their information security career.

Information security is a body of theoretical knowledge that brings together diverse fields of IT. Usually when you find someone who likes IT, they will love security, or if they do not have any actual experience, they will at least find some affinity with the idea or concepts of theoretical information security.

There is security as a body of research and knowledge, and then there are jobs in security. If you look at how security is practiced in large organizations these days, it can seem at times as though the two (security and jobs in security) are mutually exclusive.

The story with vocational information security is not all doom and gloom. I do see signs, backed up by reports from recruitment agents, that at least some firms have recognized that they need to be more practically oriented in security. The problem is that security has been largely nontechnical for too long—and now firms do not know how to get technical again, what skills are needed, or how to deploy the skills.

The most common approach to the skills problem is to try to find security experts who are also IT operational "hands on types"—but the plan is for them to join IT operations, not security. Under interview, the candidate can prove their IT operations experience by answering some applicable questions, but how do they prove their security expertise? Are they an expert because they have Certified Information Systems Security Professional (CISSP) accreditation? This goes back to my earlier comments about the lack of standards in security, and if the security industry has got the skills deployment wrong for more than 10 years, who will be in a position to decide whether or not a candidate is a security expert? In these hiring cases, the candidate will usually be a systems administrator but with CISSP accreditation (i.e., questionable security experience—really just a sys admin as opposed to a sys admin with benefits).

Migrating all technical security functions [e.g., firewall configuration, server vulnerability management, security information event management (SIEM), and so on] to IT operations is a common scenario—one that is often engineered by the security team themselves. But there is a difference between the technical security skills that are required for IT operational/administrative roles and the Hacker-type skills I described in Chapter 2. I explained in Chapter 4 why the devolvement of tech functions to other IT departments is to our detriment.

Such confusion is expected. Security is still so young. In practically every aspect of security, there are no internationally recognized standards, and security is not like any other area of expertise. There are overlaps between security and business analysis—so what you have is a service provision unit that is kind of IT, only not. Security is not like anything organizations ever tried to do before, and not surprisingly, there will be a learning curve. C-levels first thought of security as an IT discipline, and then they thought they got it wrong and decided it was more of a service management area. In reality, it is mostly IT (but the IT content of the security offering has to be unique as compared with other areas such as development or systems administration), but there is some overlap with other areas of a business. Security is security; it is not like anything else— it is a totally new species.

This chapter can seem at times as though I am talking more about the state of modern security practices as opposed to jobs in security, but the focus is on archetypal roles and responsibilities, and more basically "the things people do" in security. In order to get a picture of the "other side" of the job (the one that exists beyond the hiring process and interviews), it can help to know some common traits that exist in modern security departments.

Information Security and Strange Attractors

What is the attraction with security? Why do people take this road in their lives? I am sure there are other reasons, but some of the more commonly reported reasons are as follows.

- The alluring image of the Hacker as one who is sufficiently clever to be able to break defenses that were designed to keep people out. This is an image-centric driver based purely on vanity. One is unlikely to fulfill the dream of becoming a hacker in a security career. Even penetration testing does not really offer such an opportunity because modern-day penetration tests are not even remotely close to being simulated attacks.
- The fast track to management: Based on what the security pro hopeful has heard from others in the field (this would be the CASE element of course), a career in security means being a manager from day one. I will discuss this point in The Instant Manager.
- The IT track: IT professionals with an affinity for IT see security as being a bridge between different core technologies, and the whole penetration testing show is an interesting and challenging path to take. I will discuss this driver in some detail in The Technical Track.

- There is also the classic example where students or even other IT professionals heard there were a lot of jobs going in security, and this is the only reason for pursuing such a career path—because there is more chance of getting a job in this field compared with others. Not much needs to be said about this premise. Suffice it to say, I would only ask that you spend some more time thinking about this because you will be spending a huge chunk of your lives in a security function. If you are not so enthusiastic about security, maybe just ask yourself if you are really under so much pressure that you have to force yourself to pursue a career in security. Is it really the case that you have no other options? People can feel trapped or forced to get into a field that has no appeal to them, whereas many times they are not really trapped at all.
- The last reason is nearly as bad as the first, and it is one that you will never hear from a security stranger. Although in many cases it is no reflection on the individuals involved, it is true that security departments do get labeled as being a place to hide—an easy option to take for those who lost their way in life. Again there will not be much discussion on this point aside from a brief qualifier to the effect that if you had this impression about security—I am sad to say that in many cases it is true. It just depends what you want to get out of life. Of course, it depends on the organization, but if you are not the ambitious type, security could be the place for you—but if you ask yourself if you do actually *want* this job, the answer will be "no" in all cases.

Specialization in Security

This section sets a necessary framework for the discussion about different perceptions with security careers.

I am a U.K. national and went to university in the U.K. However, when I left university with a degree in computer systems engineering (in 1991), it was the middle of a recession and graduates were not securing "graduate jobs," so to speak. I spent the earlier part of my working life overseas, first with a few years in seismic/geophysical exploration around the Middle East, and then IT programming and system administration in Asia–Pacific. Then later in the 1990s, I returned to the U.K. and started working with IBM, not sure what to expect from my first U.K. "real job."

One thing that surprised me was the level of specialization in the job functions. From my experience of working in Asia, and as I believe is the case in most of the rest of the world, a database administrator (DBA) is a job title that one did not hear very often because IT managers did not see a justification in dedicating a person for this role (this area was not seen as being sufficiently challenging or carrying with it sufficient "intellectual property"). System administrators were also DBAs, on top of their other functions.

I later became aware that some of the bigger banks employed a dedicated DBA. In the U.K., DBAs were not DBAs in the generic sense; they were Oracle DBAs, Informix DBAs, Sybase DBAs, and so on. Instead of employing one person to handle a DBA role, larger U.K. firms were employing several DBAs with specific skills. My first impression was that this specialization strategy carried with it a lot of resource wastage, but later, I came to see that this was the way to go in mission-critical situations. IT change management system changes and regular Business As Usual administration tasks did seem to run a lot smoother with the diverse specialization situation as compared to the single DBA operative situation.

How about information security? Does this specialization situation apply to security also? In the U.K. it does, very much so. I believe this is also the case in many other places, although not to the same extent.

Back in the earlier days of the late 1990s, security pros were Hackers (usually with a title of security analyst), as described in Chapter 2, or security managers. These days? There are specializations in so many different areas. Some of the more noteworthy are "PCI-DSS expert," "privacy expert," and "standards and policies expert."

In most cases, "privacy expert" in the sense of the job description is a role where expertise is sought in privacy standards and regulations—often a very specific regulation. The challenges faced by organizations are in first knowing the requirements of the regulations and then in meeting the requirements. So where is the specialization here? Is it knowledge of the privacy law or regulation? It is hard to believe because the document that describes the regulation is usually publicly available and anyone can read it. Surely the real challenge of compliance is in the IT challenges faced by security and IT—and the security skill set required to meet this challenge cannot really be generalized any more than "security." A security expert (with some management guidance) who can speak the language of IT and actually work effectively with other IT departments is the person needed to fill this role. However, in practice, the candidate who can demonstrate knowledge of privacy regulations is more likely to get the job as compared with an analyst who has broad IT and practical security experience.

The same can be said with the Payment Card Industry Data Security Standard (PCI-DSS). Security departments in large organizations send out these requirements to headhunters who then go searching for people with the keywords "PCI" and "DSS" in their CV somewhere. There is a good chance the wrong person will be hired. The PCI-DSS is publicly available—anyone who has the ability to read is a PCI-DSS expert. Meeting the requirements of the audit is where the real challenge lies.

Why am I talking about this? If you respond to one of these ads and secure one of these highly specialized positions in security, chances are you will be filling a role that not only bores you to tears but also somewhere down the road, perhaps after a year or two, the management will realize they made a mistake, or the position becomes redundant, and you will be out of a job.

In security there is no place for this kind of specialization of roles. What about penetration testing as a position? This is more of a specialized role than just plain old "security analyst," but does it deserve its own specialization? Nope. Security analysts are penetration testers. If they are not, then they are not security analysts. Not all security analysts need to be expert penetration testers, but they must have some familiarity with this area.

And then there is "business continuity/disaster recovery expert." The way the industry handles this area is also suspect. I recall once, around 2008, being at a training center, and in the next room were some BC staff from different firms attending another course. I remember how "civilized" they looked. Let us just say they did not look like Hackers. They were clearly of management material, mostly in their upper 30s/early 40s, appearing confident and superior to menial IT workers in every way. However, I would once again comment to the effect that BC/DR is not massively dissimilar from other security areas.

BC/DR is often a separate department in firms, completely isolated from IT. I think there are various reasons why this happened, mostly connected what I have mentioned in various different parts of this book about the lack of confidence displayed by security department staff. Basically I think the management stance was something like "there is a lot of bad stuff happening in the world and we are told we have to ensure the survival of the business. We see BC/DR as being more business-oriented compared with other security areas. Those people in security don't know our business goals, so we'll get some people who can understand this stuff." Whereas their premise about the security department may be correct, to isolate DR/BC from IT is an extremely bad idea—and a cursory glance over the CISSP course material in this area should be a sufficient indicator to that effect. DR/BC is not more "business'y" than other areas of corporate security, and just like other areas, if you want to meet DR/BC challenges, you have to meet IT challenges. If you want *information* to be available after a disaster, then some involvement with *information* technology is needed, unless you still run your business with pens, carrier pigeon, paper, and filing cabinets.

The security industry is fickle with job titles. Mostly job titles are created in a momentary lapse of reason. There are self-proclaimed subject matter experts, my personal favorite: "evangelist," and the Swiss Army knife of all security position titles—"architect." There are no professional accreditation schemes or paths that if followed successfully can lead one to become a "security evangelist"—these titles are entirely self-proclaimed.

An evangelist (his actual job title was "security analyst") once told me with great confidence that there is no threat from outside the network; threats are all internal, and the challenges in security are all to do with employee awareness. I would like to ask HBgary, Google, Morgan Stanley, and so on ad infinitum (all firms who suffered externally sourced security incidents around 2010 into 2011): "is there a threat from the public Internet to your organization?" And "advanced persistent threat (APT)," the most prevalent buzzword of 2010 through at least to 2011, is not an external threat?

So unfortunately, one cannot read anything from job titles or positions or name cards in security. This makes it hard to figure out what a job entails. Security positions are advertised such as consultant or architect, but there is often no consulting or architecture element in these roles. Of course, there are detailed job descriptions, many of them very technical sounding, but these are really only job descriptions that the hiring organization conveys so as to appear diligent in security. The reality of the roles and responsibilities is in most cases very far from the job description given.

The opposite of the U.K. situation was the one I encountered in HELL. British staff managed our HR team in Prague, and when they went into the market looking for security analysts, they drew a total blank. HR even extended the search further afield to other eastern European markets and Russia. Still, the candidate profiles sent to us by HR were mostly those of completely inexperienced candidates. In the end, the only viable CV sent to us by HR, after five months, was that of an Australian national who happened to be living in the Czech Republic and had security experience from Australia. So much for moving the data center from Heathrow in order to exploit cheaper labor markets!

After a few months, I realized what was going on—it was clear that the HR searches were by job title rather than specific skills. I was aware that there were plenty of security enthusiasts in Prague and very able security enthusiasts to boot—certainly to the level of the Hacker skill set I described in Chapter 2. It was just that the local Czechs did not put themselves in the same boxes as we did in the U.K. A security analyst in the job function/area of expertise sense was not necessarily a Security Analyst (uppercase "S" and "A") in the job title sense. He or she was more likely to have a title such as "IT administrator" or something very general to do with IT engineering/administration along these lines. There were an abundance of Hackers in the Czech Republic.

In the Czech Republic, and certainly in the country that has the reputation for it—Russia—there are so many Hackers, many of whom are very skilled. The more popular theory on this is that education in analytical fields such as math, computer science, and physics is good in these places, but there are also very few jobs for graduates to find. So what you have is a huge backlog of highly skilled, mentally very active computer enthusiasts with plenty of time on their hands to find alternative sources of income other than from paid jobs in "reputable" firms.

So for any multinationals looking to find local talent in Slavic countries in general, and the same probably applies to many other places as well, be wary of doing CV searches using the same job title keywords as you use in your own country. Sounds obvious? I would guarantee that many firms make the same mistake as was made in HELL.

Another noteworthy point for those considering security as a career: the industry seems to be quite enthusiastic about industry sector specializations, and it is good to be aware of this. I mean, if a potential candidate who was never employed in the finance sector comes across an open position for an information security analyst "with finance industry experience," the candidate need not be too discouraged.

Banks can ask for a security analyst with "extensive finance sector experience," but this serves little benefit for the business. Perhaps finance sector firms use specific applications? Well, they do, but again, to an experienced security analyst, an application is an application is an application. Whenever applications are assessed for security, the analyst has to understand the function of the application (i.e., how the user engages with the graphical user interface and so on). All applications are different, but the principles of application security assessment and vulnerability classes are the same. The finance industry is not patron of its own class of vulnerability. There is no "finance sector cross-site scripting vulnerability" and "insurance sector cross-site scripting vulnerability." TCP/IP networks are still TCP/IP networks regardless of which industry sector hosts them, and when everyone finally moves to IP version six (IPv6), the IPv6 network will not care which industry sector it is in. Of course, the business objectives are different from one sector to another, but even security managers are adaptable creatures. They can "evolve" to understand new business objectives. The main cores of ideal security roles and responsibilities are the same regardless of industry sector.

The Instant Manager

If you were under the impression that security jobs have more in common with management than with security analysis, you would be correct. But also, it is not usually the case that a job in security gives you a fast track to a management career. Many would-be security pros see the word "management" in security job ads and make the connection with a job function that is somehow more "mature" or "advanced" than a tech position, and therefore more like actual management, as in a position that grants one influence or control over people or business processes. However, the reality is some way off from this picture.

If a company hires you for a security role on the basis of your MBA alone, regardless of your background, you will be a CASE as described in Chapter 3, and with this, there will be some formidable challenges and hurdles if you are actually to become a "real" manager with people reporting to you and so on.

If you are coming into security under the expectation of getting into some form of management, not necessarily security management, then it goes without saying your daily activities should be more about talking and networking than anything else—and herein lies the problem.

I mentioned in previous chapters about the gap between security and other IT departments. Security can find themselves cut off from other departments frankly because security is seen as failing to offer anything of any value, while imposing restrictions and compliance requirements, with weak or non-existent business and technical justifications business or technical justification.

The other problem is about language, and I am not talking about your ability with foreign languages. Whereas the IT world has precise terms and phrases such as "TCP/IP," which leave no room for misinterpretation, the modern security world has no such standard nomenclature.

Many terms bounce around, such as risk management, vulnerability management, and enterprise architecture—but to satisfy the requirements of these, vulnerability assessment in the form of penetration testing will be needed. People can easily understand what penetration testing is, and there is little room for misunderstanding. "Vulnerability management" though? IT governance? There is no official definition.

The most recent buzzwords get bandied around in security, and if they are not based on anything technical, everyone will have a different version of the meaning of these terms. The most recent buzzword at the time of writing is APT, and even though many security folk will not know the details of any of the forms APT can take, they will at least have a basic idea, and it is a topic that can be safely discussed without too much misinterpretation. Why? Because APT is described in the language of computing and networking—fields that *do* have standard terms and definitions.

Technical discussion involves using words such as router and TCP/IP. There are standard definitions for these terms, and there is little room for misunderstanding. At the simplest level, TCP/IP is a "network language," the same as French and Russian are spoken languages. Senior managers with no hands-on experience can understand roughly what TCP/IP means. But senior managers, and more importantly, IT strategy decision makers all have different ideas of what is meant by IT governance. How does ISO 27001 relate to IT governance? If we implement ISO 27001, we have covered part or all of our responsibilities in IT governance, right? That depends on your definition of IT governance.

Etched in my memory is an interview I had with a big four some years ago. From the very beginning, the interviewer was verging on confrontational. The questions were entirely of the high-level, ISO standard/CISSP study guide type of questions with no relation to any practical aspects of security. For example, I was asked to give security requirements for a software development life cycle, and the answer had to be exactly in the way it was described in the book he had read, or the answer would be wrong and the person giving the answer was a numbskull, a completely useless security professional. He actually seemed to be quite insulted if the answer was not exactly as it was written in whichever book he read, and when he recited his version of the answer, he claimed he was using "industry standard terms."

Many times I have witnessed CASEs seething with anger in meetings with other CASEs. They start by discussing points on the meeting agenda, but after a short while, the conversation takes on a roving disposition. What happens is that different CASEs will use different phrases to describe the same principle, with the result that they end up talking about completely different subjects until such time that they figure out there has been a misunderstanding. Anger results because one CASE believes his or her version is the correct version, while the other one believes his or her version is correct. They both understand the principles under discussion, but they read different books on the subject.

The main specialization with CASEs in modern-day security departments is actually security management principles. So what you really have is a department full of managers except nobody reports to them. They understand principles of security management but are unable to help their organization implement any of the management principles. The principles are delivered to other service provision units in checklist/"best practice" form with no practical bearing, and therefore no real usefulness.

The Big Four security team of which I was a part actually had more "managers" (that was the job title) than consultants. How much involvement in client relationships did the managers have? Not much because, quite frankly, they had so little to offer (and that is no personal attack on the managers; it is just the case that purely as a manager in security, there is literally nothing to offer that clients will not already know). It is not as if the clients had not themselves taken the CISSP exam and familiarized themselves with ISO 27001. Does this manager position in Big Four sound like a fast track to upper management to you? The stairway to heaven (it is something like consultant, then manager, then associate director, then director, and then partner) is climbed by building client relations and using these relations to generate revenue for the practice. But in your capacity as a CASE, you will find it very hard to do that, other than by resorting to politics, general skullduggery, and violation of the employee code of ethics.

Clients of Big Four would contact consultants directly whenever they had *any* query. This is because the consultants at Big Four were at least experts in application security; their knowledge in this area surpassed that of their clients, and they had built trust with clients just by giving straight answers when they knew the answer, and when they did not, they would reply "I don't know" and go back and do some research.

The conclusion: jobs in infosec are management oriented in that they are highly *security management* oriented. But does this type of career give one a fast track "up the ladder"? No, it certainly does not; in fact, it is more likely to lead one to consider an alternative career.

The Technical Track

One of the more common drivers for graduates seeking a career in information security is the technical challenge.

I discovered the joys of programming BASIC on my Commodore 64 at the age of 14 and never lost my appetite for coding. I got into security at a hobbyist level when I was around 27 and started working with TSAP in my first actual dedicated security role when I was 29 (the year was 1999). Previous to this time, I had two main jobs in IT and I loved them both.

IT in general, especially software development, brings out the creativity in us and gives us stimulating challenges and problems to overcome. I was first a software developer in my life as an IT professional, and then later I was a Unix systems administrator, also responsible for third level support with some major applications such as Oracle's database server and Lotus Notes/Domino Server. These positions were predominantly third line support positions, but it was not all about problem solving. In between support calls, there were changes to be planned and implemented, plus the "IT specialist" position carried with it free reign to dream up solutions for improving reliability and so on. There were always plenty of challenges and opportunities for creativity (with Perl and Shell scripting), and one never stopped learning in this type of position.

Security to me was an opportunity to take all this turbo-charged learning, creativity, and self-testing to another level. Security was not just about Unix and a couple of other major applications—it was every major operating system, Cisco, networking, and other applications. This was the allure of security for myself and for many other budding security pros—it was a technical arena like no other.

In 1999 in TSAP, security was exactly as I have just described. If one was looking for the kind of technical playing field as I described in the previous paragraph, one could have found it in one of the security service providers of the time.

To say that security went through a change in the early 2000s would be the understatement of the century. A major paradigm shift in security was seen in 2002 onward that took on biblical proportions.

Outsiders and graduates not familiar with the industry may well have the idea or impression that entry-level jobs in information security are heavily IT-oriented (especially as many job adverts make it seem so), but the reality on the ground could not be further from anything to do with IT except perhaps use of a word processor/spreadsheet application and an email client.

Even with a job description that is so obviously technically oriented such as penetration testing, someone coming into this field with a taste for IT will be disappointed in all but a few rare cases (perhaps exceptions would be government-sponsored "research" facilities or some niche areas of the industry). The mandate of most firms who offer penetration testing as a service will merely be to act as an independent third party in remotely assessing the perimeter security of a client—for the sole purpose (and nothing more) of helping the client meet their regulatory compliance/audit requirements. Such firms are a production line for penetration tests and cannot afford to be analytical—moreover, there is no mandate for them to be analytical. The clients just want the scan out of the way ASAP with minimum fuss/cost. Autoscanners are used heavily with modern-day service providers with some cursory false positive checking, which is a little more than filtering out the obviously ridiculous false positives such as sendmail vulnerabilities reported for Microsoft Exchange Server.

If you ever visit a service provider office and meet the analysts, you will not see too many smiling faces. There will not be an atmosphere of positivity. There will be very few "cups half full" in these firms. There will, however, be a lot of insecurity that comes with the analysts' knowledge that their job is not really a specialized position—and therefore there will often be plenty of political problems. Because there are no real measurable aspects of an analyst's skills (I discuss professional accreditation aspects in Section 4), as a facet of human nature, at least some of the analysts will feel pressured to use other means to prove their worth to their manager.

The majority of these penetration-testing positions are exactly as I described previously—the analysts' job is to run an autoscanner against client IP ranges and then skim over the results for obvious false positives. There is very little intellectual capital required for this position—perhaps it helps if you know what an IP address is. If you come into security and occupy one of these penetration tester seats, chances are that you will be bored senseless.

The inspirations in security changed along with the skills deployment shift from Hacker to CASE. When I joined TSAP, my Hacker colleagues inspired me and I pushed myself to read, code, research, and test outside of my normal working hours. Things changed so much from 2002 onward.

From 2002, service offerings in TSAP were no longer of a heavily analytical bias, and there were no Hackers around anymore (they had been fired because they were supposedly no longer economically viable), so where was the inspiration for new hires? Analysts were intensely bored and started finding ways to fill the void—usually with politically oriented activities. Where was the inspiration? One line manager in particular seemed to be busy and active (although this was just a mask—the company had too many managers and very few client relations to manage), and when the analysts saw how busy he appeared to be, they wanted to be like him—engaging with clients and effeminately using his stylus to mark in calendar entries on his pocket PC that made a beep every time a spam mail was received. The message here then is that it is unlikely, in your career as a security analyst, that you will find any technical inspiration from anyone. If you do find inspiration in your career from nontech sources, it is likely you will be taken down dark alleys and wind up questioning the source of your original inspiration.

Big Four had a reputation for service quality, and therefore a person wishing to join Big Four might expect to find some technical inspiration while working there, but sadly my own experience lays waste to that theory.

Before I joined Big Four in Thailand, I was at TSAP, also based in Thailand, and I had become aware of what our competitor had to offer in terms of quality of service. Big Four was a force to be reckoned with at that time, but what I did not realize is that the service quality was coming from only one individual who was fired around 2005 or so. When I joined Big Four myself a few years later in 2007, I was shocked by what I found there.

Big Four did have one excellent group of Web application testing consultants, also within the Thailand practice, but globally I saw no other evidence of quality in service provision in my time there. There were internal forums for knowledge sharing, regularly accessed by several hundred consultants and managers globally.

There was once a posting on the board related to an on-going remote penetration test that was being performed by a U.S. analyst. Their autoscanner tool found a banner indicating the presence of an old Checkpoint Firewall-1. The scanner flagged intelligence vulnerability with the SecuRemote service. Originally discovered by Haroon Meer of SensePost (http://www.sensepost.com), this issue supposedly affected Firewall-1 version 4.1 SP4 (not at all a recent version), whereby it was supposedly possible to issue a client request and receive a response that showed internal network addresses "behind" the firewall. The consultant was asking for a false positive check for this issue. The post was already 10 days old, and among the comments and queries bouncing around, there was no sign of any useful input. The time frame of 10 days was disturbing because this vulnerability was well documented publicly, and it is covered in Chris McNab's *Network Security Assessment* book, which I consider to be the bible for start-up penetration testers. A quick 10-minute search engine effort turns up several write-ups about this issue (plus the exploit also from SensePost, which is a perl script of 130 lines including comments; see http://downloads.securityfocus.com/vulnerabilities/exploits/sr.pl).

The client's Checkpoint was much more recent than the vulnerable version, but I found it quite shocking that after 10 days there was nothing of any value contributed by anyone. There were plenty of other issues similar to the Checkpoint vulnerability. From where was Big Four finding these people? It was almost as if the consultants had no actual educational or vocational IT experience at all—and Big Four was charging the consultants out to clients at astronomically high rates.

Another quite scary anecdote from 2006 is related to a major multinational bank I came into contact with while working as a freelance consultant in London.

I mentioned before about how the actual job function of a "security analyst" can differ radically from what is written in job descriptions posted by headhunters. There are numerous examples of these discrepancies that I have come across, but there are few as alarming as the case I witnessed in London.

The jobs advertised by the bank were contract positions (rates were above the average, so we are talking several hundred pounds sterling per day) and even though they were absolutely nontechnical in nature, the roles were spec'd out as highly technical in nature, something along the lines of application security assessment type positions. Recruitment agents would tout the job as technical in nature, and also candidates would get the impression from their interview that the job was of a technical, hands-on assessment disposition.

The actual mandate for the application risk assessment team was really more of an administrative function than anything to do with IT. The bank was rolling out new applications at a huge rate, all of which had to be subject to a "risk assessment"—and this was the team's core function. But there was no actual technical testing or architectural review for new applications. No, the team members used an internally created process/flow chart whereby nondetailed audit requirements were ticked off from a risk assessment form, and where there was any doubt about whether the application was compliant with an audit point, the team members would merely call the relevant project manager and get them to sign off on a risk exemption form with as little fuss and discussion as possible—anything to get the application into production ASAP.

So the bank's risk assessment process for new applications was really just an administrative formality, and the team members' key performance indicators (KPIs) were based on how many new applications they had processed in the year. If they held up an application release to production by performing some nasty security analysis or asking difficult questions of the development teams, their performance indicators would suffer and they might not get their bonus at the end of the year.

Several contractors had walked offsite on their first day when they saw what was going on with this "risk assessment" team. Apart from the fact that the bank was knowingly releasing applications into production with gaping security holes, if they were really happy to continue in this vein, why spend massively for a production line of twenty security staff, when really they could hire junior administrative staff members at slightly more than the minimum wage depicted by U.K. labor laws?

As a penultimate note on tech security jobs, when people think about careers in information security, they should be aware that a security position may not be a position under a security department umbrella—their mandate could be to supplement the security offering of an IT operations crew. Does this type of security/operations position typically offer the IT-oriented security pro the type of challenge they are looking for? In most cases, the answer will be no—but also it should be said that if a prospective new hire was looking for a technically oriented position in security, they are more likely to find it in IT operations as opposed to a dedicated security department. I discussed the rationale of passing analysis function to operations in Chapter 4 in Migrating South: Osmosis of Analysis Functions to Operations Teams, and from this section, one can glean some indicators of what it is like to be a security analyst under an IT operational umbrella.

There are a few niches here and there in security where real attention is paid to detail, where the risks stare the management in the face to the extent that they realize they cannot sacrifice quality for a quick buck. Although I could not put numbers to it, I do believe that these niches are growing and becoming quite sizable islands, but the security industry has been a low-skilled affair for so long now that the people do not exist in the industry that would know how to improve the situation. The question "can security improve?" has a similar theme to "can a leopard change its spots?" Change will be difficult because it has been more than 10 years since appropriate knowledge left the industry. For security strategists, the maps that lead the way to more effective security are now at least rare, perhaps even lost to the ravishes of time.

From what I hear, requirements for skilled architects, application testers, and forensics experts are on the rise, but I would not trust the numbers I have seen in this respect, and certainly I do not have any reason to believe that information security risk profiles will improve as a result of these newer hiring trends.

Overall then, what are the chances of your finding your dream technical challenge in a job in IT security these days? Without a shadow of doubt, the chances are, shall we say, very slim. Security is a wonderful thing, but jobs in security? That is different.

Summary

People are attracted to security for a variety of reasons. The two main reasons I have focused on here are the "instant manager" (as in there is an idea out there that a career in security means being a manager from day one) and the technical track attractors, but more generally, I try to give a picture of what it is actually like to work for a security service provider or end user such as a bank or insurance firm. If I give an honest appraisal of how security is really practiced in larger organizations,

I can hopefully cover concerns held by many would-be security pros, regardless of their motivation for wanting to enter this field.

Security pro wannabes should be aware of the specialization of security positions as advertised by firms and recruitment agencies. Specialization is certainly a common phenomenon in the U.K. security jobs scene, as well as many other "developed world" economies such as the United States and Australia.

Be wary of job titles such as "privacy expert" or "PCI-DSS expert." We have to ask ourselves where the expertise in these positions is. The challenges faced by firms are not in the understanding of privacy laws/ audit requirements or PCI-DSS requirements (PCI-DSS requirements are publicly available as online documents—anyone who wants to know what is required for compliance can read the documents). The challenges are in meeting these compliance goals, and the challenges faced by other IT departments plus security therein.

Some markets around the world, the U.K. is an extreme example, will divide security up into boxes into which to place people. The theory behind this is the same as with other IT areas, in that if you want a job carried out properly, you have to focus staff in specific areas so that they will not be distracted. So if you want to change a light bulb, you have one expert at unscrewing the old light bulb, another one for disposing of it, and then another one inserts the new light bulb while a "ladder holding specialist" holds the ladder. In the U.K., how many security experts does it take to change a light bulb? The answer is "many, depending on your budget."

While this specialization works in IT areas in large organizations such as database administration, it should not be applied to security. Why would you have a person dedicated purely to forensics (for example) who is not required to do anything else, and their core skill is purely forensics and forensics alone? Aside from excessive resource wastage, this also makes for some fairly tedious job functions in security departments. Security should not be divided up into penetration testing, forensics, incident response, and so on because the same core skills are needed to perform each role. These areas are only marginally distinct from each other—they overlap heavily. A role in incident response requires a high level of IT expertise to carry out the required responsibilities effectively. The knowledge particular to incident response can be covered in a two-day training course.

With penetration testing, some may see it as a specialization, but in reality, if security analysts have no penetration testing experience, or more particularly knowledge of threats and attack vectors, they are not going to be very effective as security analysts; likewise, someone who deals with forensics cases is not going to be in a position to decipher what happened in an incident if he or she does not know the details of how systems and networks function or how attackers think.

The extreme cases of specialization are the ones I mentioned previously such as "PCI-DSS" expert and so on; these are to be avoided because they will bore the new hire to tears, and also the position will not be so stable (if there is such a thing these days). One day the management team may wake up and realize they made a mistake and just phase out these specializations. Something like PCI-DSS is a good example because it is only a service that sells while there are firms around who need to comply and pass the audit; but as markets become more mature, the number of firms that allow Web visitors to pay with credit cards and also are not yet PCI-DSS compliant becomes less and less. These audit-related requirements are merely fads (or just buzzwords) that pass with time, whereas security analysis is something that has a shelf life of at least one or two decades.

Many will site a fast-track to a management career as being their driver for getting into security, in that security is "at the center" of an organization and links to all other departments—thereby making the analyst more "visible" to others in the firm as opposed to something like a job in IT operations.

It is true that most security positions with end users are CASE positions, not at all analytical, and closer to a management position as compared with an IT vocation. But in reality, how much like a management position is it going to be? Yes, as a security analyst, especially one who performs internal audits and risk assessments, you will get to meet a lot of people in other departments—but the problem is, as a CASE with little to offer the firm except baseless rules, regulations, and standards compliance checklists, you will not be very popular—people will avoid you like the plague. In fact, this type of security position where your skill set is closer to a manager than an IT expert actually works against you if you are trying to climb the ladder fast.

So how about the technical track? How likely is it that you will find your dream technical challenges in security? Much of what I have already covered in this book to this point will give a fair indicator—but more detail is needed.

In the late 1990s, with the Hacker ethic predominant in security, the service delivery was of a decent level of quality, albeit absent of business acumen. Security presented a technical and creativity challenge for IT enthusiasts, and Hacker work colleagues inspired one to make security something that was lived and breathed, inside and outside of normal working hours.

The security vocational scene changed radically since roughly 2002. Hackers were no longer seen as economically viable, and security became more of a management function than an IT function. Security departments these days specialize in checklists and standards, and there is no real analysis performed along with the checklists.

Security departments are usually very political because there is no measurement of failure in security delivery and no meaningful measure of performance. KPIs are usually geared around something like closing off audit compliance as a fast as possible, and "as fast as possible" in these cases means really "using as little analysis as possible." Technical is a four-letter word in most security departments because it implies analysis—and analysis is bad for KPIs and therefore bonus payments.

So I think it can easily be gleaned then that one is unlikely to find the technical dream world that he or she might have thought existed in security. Penetration testing is an area where one may expect to find a technical challenge; but apart from a few niche areas, even penetration testing has been reduced down to production line running of autoscanners (please see Chapter 5) and cutting out analysis so as to maximize profits and reduce costs at the expense of quality. Penetration testing is mostly performed by service providers for clients who merely have a requirement for a trusted, independent third party to run a penetration test as a compliance requirement. The expectation on behalf of the invoice-paying client is usually only that the penetration test is conducted with minimal analysis and therefore time.

So where will the inspiration be in security? Will there be inspiration that leads one to self-improvement and self-study? Not likely. With today's status quo, there is no security "intellectual capital" that has any value to organizations. The little bits that security pros will latch onto are items that impress in meetings, such as knowing what "nonrepudiation" and other buzzwords mean. The "CIA triad" (as in confidentiality, integrity, and availability of information assets) is so often quoted in meetings, but who will be able to help the organization to preserve the CIA of critical information assets?

The majority of larger organizations migrated their technical security analysis functions to IT and network operations teams, and for the potential newcomer to security, this is something to be aware of because the security position, if it does have any analysis mandate at all, is likely to be an IT operations position.

If a person comes into security looking for a technical challenge, he or she will find something closer to a challenge in an IT/network operations security role as compared with a position in a dedicated CASE security department; but it pays to be aware that there is a big difference between the typical IT operations skill set as compared with a Hacker-like skill set, or something closer to the ideal security analysis skill set.

Security initiatives such as vulnerability management, SIEM configuration and operation, firewall configuration, identity management, risk assessments, and other areas will be handled entirely by operations teams, with no direction from security at all.

"Security is so boring," "I get tired of giving the same message," "Why do we do this? This checklist never changes and everyone knows that," "I have no value in this firm," "What am I doing here? Surely I'm over-qualified for this," "I need to find ways to deal with the boredom. In the end I just realized it's better to laugh than to cry. I just have to laugh at my company because I know that this vulnerability management suite they bought is as useful as a chocolate fireguard and it cost them 30000 dollars just for the license." I heard quotes like these so many times from security professionals. Granted, when things are not managed very well, the same ridicule can be found in other business areas. But security as it is practiced today does rather lend itself to such stories.

Many security professionals are OK before they get into the field, and then the psychological pressures of modern-day security practices drive them insane, or they become raving politicians or just manic-depressives. Most security professionals are in denial of the futility of their positions and react quite angrily to any suggestion that the role of the modern security professional does not actually help their organization to manage information risk.

For the aspiring newcomer, the accreditation picture in security is worth a bit of discussion. Many security professionals will latch onto things such as CISSP accreditation as being something that distinguishes them, but inwardly, they are aware of the weakness of this position.

The reality is that these accreditations in security (not just CISSP—the same can be said for most, if not all, of them) prove little more than the ability of the certificate holder to see a task through to completion. So many security professionals are certificate hunters in that they will try to get as many letters after their name as possible. Whether or not this helps them to secure job positions or gives them a competitive edge is subjective. In some cases, it will help them to secure a new job—it depends on the perspective of the hiring manager. But really the candidate with a thousand letters after his or her name can only use the certificates to show he or she is a fine upstanding, hard-working citizen who can see a task through to completion—or as many tasks as the number of certificates he or she has gained.

The (ISC)² CISSP certification covers some management principles (and more detail in a few areas) that are useful as high-level guides in security in the same way as ISO 27001 is effectively a security management standard—but the key word here is *management*, in the way that these bodies of knowledge are useful for *security managers* and not so much for those who are responsible for dealing with the ground-level challenges of information risk management. It is a shame that the only really widely recognized accreditation in security is a *management accreditation*. So for analysts, consultants, architects, and so on, their only distinguishing accreditation is one that (partly) qualifies them to perform a job function other than their own.

Discussions about certifications nearly always go south very fast, with a lot of angry comments being merrily distributed—"you're only jealous that I have so many certifications" and so on. There is this religious attachment in security to matters such as these. I mentioned in Chapter 5 about religious views on autoscanners. There are many such areas where security pros get easily angered or offended because frankly, in our lives as security professionals, we spend at least 35 to

40 hours per week doing this stuff. Many do not want to acknowledge that what they do has no value because that could mean that *they* have no value. Much of the anger comes from ego and so on (I mentioned in the introduction of this chapter about motivators for entering into a career in security, one of which is purely just vanity), but generally there is a lot of insecurity in security—from both a network and a personnel/psychological perspective.

I remember from the few times I attended a training course in some security area (for the purpose of attaining professional accreditation) how miserable the other attendants seemed to be. Unless you are at a Blackhat event or something similar, it is noticeable how most other security pros you meet seem to be a bit down in the dumps. This is a great pity because if security is where it should be, jobs in the field would be far more challenging, involve some creativity, and reward hard work and professionalism. These factors would certainly help to bring smiles back on the faces of security professionals.

We have some way to go before security is a fun place again. In the meantime, I can only urge the more technical pros to stay true to their principles and *stay technical*. I would urge against abandoning all hope and succumbing to the unchallenging world of checklists and standards. Checklists, standards, and audits will be a major part of your job function, if not your only job function, but do not let checklists, standards, and audits define who you are. If you have some tech skills in security, make sure you at least hang on to them.

Maybe do some reading and research in your spare time. There are plenty of security hobbyists who are deeply enthusiastic and who also write about security and share their work. I would not necessarily advocate quitting security altogether. If you have opinions based on your extracurricular analysis of internal security controls, do not be afraid to voice them just because others in your team will not like it—but also be prepared to confidently back up what you have to say. If others disagree with your opinion, respect their opinion but also ask for proof that you are wrong. If no such proof is forthcoming, then the objections are probably just based on emotion or politics or both.

For line managers, I sympathize with any security professional that is not allowed to have a sense of humor. The job is boring enough as it is, without having some management culture that makes a nonsensical connection between being professional and also never talking about anything other than work. If laughter is banned from the security department, reconsider this directive.

I would urge everyone in security to abandon insecurity and pride. Try to make the disconnect between the value you contribute to the organization and your value as a human being. Try to avoid competing with your work mates over matters such as numbers of certificates or whether autoscanners are great or not. By voicing your disrespect for others' opinions, is it likely you are going to actually change anything? These things will "all come out in the wash," as they say. At least in the meantime, regardless of which side of the fence they sit, if you get along well with your work colleagues, your job will be more fun. Like so many other jobs, the security job is only as good as the people you work with.

7

PENETRATION TESTING—
OLD AND NEW

Thus far in security de-engineering, I have covered the dilemma faced by the networked business world in the area of information risk management skills. The skills issue is applicable to all facets of the delivery of information security in the majority of larger organizations.

With regard network penetration testing, in Chapter 2, I covered some aspects of the older style delivery of penetration testing, but the focus was on the skills involved rather than the methodology. In Chapter 4, I looked out how cheap/free automated testing tools replaced the Hacker ethic in vulnerability assessment in general. In Chapter 5, I looked into the details of autoscanners and Web autoscanners first in terms of how they function and then with respect to the expected return on investment.

Since roughly 2002 onward, much of the penetration testing marketplace was only in existence because of the audit stipulation for penetration tests to be carried out by "an independent third party." Even if service providers could lay their hands on advanced penetration testing skills, very few of the penetration tests will actually deliver any value other than the tick in the box on the auditor's score sheet. The methodology will have been "dumbed down" because to be too analytical slows things down, and that can mean that both service provider staff and their clients miss their key performance indicator targets with the resulting impact on year-end bonuses.

In the aforementioned cheap penetration tests where quality is sacrificed, there is probably (I say "probably" because I cannot really read the mind of the decision maker) a perceived lack of a threat—and so from the perception of the service provider's client, it is OK to just get the tick in the box and carry on. There might be some question marks over the quality of the delivery of these tests, but it does not pay to badger the service provider for information on testing methodology.

In the previous three years running up to 2011, there has been an undeniable increase in the number of financially damaging incidents originating from the "outside" (the public Internet). So just from intuition, one may believe that there is now more focus on the actual technical quality of penetration testing, and perhaps more organizations are starting to question the return on investment of these exercises.

Personally I cannot say if organizations are now seeking to gain more from their penetration testing investment other than just compliance, but I am willing to go with the assumption that there are indeed more than a handful of security managers who have recently been sleeping less comfortably at night as a result of the increasing levels of skullduggery "out there."

This chapter is for those who *do* want to see more value from their penetration testing. I aim to explain the differences between the older (more effective) style of unrestricted penetration testing as compared with the highly restricted offerings of the last decade or so.

There are a lot of misconceptions in security about penetration testing. Many see penetration testing as the one sure-fire way to assess network security. With this in mind, I also aim to take a slightly higher level/bigger picture view: even if Hackers deliver penetration testing under utopic testing conditions, what can we really expect to get out of it? How often should the tests be delivered and how long should they last? Where should penetration testing fit in the overall scheme of the information risk management strategy?

Testing Restrictions

The penetration testing landscape changed quite radically from the 2000s onward. Earlier penetration tests were conducted almost entirely as per the Hackers' rule book, and as you probably have gathered from previous comments on the Hacker paradigm, that basically meant that the only rule was that there were no rules. The only rule to speak of was one of basic ethics and to avoid compromising targets in private networks other than that of the organization under testing.

In the very early days of the Internet through to the dot com boom, security service providers called the shots on everything in security, but then the clients started telling the service providers what to do—and this included imposing restrictions on penetration tests. The client-driven restrictions came about partly because of a perceived lack of any real benefit from the testing and also partly because in most cases there was a genuine lack of quality in the delivery. Why bother about potentially troublesome issues [such as intrusion detection system (IDS) false alarms being triggered during the test, servers crashing, and so on] with penetration tests when the value returned from the testing was either not seen or nonexistent?

With regard to penetration testing engagements from around 2001 to the time of writing, apart from a very small niche market, the testing was throttled to the degree that the test had almost no value for the client apart from the port scan results.

Today's tests are conducted with the following approximate restrictions: the source IP address range for the testing must be prespecified and must not change throughout the testing window, only the specified range of targets can be tested, "potentially disruptive" exploit testing will not be attempted without prior arrangement with the client, no denial-of-service (DoS) testing will be performed, no social engineering attempts will be made, and in some cases the documentation and logging requirement for clients can take around two hours per day out of the testing window.

Restriction 1: Source IP Address

The early 2000s saw a significant improvement in firewall configurations, and in penetration tests during this period, a port scan may reveal only one or two open ports such as the Webserver HTTP ports (usually 80/443 TCP).

Several times during early tests with TSAP, there were cases where intelligence mining would indicate that at least one perimeter device could be running a service such as a mail or DNS server, but in initial port scanning, these services were not found. The client's firewall in these cases was only permitting connections to the services from specific source IP address(es). Very often the IP address of the DNS server or mail server could be gleaned from dumping the DNS records from the authoritative name server for the client's domain. In another case, a "hidden" File Transfer Protocol (FTP) service was found from a Google search.

Very often, the device, or range of Internet protocol (IP) addresses, permitted to connect to the DMZ service was colocated in a data center, or it was hosted by the client's ISP, or it was just located in another one of the client's global premises. Right or wrong, TSAP Hackers would often find a nondisruptive way to compromise these intermediate hosts and so "exploit the trust relationship" offered by the client's external firewall. Most clients saw this method of punching holes in firewalls as purely mythical, but as we demonstrated, it can happen, and it does happen—it is not just theoretical.

Usually there would be a few score other ways to compromise the client's network without resorting to these "variable source address" methods. But there were a few times when clients had their firewall configurations well nailed down, and these "bounce" methods came in handy. There are some slightly more exotic but frankly only theoretical ways of "bouncing" port scans and attacks through intermediate hosts without actually having compromised them. An example of this would be a method such as "FTP bounce" (even included as an option with the nmap port scanner). I have never seen any of these methods work, or even attempted.

Also with the bounce method, as a common scenario, attackers will not need to maintain a permanent "presence" on the compromised host. Their attacks can still be staged from their own machine(s). They just set up a netcat tunnel or install some bounce software on the compromised intermediate. We were in a situation in a TSAP penetration test where we needed to bounce through a Windows host. One of the Hackers knocked together a "bounce.exe" program in 30 minutes that echoed commands from our testing lab through the Windows intermediary host to a target specified as a command-line option.

IP source address spoofing is another story. The previous bounce examples I mentioned are not to be confused with source address spoofing. When you are actually in control of the intermediate bounce host, your source IP address is not spoofed; it is "real" (i.e., it is the actual or NAT'd IP address that reflects your address on the public Internet). IP source address spoofing is when one actually fakes their IP address in a TCP/IP transaction.

To fake the source address is trivial—there are so many ways of doing this. But of course the way TCP/IP works is that the destination end of the transaction answers to the source address in the packet header. So if your source address was spoofed, you will not get an answer, which is OK if you do not need an answer (I mentioned in Chapter 2 about spoofing Simple Network Management Protocol requests in order to get a router to send its configuration file to your Trivial File Transfer Protocol server). Source IP address spoofing is common with worms, DoS attacks (such as SYN Flood), and other malware where basically the author is only trying to cause damage— they do not actually need to see any response from victim hosts. But from my own experiences, IP address spoofing is not a common activity in penetration.

Restriction 2: Testing IP Address Range(s)

TSAP Hackers were very much in the attack simulation mindset when engaged in penetration testing, and as I mentioned before, the only rule was that there were no rules.

Penetration testing engagements can be "black box" where very little or no information about the client is given to the testing team beforehand apart from the company name and location. I have commented several times about the real objectives of modern-day penetration testing, and from this, it should be clear that black box network penetration testing is something of the past. The "white box" approach is far more common now. The client supplies the target IP range and stipulates that even if they own other Internet subnets, the testing team must stick to targeting the range given under all circumstances.

With testing ranges, it all comes down to what clients expect to get from a penetration test. If they do actually want a simulated attack, then they should at least be aware that restricting testing to a subset of their Internet-facing addresses is not a simulation. Attackers who target an organization will not care about the status of the extra-testing range targets, and the whole network can be compromised from these. They will get a list of IP address ranges from "whois" and search engines, and just probe everything under the organization's ownership until a weakness is found.

To illustrate the potential dangers of limiting target addresses, and also to cover a general point about customer attitudes to penetration testing, I recall a case with an online gambling firm in Hong Kong. From Google searches and "whois" Internet domain registration information, the client owned at least two class C (up to 253 individual host IP addresses) address ranges but limited the testing to 10 "live" IP addresses. The 10 targets given were purely Webservers for which the client's firewall exposed only ports 80 and 443, and the TSAP Hackers did find some X-site scripting, server-side parameter validation problems, plus a glaring Structured Query Language (SQL) injection issue. Additionally though, in the initial port scan, it was clear that there were other live IP addresses (outside of the testing range) with "visible" listening services. The TSAP Project Manager in charge of this Hong Kong project unfortunately neglected to inform the Hacker team of the testing restrictions, and generally Hackers need no second invitation when they see a down-level Berkeley Internet Naming Daemon (BIND) service. Exploit attempts resulted in a server crash with one of the off-range targets, so the Hacker team focused on another unpatched BIND service in the off-range subnet. The second exploit attempt was successful and super user access was attained.

More often than not, because of poor internal security controls, when one host is compromised, the rest of the network is wide-open. The attack effort in this case was taken no further, but from port scanning and probing, it was clear that other targets (some database servers, for example) in the network were effectively wide-open.

The DNS server issue had a high impact on business risk—but the client was not interested at all in this finding. The client's only concern was that we had strayed over the acceptable testing boundaries. Was the client already aware of these BIND issues or even the wider picture of perimeter security? Certainly they were not aware, but it also did not matter to them—they raised no concerns over the findings and did not ask us how to initiate an emergency fix/workaround for the problem. Even three months after the findings report was issued, no attempts at reducing the risk had been made.

In reality, not so many clients would be as lapse as the aforementioned case, but also I would say that this story does give an indication of how the perceived value of penetration testing (and information risk management in general) was heading. If penetration testing was seen as being a completely valueless exercise, the point about testing range restrictions is of course mute.

The situation with the Hong Kong client played out with the client firing TSAP and going with another vendor. The violation of testing restrictions was seen as the most pressing issue here, rather than the critical finding to do with perimeter security.

Restriction 3: Exploits Testing

As a further restriction in modern-day penetration testing, the organization will often dictate against exploits testing in a live penetration test. Aside from the reasons I have given previously about the lack of a perceived business case for quality in penetration testing, there is also the fact that many exploit attempts can result in services crashing or maybe just entering an unresponsive state.

The exploit-testing restriction was something that came into fashion soon after the turn of the millennium. Prior to that time, Hackers would merrily conduct penetration tests and conscientiously try to avoid server crashes, although the nature of the beast does dictate that services can become unstable or just completely die as a result of exploit testing. Obviously this can be a business problem with live production systems, but security service clients never had severe reservations about these service outages up until 2001 or so. Prior to this time, during a penetration test, clients would have administration staff on 24-hour standby, and they were aware there could be outages during the testing window. Services would rarely need a manual restart anyway, and when they did, it could mean the service was unavailable for 15 minutes as a maximum. The worst case where a server needed to be rebooted never happened on my watch, and I am unaware of such a circumstance ever occurring. Furthermore, penetration testers were usually given a hotline number to call if there was a problem during testing, so that they could themselves alert the client's IT staff to any availability issues.

After the period where restrictions started to be imposed, penetration testers either were completely blocked from running exploit tests or were forced to run the tests at some unearthly hour, perhaps in the middle of the night during a "maintenance window." Penetration testers were given a contact number to call in the event they saw fit to try out "potentially disruptive" exploits, and often the responsible person was unavailable or uninterested, so the test would just be skipped over.

A semirelated issue was about installation of code on client production servers. Again this client-imposed requirement has the effect of dramatically reducing the efficiency (and therefore the value) of penetration tests. Some exploit attempts can be said to be nondisruptive, and when performing these tests, one did not need to inform the client for availability reasons, but many exploit attempts involve uploading some sort of code on servers. Generalizing radically: first there will be a remote compromise which usually doesn't involve uploading code (although the code may be temporarily resident in memory) but in order to further explore attack opportunities (after a successful first stage compromise) it is helpful for testers if they can upload code such as compilers, debuggers, port scanners, netcat, sniffers, and others. If the testing team is prevented from doing this, then it is not a penetration test that is delivered for the customer; it is something with considerably lower value.

Then there is the exploit code itself. One of those religious arguments in security used to be about the deployment of "zero-days" in penetration testing, as in exploits for vulnerabilities that have not been publicly announced by the vendor. There is a lot of talk about ethics in these cases. Other points are raised to the effect that there is no actual benefit in use of zero-days in commercial penetration testing, with the reasoning that if the vulnerability is unknown, there will be no mitigation for the issue (such as a vendor patch). This is not an invalid point in that by using zero-days, the service providers are testing the client's ability to defend themselves against a threat for which there is no defense. But a penetration test is intended to test an organization's defenses against issues such as software vulnerability, and there is the concept of "layered security." If it really is the case that one single successful exploit using a zero-day means game over for the organization, then this is clearly a serious problem that needs highlighting. In the real world today, so many new incidents are committed using "zero-days." I am led to believe that there are reams of undisclosed vulnerability "in the wild" with popular software packages. So the issue of zero-day testing is becoming more critical with time.

It is most certainly in the paying testing subject's interests to know their level of vulnerability to *any* software vulnerability, not just public-declared vulnerability. Bad guys do not care whether or not the attack code they are using is for public domain vulnerability or otherwise. They are focused only on results, and how they achieve those results does not matter.

In TSAP, we had several lengthy discussions about the subject of zero-days. Several times during two-week penetration testing windows, the Hackers had discovered new vulnerability in commercial products and subsequently developed an exploit for the discovered vulnerability within the testing time frame. In all of these cases, without fail, we informed the vendors who duly ignored us. We had an agreement between ourselves not to use our own zero-days in client penetration tests unless the vendor had not acted on our communiqué (i.e., released a patch) within a two-month time frame.

How about the situation where we (TSAP Hackers) became aware of zero-days from other parties? Whenever vendors were informed of security bugs, there was an empty void where a response should have been. Should we use these exploits in client penetration tests?

Any security hobbyist who is active in forums and blogs will come across undisclosed vulnerabilities that were ignored by vendors. Many security practitioners feel decidedly uncomfortable with these cases, and there will be a long queue of those who talk of "ethics" waiting to beat the analyst who uses zero-days with a rather big stick. Clients may raise an eyebrow (most likely there will be some thoughts along the lines "if they have access to this code, what else do they have access to?") if they know you have access to a zero-day or two, but in possessing knowledge of zero-days, you have not committed a crime. If you have not committed a crime, there is no basis for any discussion about ethics here; nonetheless the ethics word does find its way into these discussions.

So for those who do seriously want to see some value for their penetration tests other than just the compliance tick-in-the-box, what needs to happen?

Certainly if penetration testing is going to be a productive use of time for all concerned parties, then surely it has to be an actual attack simulation. If a penetration test is nice and "ethical," and caters to all of the target organization's most minor concerns, then it will be very far from being an attack simulation. If you are going to pay for a penetration test, why would you want your end product watered down at all? Sure there might be some business risk from having services crash on you, or there could be IDS alerts raised, but these things happen in real attacks. When a service crashes under exploit testing, it is not the result the attacker is looking for, but it does indicate vulnerability nonetheless. And if you want to assess the effectiveness of your IDS, surely a penetration test is an ideal time to do so.

Taking the three main restrictions in order: limiting the testing to particular source IP addresses does not actually achieve anything for the organization under testing. If I remember correctly the first time I came across this restriction, it was because our client wanted to enter an IDS exclusion for our source IP addresses. Other reasons could be merely to do with accountability (perhaps they wanted to log our actions?). Whatever the concerns, it is clear that a penetration test from a fixed source IP address (from the target's perspective) is a diluted penetration test. Attackers really can and do "bounce" through intermediate hosts and set up command pipes and tunnels, and obviously if a testing subject denies the opportunity for penetration testers to attempt these tricks, they could be denying themselves return on investment. I described in Chapter 2 about a penetration test with TSAP for a Korean telco whereby as a first "network unlock," router access control lists were bypassed by forgery of our source IP address, not exactly "bouncing" but the principle was the same nonetheless. From the client's perspective, we had attacked from a source IP address other than the one stated in our testing specification document (not that they would have noticed—all of the compromised devices even had the default logging settings nullified).

In terms of the effect on penetration testing quality, the third restriction related to exploits testing is more damaging than the other two. The first two of the three restriction cases will not have a negative effect on the test quality of *every* penetration test (it depends on the actual scenario; in many cases, the testers will not need to bounce, spoof, etc.), but I can say that these attack methods are real in that they do actually occur in the wild. The third case is different. In many cases, the restriction of the usage of "potentially disruptive" exploits (nearly all exploit testing can potentially be disruptive) means the penetration test is not a penetration test—it is the equivalent of an autoscanner (see Chapter 5) test, and really speaking, the organization should not actually *pay* for this as such. There may be "testing windows" where the testers can attempt potentially disruptive exploits, but the overall efficiency of the testing will be reduced to a level where little can be achieved in the time available.

If the organization under testing wants to see some return on investment, then penetration testers need to be allowed to carry out whatever tests and tricks they deem fit, and the tests need to be performed without worrying about waiting for client permission. Older style, pre-2000s penetration tests did not follow any strict pattern as such. A number of tests were performed based on the results of other tests, and based on those test results, more tests were performed. Hacker testing teams would work 20-hour shifts, then sleep 10 hours, and then start all over again for the entire testing window. When penetration testing is "done right," the testing flow takes on a life of its own, and it should not be interrupted or restricted if the paying client does want to see maximal value from the exercise.

Penetration Testing—The Bigger Picture

I commented on the skills involved with penetration testing and security in general all through this book, but Chapter 2 gives a better indication of the skills portfolio required for penetration testing. The skills involved with penetration testing are one aspect, and then there are the restrictions on testing—I covered these in the previous subsections of this chapter.

How about the situation where we have both the skills and restrictions bases covered? Taking a step back and looking at this area from a wider, information risk management program perspective, how should penetration testing fit into the jigsaw of the whole information risk management cycle? I will attempt to answer this question in this chapter.

For some years now, there has been a common perception in security departments that penetration testing (or use of autoscanners) is really the means to an end in terms of vulnerability assessment. There is a communal belief to the effect that if network vulnerability is to be evaluated, then some sort of remote scan is the only way to do this. Internal methods of assessment also include some sort of network-based scanning; usually a commercial vulnerability management suite is used.

With the recent upsurge in the frequency of major incidents, there has been a renaissance for the penetration testing marketplace, perhaps even with some attention paid to the testing methodology and results.

Furthermore, to cover this section in a modern perspective, it seems pertinent to talk about the Advanced Persistent Threat (APT) phenomenon and what it means to larger enterprises.

APT is not exactly a new phenomenon, and just like other phrases in security, there is no universally accepted definition, but it is the most widely touted buzzword in the industry at the time of writing, with new players on the security service provider scene who claim to specialize in this area.

APT is usually associated with attacks by a group, such as state sponsored attacks (China is often the state associated with these activities), or even attacks by individuals. Sometimes APT is used to refer to intellectual property theft, and other times, it is used in connection with large-scale distributed DoS attacks. The persistent part seems to be missing in many of these incidents that are linked with APT. As the "P" part suggests, the attacks are not one-off incidents; they are repeated over a number of months or even years.

I suppose also the "A" part ("A" for advanced) can be a misnomer in many of these cases. Many of these APT attacks are kicked off by use of a very simple malware-related incident that comes about as a result of users clicking on a link they should not click. Social engineering can also play a leading role in APT events.

APT events are of course primarily economically motivated attacks, and cyber cartels are rapidly surpassing drug cartels in their impact on global security. Supposedly Russian mafia made more money in online banking fraud last year than what the drug cartels made from selling hard drugs. As long as these economic incentives for APT exist, the threats will not dissipate. The attacks may change in nature as the network defenses change. In the past, the easier path to compromise networks was seen as remote intrusion by remotely exploiting software vulnerability, but then as firewall configurations and patch levels improved, the attacks changed to be more malware-oriented in nature (and the malware is often capable of network assessment and multistage vulnerability exploits—we are not talking about the "I love you" virus or Code Red here). Very often the malware enters the network by exploiting lack of employee awareness (e.g., the user is tricked into following a link and installing malicious code) or by use of some sort of social engineering.

The usual pattern-based malware detection and software vulnerability defenses have become increasingly less effective. Malware is released at such a huge rate that pattern-based defenses cannot keep up, and patches can only be written to mitigate known vulnerabilities. What if the vulnerability is not yet public knowledge? Many of the incidents you read about these days will include the "zero-day" phrase in the article somewhere.

The malware attack is only the first stage of the attack in some cases. In other cases, the malware show may be enough by itself to create a nice encrypted tunnel through which intellectual property may be sucked from the network—it depends a lot on the network architecture, and firms who never gave a hoot about this issue are living under serious financial risk.

The economic motives are various: identity theft for online fraud, business intelligence for competitive advantage (corporate espionage is a matter that has been brought to the attention of Western governments by defense agencies), and theft of intellectual property (e.g., Italian fashion designers have their copied products on the shelves in China before they are officially released for retail in Italy).

Still in connection with APT, with software patches, we can patch a zero-day issue today, but a new zero-day mass-attack will be widespread tomorrow. The attack surface never really reduces in size. Patches have never been a means to an end for all security problems, but the common corporate perception has been, for more than a decade, that if you are all patched up, you are safe. In fact, through the earlier part of the 2000s up to around 2009, there was not so much security media focus on zero-day attacks, but that has all changed dramatically these days.

If software patches and antivirus and other blinking "heuristic" magic box defenses are not so effective at keeping bad guys (and girls) out of good guys' (and girls') networks, then why should penetration testing ever be on the information risk management agenda anyway?

I have heard frequent comments from security professionals lately amounting to what could easily be mistaken as raising a white flag in the face of seemingly uncontrollable risks. Some are even questioning the need for firewalls. The common Checklists and Standards Evangelist response when they have been subject to an incident on their watch (which came about as a result of a trivial privilege escalation after a remote exploit for a known vulnerability) is, "I have been telling you for years, there is no *silver bullet* for these security problems."

I will talk more extensively about solutions in Section 4, but for now, I will focus on the penetration testing side of things. Given the constantly evolving APT threatscape, is there even any incentive for penetration testing these days? If the bad guys are always going to win regardless, why bother at all with penetration testing? In the remainder of this chapter, I make an attempt at answering these questions.

Firstly I will discuss briefly about the testing conditions, and then go on to discuss the skills aspect of penetration testing and what is required if we are ever to see effective penetration testing. Lastly in this chapter, I will talk about potential changes in penetration testing in line with changing threats such as the APT phenomenon I discussed previously in this section.

With regard testing conditions, an important consideration is the duration of the testing window. If it is decided to go ahead with testing, how much time is required to perform an effective test? This is a question that is frequently asked of service providers, and the answer is that there is no definitive answer for this question. A really talented Hacker team can continue to find security issues for weeks after the testing start date. But we can say that the number of reportable findings per day will taper off after the first week and then diminish to zero over an infinite testing time, or until the Hackers get bored. How many man-days should be allocated for testing? It depends on the size of the target and the financial importance of information assets and applications therein. Usually the intuitive 40 man-days is about right, but the end user must be aware that security problems may be missed (i.e., there *will* be false negatives).

Another consideration with regard testing conditions is the black box versus white box issue. Use of a completely uninitiated third party in penetration testing is critical. The testing team cannot know anything about the target network configuration apart from perhaps the IP address range(s). If the test is specifically a Web application test, it can help if the testing team knows the business purpose of the application and how it is actually used by an authenticated user. Often a Web application testing team will be given authentication credentials after a few days (if they cannot find a pair by themselves).

Thus far, I have discussed testing conditions as in white box and black box, and also I have covered the testing window length question. These are matters relating to how the testing should be performed. But what about the rationale for testing? In a perfect world, is there a place for penetration testing, and if there is, what are the expected deliverables?

The perfect world penetration test has two components. I commented earlier in this chapter about testing restrictions–with the conclusion that restrictions are bad. Then there is the second component which is about experience and skills: the skills held by both the tester and the testing subject.

When penetration testing is restricted or carried out with limited skills, as has been the case over the past decade and more, it will always be a waste of time and resources. If you have a situation where you hire a limited-skills third party to try out some exploits on your network somewhere, this is the same as paying a hooligan to come and break your windows (destabilize or crash services), leave, and then tell you that you missed a security patch somewhere, something that IT operations were probably aware of anyway.

Then there is the second aspect I mentioned: the skill levels in the security department of the organization under testing.

The key to the whole "need for penetration testing" enigma (apart from the all-pervasive regulations compliance driver) has historically been connected with the level of knowledge that internal staff have of their own security controls. If you are an internal security staff member, how likely is it that a penetration test will reveal something you do not already know? If I do not know anything about my own network security, then it is possible that everything uncovered in the penetration test will be something that I did not know *before* the test, and therefore the test is seen as being highly valuable. The associated thought that usually comes with this is something along the lines, "Penetration testing is a means to an end in terms of network security assessment." The thinking is that if a penetration test returns a clean bill of health, then there are no false negatives and everything is fine. Likewise, if the test uncovers some issues and those issues are fixed, then from the security department perspective, everything is fine.

The aforementioned philosophy is common in security and also deeply flawed. Penetration testing results from a third party should never be relied on as the single source of information on the status of network security.

Penetration testing costs are certainly less than they were in the late 1990s/early 2000s, but they are also nonnegligible. Usually a test that is supposedly "manual" will be billed out to cover a maximum of two calendar weeks and up to 40 man-days of testing (10 calendar days with four security analysts). If an organization is using a third-party penetration testing team to substitute internal security expertise, is 40 man-days enough time to give even a semi-accurate picture of the network security posture? Given the complexity of systems and applications, certainly this is not enough time, even with a highly skilled testing team. Realistically even a 1000-man-day test will not be enough.

If we talk about the skill levels of the testing subject, the perfect world is one where internal security staff are literate in the microscopic configuration details of operating systems, routers, switches, hubs, load balancers, intrusion detection system (IDSs), redundancy devices, mobile devices, virtual private network (VPN) gateways, firewalls, applications, databases, and so on. They have conducted internal risk assessments, and they are aware of vulnerabilities, threats, and attack vectors with the network, and of course at least one person in the security team knows how all these pieces of the jigsaw fit together (i.e., they know the network architecture and data flows therein) and the dependencies between applications and other information assets.

In such a world where security pros are aware of the configuration details I described in the previous paragraph, a penetration test delivered by outsiders is really only performed to catch a misconfiguration or bug they may have missed from their own risk assessments. If the security team is aware of the organization's information landscape to such a degree, they are in a position to make an educated call on the potential usefulness of a remote penetration test (and also the potential usefulness of the remote penetration *testers*)—and frankly this is the situation where the check-signatory gets the maximal return on investment from a penetration test. The test may result in a blank report (i.e. no vulnerability worthy of mention was found), but under the aforementioned circumstances, this is perfectly fine. If the testing subject sees a blank report under these conditions, it really is good news.

Of course, if we are talking about complex applications developed by a third party (or by an in-house development team), then even if highly skilled internal analysts have assessed the application, there will not be many situations where it is *not* a good idea to get a skilled third party to cover at least 20 man-days of security testing on the application.

The answers with regard the rationale behind penetration testing come from common sense and good knowledge of the corporate network, and from taking into account the changing global threatscape.

As well as the prequalifiers for penetration testing to do with testing conditions and skills and so on, there are other considerations that I will cover in the remaining paragraphs of this chapter, not least including some coverage of the testing of the configuration of security "layers." The threats are different now, and we need to consider changes in penetration testing in line with these newer threats. Also our perimeter is no longer formed by our border firewalls and DMZs. We need to take this point into consideration when we look at the value offering of penetration testing.

If we ignore the regulatory compliance driver for a second, five years ago, it would have been a questionable idea to pay a third party to do an external perimeter penetration test if the organization exposes only Web-based services to the Internet and patch levels are current. These days? There has always been a threat related to undisclosed vulnerability (I call these "zero-days" here, although there is a lot of discussion over the terminology), but the threat seems more real these days in that there is apparently more zero-day activity in the wild. Organizations need to deal with the zero-day threat by use of nonspecific measures. If a remote attacker can gain low-privileged access to a DMZ device by exploitation of a previously undisclosed vulnerability, then at least internal staff need to try and make it hard for the attacker to raise his or her privilege level. We hear a lot about "layered security," so if we want to test how effective our "layers" are, we need to ask a penetration tester to assess our layers; maybe when we were configuring our layers, we missed something? Layers on a DMZ device can include operating system file system permission controls. A "layer" for an employee office space subnet could be network access control between the subnet and critical infrastructure subnets.

With APT in general, organizations now need to shift the emphasis. Before, the perimeter was clearly defined. With the mix of unaware employees and Microsoft Windows laptops and desktops (this is not a Microsoft slur; the majority of malware affects only Windows mostly because it is the most widespread corporate operating system), home users, and a mobile work force, you have a security problem that is very hard, if not impossible, to fix. So where is the perimeter now?

More than ever before, organizations could give some consideration for internal manual penetration testing, perhaps from a source IP address of an employee office/desktop PC subnet. Because of the highly elevated risks from malware, mobile devices, and removable media (thumb drive born issues, e.g., Stuxnet), organizations need to adopt a strategy that says "we *will* suffer security problems from employee subnets, so let's plan for this eventuality and try to limit the overall financial risks." It is far from advisable to rely on the automation of the vulnerability management suite for assessment of the internal security posture (I covered this point in more detail in Chapter 5).

With malware/APT, in some sectors, there has been a white flag raised with regards technical prevention, and a shift toward post eventus/forensics techniques in some sectors, with the idea that if the malware can be traced to an individual or group, perhaps the organization can deter further attacks, and if knowledge can be gained of the details of the malware behavior, then perhaps we can alleviate the risks based on past behavior. This is all well and good in some cases, but we should not give up on attack prevention. The "attack surface" *can* be reduced in line with business risk. We can at least make it harder to stage successful attacks, and then perhaps the efforts will shift to easier targets, perhaps the firm down the street rather than our own.

Summary

Network penetration testing has been predominantly a regulatory compliance affair since roughly 2002 onward. Larger organizations engage the services of a "trusted third party" to give them a tick in the box to the effect that their perimeter is free of security vulnerabilities. If not for the compliance driver, the market for commercial penetration testing could be at least 90% smaller.

As a result of hacker activities, Sony's online gaming PlayStation network was made unavailable for more than four weeks in 2011, and the public was informed by Sony that millions of user emails, passwords, and credit card details were pilfered. This was just one of many large-scale corporate incidents reported in the previous two years up to mid-2011.

I have reason to believe that some organizations are now starting to revisit their penetration testing philosophy on the back of this new spate of incidents. After all, if you are going to pay for penetration testing, why not get something more for your money other than just compliance? With some attention to detail, you can pass the audit and as a bonus you can get some security also, all for the same price ("passing the audit" is in most cases not the same as improving security).

I mentioned in this chapter about how penetration testing methodology changed from the late 1990s through to today, and one of the major changes was the introduction of restrictions on testing methodology.

Clients of penetration testing service providers started to demand that the testing team specify their IP source address(es) and stick to that range throughout the duration of the testing window. During penetration tests, client IDSs were sometimes triggered during testing, and staff were woken up in the middle of the night (clients took the approach of adding penetration tester IP addresses in their IDS configuration as an exception). Systems would sometimes become unstable or crash, and even though clients were not actually logging much in the way of system-generated events, they would ask penetration testers to stick to a constant source IP address for accountability.

Attackers in reality do "bounce" or "tunnel" through intermediate devices. They sometimes "spoof" their source address also. These activities are real and are used in actual attacks. In TSAP penetration testing engagements, such bouncing, tunneling, and spoofing techniques were often deployed to great effect. So by preventing these activities, clients of penetration testing services are losing a lot of value from their deliverables.

Another restriction that was imposed was in regard to testing target ranges. The service provider was given a range of IP addresses to assess, and they were asked not to deviate from that list. Although there may be live services exposed to the Internet on other servers under the client's ownership, these services were not to be the subject of penetration testing. Even if there was a wide-open server in the same subnet as the testing targets, the testing team was prohibited from so much as port scanning the device unless it was in the specified range of target addresses.

The restriction that had the most damaging effect on penetration testing was the imposition of exploits testing restrictions. From 2000 onward, increasing numbers of clients demanded that if exploit attempts could result in service instability, then the exploit test was either not performed at all or the service provider had to try the test Out of Hours, usually in the middle of the night. Unfortunately, very many exploit attempts could potentially result in service outage.

Prior to the exploits testing restrictions, service providers such as TSAP would be in constant communication with clients during penetration tests. Clients had IT support staff on 24-hour availability anyway. Usually we were given a hotline with which to call the client if we noticed any service availability issues during testing. Clients' IT staff were aware of the dates of penetration testing windows, and they also had a hotline with which to call us. Generally, there was seldom any incident where client services were significantly disrupted during penetration tests, unless the testing was actually designated as DoS testing. Moreover, clients understood that if a service was disrupted during testing, this in itself was something worthy of attention from a security viewpoint.

All of these restrictions have a massive impact on the quality of penetration tests. Surely a penetration test should be a simulated attack if it is to have any value for organizations. Penetration tests, when carried out by Hackers, take on a life of their own; the testing methodology cannot be generalized. Tests are carried out, and then other tests are carried out based on the results of the first tests. Hackers may be multitasking between 30 different activities during a testing window. They test for 20-hour stretches, sleep 10 hours, and then start all over again. Usually the testing window is only two calendar weeks as a maximum. This is usually not enough time, and if things are even more retarded by imposing testing restrictions, then there is a good chance there will be critical false negatives.

How did all this restriction business come about? I think it was a combination of two major factors: one was the "just get us through the audit" phenomenon that I described in Chapter 4. The other was a fall-off in testing quality on the service provider side and also a lack of appreciation/understanding of testing quality on behalf of the testing subjects. If the penetration test was seen as not delivering anything of value other than regulatory compliance, then it made sense to completely avoid situations where IDS false alarms could be triggered or service availability could be impacted.

With the subject of return on investment from penetration testing, there are two aspects to consider with regard skills: there are the skill levels of the testing team, and there are also the skill levels of the testing subject.

I mentioned in this chapter about the perception of penetration testing as being the one and only way (on top of fully automated internal methods such as vulnerability management) of assessing the risk posture of a network. This perception comes hand-in-hand with a situation where a security department has limited knowledge of their organization's infrastructure, and under these conditions, penetration testing is used by the security department to compensate for a lack of knowledge of the configuration of IT systems. Of course, such a scenario is inadvisable from a standpoint of risk. The landscape of internal systems and networks is too complex to be mapped in a two-week or even a 100-week penetration test. Security teams need to know their environment in detail, and they need to be performing their own risk assessments.

Internal security staff of an organization should be literate in the microscopic details of corporate infrastructure, information assets, and applications. They should also be aware of vulnerabilities, threats, and attack vectors (and therefore risks). If internal security staff are aware of the configuration details of internal systems and networks, then a penetration test is only performed to catch a misconfiguration or bug they may have missed from their own risk assessments. If the security team is aware of the organization's information landscape to this degree, they are in a position to make an educated call on the potential usefulness of a remote penetration test (and also the potential usefulness of the remote penetration *testers*). Organizations see the maximal return on investment from penetration testing when their own internal security staff are clued in on the IT architecture. In this situation it will also be clear how often testing should be performed.

Usually monthly is too frequent, and bi-annually is too infrequent. There is no fixed answer here; it depends mainly on how often configurations change.

With regard penetration testing teams skills, if underskilled analysts deliver penetration testing, or the tests are restricted, then the return on investment will be nil or just purely the value of regulatory compliance. In this chapter, my reference point is to talk about unrestricted penetration testing delivered by Hackers.

This chapter covered the testing restrictions, testing conditions, and then the required skills from the tester and the testing subject. Do we also need to consider changing penetration testing methodology as a result of changing threats?

Recent changes in the threatscape "out there" and the associated birth of a new buzzword—APT—have led to what should be a change in thinking on penetration testing and information risk management in general. Because of the potential for revenue generation for the bad guys, APT has been and will be around for a long time to come yet. APT does not cover specific vulnerabilities as such; it is used to describe the type of attacks used by organizations such as states or criminal gangs. The attack motives can be large-scale identity theft, intellectual property theft, or other forms of corporate espionage/cyberwarfare. More and more we see use of undisclosed vulnerability (I call it "zero-day" here), malware (that potentially uses zero-day exploits), social engineering, and classic attacks on custom-developed applications such as SQL injection and cross-site scripting.

With the increased prevalence of APT, traditional defenses against malware and exploits such as antivirus and patches do not give us the risk mitigation we hope for. Malware is being generated at such a huge rate that we cannot rely on pattern-matching techniques, and how does a software vendor write a patch for a vulnerability that has not been publicly declared?

Also we now see a change in the corporate perimeter. Employees are mobile and use mobile devices, they work from home, and there are multiple VPNs for vendors, business partners, mobile workers, clouds, and so on.

With modern threats to desktop PCs and laptops, it could make sense for organizations to consider internal penetration testing. The hard reality is that it is now very difficult, if not impossible, to defend against risks to employee computing devices from malware and "clicking on the wrong link." So organizations need to take the strategy that says "we will have malware issues on our employee subnets, so let's plan for this eventuality." Just because a zero-day, social engineering, or malware attack is successful, it does not have to mean "game over" for the organization. It could be useful in some cases to stage penetration tests of the corporate critical infrastructure from areas such as employee office space subnets. If an organization does use "layers" of security, then it might be a good idea to test the configuration of the layers.

The focus of this chapter was mainly network infrastructure penetration as opposed to Web applications. Of course, with complex custom applications, there is nearly always scope for extensive security analysis by skilled analysts, depending on the financial exposure.

So hopefully this chapter has helped in shedding some more light on penetration testing. It is possible to do the testing in such a way that more value can be seen from the engagements than has been seen thus far in the information security story.

Penetration tests must be unrestricted and delivered by analysts with advanced skills. The testing subject's internal staff must possess highly detailed knowledge of their IT environment. With these two prequalifiers in place, the testing can be delivered under the rationale of finding loopholes or misconfigurations that the in-house analysts may have overlooked, and it is only under this scenario that the testing subject will see return on investment other than base regulatory compliance. If either of these two prequalifiers is missing, penetration testing (other than for compliance) is inadvisable. The levels of knowledge and experience with the testing subject are as important as the levels of knowledge with the testing team.

If we take into account the testing restrictions, plus the internal and external skills issue, and then we also take on board the concept of testing the efficacy of layered security defenses, then penetration testing has the potential to be a valuable service for the connected business world. Security professionals now have a choice to make: they can continue billing customers in helping them find regulatory compliance, or, for the same price, they can help their customers to be compliant, with the added bonus of enabling business to be conducted under an acceptable level of information security risk.

8

THE LOVE OF CLOUDS AND INCIDENTS—THE VAIN SEARCH FOR VALIDATION

So far in this book, I have lamented on the state of information security offerings in the commercial world. I have commented heavily on the deployment of inappropriate skills in the industry, and from this, one can derive a host of problems that lead to other problems, which leads us to a conclusion: the majority of corporate networks are wide-open to attack, and chief executive officers (CEOs) have never been well-advised in security.

I commented in Chapter 3 about how the skill sets of security analysts have been reduced down to the level of parrot-fashion recital of checklists of security standards and so-called best practices—minus possession of the necessary intellectual capital to be able to connect "best practices" with actual real practices in the information landscape.

The world of the modern information security professional [the checklists and standards evangelist (CASE)] may seem to be a bleak one as I have described in this book, but this is the reality of the situation in most cases.

Self-recognition of the futility of the security department's offering can lead to some fairly heated forum discussions on subjects such as the relevance or value of Certified Information Systems Security Professional (CISSP) accreditation. There is a lot of emotion with these subjects because so many in security feel the need to use certifications to validate their existence. In their own mind, they see themselves as offering sparse micropockets of value to the organization, and this can affect self-esteem. Many security professionals feel the need to distinguish themselves somehow, and they see the only avenue available for this as being the certification path, or office politics, or both. So when someone questions the value of accreditations, the security pro with a mash of letters after their name will react angrily. The anger reaction is based on the fear that the critic is correct in their observation.

I have commented before in this book about the state of the security industry and the plight of security professionals therein. The defensive, angry CASE bloggers are victims of the failures of the industry. There should not be any need to find validation. The gap between security as a theoretical area of IT and corporate security is huge, to the point of being mutually exclusive. Likewise, the gap between where jobs in security are compared with where they should be is huge. If the gaps in these two areas were narrower, we would not be suffering so many incidents, and security pros would be considerably happier in their daily professional lives.

In this chapter, I will discuss two further ways in which security professionals seek to validate their existence. One such way is in the dream of the creation of a global database of incidents statistics that can theoretically be used to provide unquestionable evidence of security issues, thereby proving the existence of a threat and, in turn, validating the corporate existence of security professionals. Many see this as the only sustainable way to prove their value and validity in security.

There are also temporary ways of finding validation in security, such as the introduction of a new audit program (Payment Card Industry Data Security Standard was an example of one such new area of intellectual capital in security that provided some companies with new projects and some professionals with a new source of income).

Another temporary validation channel comes in the form of the security aspects of new branches and developments in IT. The more recent macrochange in IT was the introduction of "cloud" migrations, as in moving applications and other infrastructure off-site and employing the services of an Internet-based cloud provider. There are of course some security concerns with the cloud idea, but is cloud security really a whole new area of intellectual capital? Is it something to get excited about in the way of a new source of self-validation for security professionals?

In this chapter, I discuss the practicalities of a central, global authoritative database of incidents statistics, and I also I talk briefly about the misplaced hype that comes with new fads in security, taking cloud security as an example.

Love of Incidents

Use of incidents as "evidence" for justifying the existence of a security department is commonplace. Likewise, security service providers get all excited with each new incident that is announced.

I recall back in my days with TSAP that there were not so many public-declared incidents that made headline news. As the first few years of security service provision drifted by, there were increasing numbers of claims by clients to the effect that our recommendations were baseless because there was no "evidence" of a threat and therefore no vulnerability. How did TSAP managers react to this? The reaction was mainly one of dejection. The managers suspected that their clients had a valid point. Why should the clients keep forking out for man days of consultancy when we could not "prove" the existence of a threat?

There is this dream in some quarters of security that revolves around the creation of a global security incidents database upon which statistics can be drawn. In this dream world, statistics would be presented to the decision makers as evidence of a need for security investment. Moreover, the incident numbers can supposedly be used to validate the existence of the security department. The CASE-held belief is that the theoretical "evidence" provided by such a database is the *one and only* way to convince the board to part with cash in the name of "critical" security projects (an example of a so-called "critical" security project is implementation of some hugely expensive enterprise-wide security software roll-out that does little for security and merely puts some ticks in the boxes on the auditor's score sheet). The "no incidents equals no corporate right to exist" mindset still finds its way into security under multiple different guises.

During my time with a Big Four company in Thailand (the year was 2007), there was an incident with a large telco where large quantities of personal data were compromised. During 2007, there were a few public-declared incidents to speak of globally, let alone in our backyard. The excitement over the news of the telco incident among the security team managers was palpable. Partners in our business division had good relations with the telco's management, and some of our number felt an opportunity existed to make some money as a result of their client's misfortune. Big Four managers knocked on the telco's door (as I understand it, there were several of them—internal communication was never one of the team's strong points) with an offer of help and were duly ignored. I did ask the managers how they intended to help the telco and got blank faces as an answer. The telco had their own CISSP-certified security staff, and they were aware of the details of ISO 27001 (at least they had a copy on a shelf somewhere). They were also trained in how to deal with security incidents. So the approach needed to be more sensitive than just wading in there with unqualified offers of "security expertise in the area of incident response" within 24 hours of the incident news going public.

One of my former TSAP work colleagues was working with another service provider based in Thailand when I was at Big Four. There was similar excitement from his firm on hearing the news of the telco incident, but the angle was different. They were new on the scene in Asia, an all-Western affair, and at least two of their number were Hackers (I was aware of them from Blackhat events); moreover, their angle on the whole telco situation was that they were Western and Hackers and therefore superior in their security knowledge. I suspect they genuinely did have something of value to offer for the prospective client, but there were several problems with their approach. Asian clients, apart from being heavily nationalist, were also very perceptive. They were excellent at sniffing out attitude and moods in general. The service provider's approach was doomed to failure.

I was personally aware of some of the internal practices at the telco, and just as with over 90% of other large organizations at the time (and still today), they were way short of where they should have been in security. But the whole premise of exploiting news of a recent incident to somehow lever open the telco's door to business was blatantly flawed.

There is first of all the problem that, as a service provider, when you get all excited about incidents, you are effectively celebrating the misfortune of potential clients. But then there is also the issue that just because a client suffered an incident, does it necessarily mean that they have made some misjudgments in their information risk management and need help in this area? Perhaps not. All security control implementation decisions are a spending versus potential risk balancing act. It is all about qualitative risk assessment. Perhaps they made a decent decision on safeguards but just got unlucky.

Service providers are in the business of providing service, and they need to poke around markets for new business. It would better serve service providers if they were careful to avoid being seen to be even indirectly connecting their solicitation with a recent security incident. Larger organizations all have a preferred security partner or two anyway. Post-incident is not the time to be trying to come between an organization and their current service provider.

Returning to the matter of the theoretical global incidents database panacea, even if the industry wrongly agrees that we need it, really how much expectation can there be that an omniscient evidence collector will ever become reality, and if it does materialize by some miracle, then will the information provided be even close to reliable?

I mentioned in Chapter 4 about a remote penetration test with a Korean telco where it was discovered that unbeknown to our client, a hacker group was using their network to host "warez," anonymous File Transfer Protocol, and Internet Relay Chat. In Jakarta with another telco, during some internal security assessment, we discovered some "interesting" code and root shells on some servers. HELL's domain name found its way into some other firms' spam blacklists because their corporate network was also part of a global botnet. During a remote testing project with a global mining giant based in Sydney, evidence of a root kit was found on one critical server. All of the aforementioned hacks went unnoticed by the respective organizations.

There are still plenty of larger organizations that have not configured logging (in fact, it is worse than that: they "deconfigured" even the default, factory log settings in many cases, so that there was a complete lack of log messages) even on some of their more critical devices, and then of course it is one thing to log events and quite another to correlate events across the network and alert on suspicious activity. Many do both recording and detection, but either or both of these are configured poorly. It is usually IT operations staff that are responsible for the configuration of logging, detection, and alerts, but they receive no guidance from the security department apart from a few less-than-subtle reminders of management-level corporate security policies. When there is a project requirement to disable logging or alerts for "a critical business reason," IT operations will carry out the requirement usually without seeking any input from security, but even if there is a content management system record for security approval, the change will be given a cursory glance over and accepted by security.

Quite common also is the configuration misdemeanor whereby an organization configures a network log server that aggregates log messages from various sources, but then disables local logging on those sources because it is seen as redundant. Unfortunately though, security incidents and connectivity outages often come as a pair. Usually there is a viable business case for local logging.

Incidents can easily escape the net of logging, monitoring, detection, security information event management (SIEM) systems, and so on, but in keeping with the theme of this book, there is also of course the matter of IT skills or lack of. It is usually IT operations that have all the responsibility of both configuring a SIEM system (for example) and also investigating alerts of potential incidents. Attackers know subtle ways to avoid their actions being detected, and they can of course disable logging and delete any existing local log trails. For example, on a Unix system, just by doing something simple like soft-linking the shell history file to /dev/null, they can hide all of their shell commands from prying eyes. If someone is going to engage in a forensic investigation, that person needs to know how an attacker thinks, and this knowledge is not usually a part of the standard skills portfolio of IT systems administrators. Even if the appropriate skills are deployed in an incident investigation, the details of incidents are often lost because the attacker destroyed the event trail.

So what can be gleaned from all this is there are a considerable number of variables involved with accurately diagnosing information security incidents. With denial-of-service (DoS) incidents, how can one be sure that the incident is really malevolent in nature? Quite often, what at first appears to be DoS is actually the result of an unauthorized change or dynamic routing misconfiguration, for example. If the source addresses in the packet headers are spoofed, then it is a good chance that the attack is actually a malevolent DoS attack, but often the verdict is not so clear-cut. In my time at HELL, a dozen or so potential DoS cases were sent to the security team for investigation that turned out to be DoS as a result of unauthorized changes/ botched admin work.

For the sake of argument, let there be a hypothetical database of incidents out there in the ether somewhere. With software bug type issues, the database has detailed information of the public-declared vulnerability that was exploited. Picture the following scene: a critical enterprise server has a severe vulnerability issue. A Hacker has identified the vulnerability and is now proposing a fix. The vulnerability is a local buffer overflow issue with an executable binary on the server. However, applying a patch or workaround breaks an in-house application, and the security change is rejected. The Hacker knows this vulnerability well and has successfully exploited the problem to gain root access in penetration tests. However, the vulnerability is not found in the global incidents database (i.e., there is no record of the vulnerability ever having been exploited). So who does the decision maker believe? The individual who rejected the change proposal, or the Hacker? There is after all no evidence of a real threat because, according to the global database, there has never been a recorded case of this exploit.

As time goes on, the volume of global incidents data in the incidents database becomes larger, and therefore, if we are calculating risks based on the information in the database, the calculations become more accurate with time. But at what point can we say the database is usable or mature? The problem is that when fiends break into systems (for example), there can be several easy "entry points" as in easily exploitable vulnerabilities. The hacker chooses one, and this is the vulnerability that gets recorded in the global incidents database after a forensics exam. What about the other entry points? They will not get recorded because the hacker did not exploit them, but they are nonetheless highly critical issues that need addressing.

Clearly it would be a big mistake to place a great deal of emphasis and credibility on information from a theoretical global incidents database within two years of data collection. How about 10 years then? Or 20? At what point can any validity whatsoever be placed on the historical incidents data?

Anyway, all of what I have discussed over the incidents database aspiration to this point may be irrelevant. Organizational computing networks and business models are too complex to be simplified down to the level of being able to judge business risk from a past history of vulnerabilities that were exploited. Company A's vulnerability may present them with a serious risk of financial loss, whereas the same vulnerability in Company B can lead to a lower risk exposure for that company. A vulnerability with a piece of software can have dramatically different impacts depending on (among other factors) the network architecture, existing security safeguards (or "layers"), and what the software is actually being used for (i.e., what is its business purpose?).

Past exploits of a specific vulnerability may have cost Company A US$2 million, whereas with Company B, exploit of the same vulnerability cost US$500,000; so what conclusion can be drawn from this? The same software vulnerability can exist in 10,000 different companies, but it will most likely carry a completely different business risk for each of the 10,000.

Corporate business models and networks of information assets are too complex, and no incidents database of past troubles with other organizations is ever going to be useful as a basis for information security decision-making.

In security, we cannot afford to wait for a global incidents database because there are just too many variables working against accurate incident recording, and to be quite honest, the whole concept is bogus. Anyway, do we actually need an all-encompassing incidents database? Do we need to rely on incident statistics just to find self-validation, justify our existence, and get security budgets approved? If we are delivering security services with a thoughtful strategy centered on provision of ground-level-up knowledge and experience, then we do not need to bang the evidence and incidents drum at all (I will discuss service delivery solutions in more depth in Section 4).

The Love of Clouds

In this section, I attempt to rationalize the hype over cloud security, and in so doing, I will cover some important, commonsense aspects of cloud security that should not be overlooked.

When information technology strategists realized that by sharing resources with others they would save cash, it led to the phenomenon that now has the associated label of "cloud computing." Applications, databases, file services, email, and others do not necessarily need to be hosted in the organization's data center with the associated floor space, power, human, and other resource requirements.

The term "cloud" is derived from the use of a cloud in PowerPoint presentations to represent a network. The network in cloud computing is the public Internet.

Cloud computing is not a new phenomenon—anyone who has used Google's Gmail or other Web-based email services has been a client of a cloud computing service provider. Some cloud computing architectures are based on virtual machines (VM—a single physical computing device may host more than one VM, and hardware resources are shared between the host and guest machines)—and this concept is also nearly as old as the stars. Software such as Vmware was well known as far back as 1998, and my work colleagues and I at IBM used this software for AIX admin work. Our corporate laptops were built with Microsoft Windows 98, so rather than access AIX with the Windows telnet (a somewhat clumsy, difficult interface), we installed Linux VMs on our laptops and gave ourselves native Unix-to-Unix access.

Among others, Larry Ellison (the CEO of Oracle Corporation), Forrester Research Vice President Frank Gillett, and GNU's Richard Stallman have criticized cloud computing hype generators. Frank Gillett commented that companies simply relabel their products as "cloud computing," resulting in mere marketing innovation instead of "real" innovation. He has a valid point. Cloud computing is far from a new technical innovation. Nonetheless, sufficiently wide network pipes are now at an acceptable level of width and price for resource sharing, whereas five years ago, this type of sharing over a wide area network (WAN) may not have been seen as offering an economic benefit. Additionally, hardware resources (such as central processing units (CPUs) with higher clock rates and more on-board random access memory (RAM)) are now more affordable for something like a VM-type model.

In the security space, cloud computing got a lot of security professionals very excited because of the marketing con that cloud computing is a radically new concept, and along with a radically new concept in IT, there is the opportunity for a further con to the effect that there is also an associated radically new concept in security—supposedly a whole new area of intellectual capital for security pros to sink their teeth into and justify their corporate economic viability.

I have commented several times in this book about the lack of any real challenge in modern-day corporate security practices where the product is rarely more than checklists of best practices and security standards. CASEs inwardly realize that these post-2000 practices leave them in a somewhat vulnerable position. The cloud security wave was jumped on by many in the field who saw it as an opportunity to find the kind of self-validation they had been seeking for so long, only to discover that once on-board, the cloud security space offered little more validation than they already had. Nonetheless while the image of cloud security as a totally new area persisted, so the image of the value-offering of "cloud security experts" persisted.

I find it astonishing that so much can be written about cloud security. There are so many new documents, standards, guidelines, and policies devoted to this area, and they are all as critical as the author would have you believe. Whole new service provider companies have come out of the woodwork that allegedly specialize in cloud security. The word "cloud" now finds its way onto the CVs of thousands of security pros, and it is seen as being as essential a search keyword as "CISSP" or "architect."

I mentioned back in Chapter 6 about the Western practice of over-specialization in the security jobs market, in that job titles such as "PCI auditor" are created where there is scant actual specialization in the job function on top of the core capabilities of a bog-standard security analyst (minus the self-proclaimed "senior" qualifier). Well, not surprisingly in recent years, there have been thousands of positions created by firms for "cloud security experts" also. How much specialization is there in the cloud security space?

By common reckoning, there are three major classes of cloud systems: Software as a Service (SaaS), Platform as a Service (PaaS), and Infrastructure as a Service (IaaS).

SaaS is something like Google Docs where you as the customer buy a subscription for a product that is remotely hosted in the cloud provider. With Google Docs, the word processor does not run locally on your PC; the software is installed and runs (mostly) on the cloud provider's computer. Your documents are also stored there, but there is some Javascript running client-side in your Web browser.

PaaS from a user perspective is the same as SaaS, but look at is as a SaaS application programming interface (API) if you will. PaaS is a platform on which users can write their own software to run on the PaaS provider's hardware. An example of this is the Google App Engine.

Finally, there is IaaS, which is basically a VM-type arrangement. The cloud provider can grow or shrink the number of VMs running at any given time. This model evolved from the virtual private server (VPS) model. Rather than purchasing servers, software, data-center space, or network equipment, clients instead buy those resources as a fully outsourced service. Suppliers typically bill such services on a utility computing basis, and amount of resources consumed (and therefore the cost) will typically reflect the level of activity.

Are there really any radical new considerations with any of these cloud architectures? The answer is that it depends who you ask. If you ask Hackers with more than 10 years of practical experience in the field, they will laugh at the idea that cloud security is supposedly a whole new ball game and it "changes the dynamics of security forever." The idea of companies spending a few thousand dollars to send security staff on a two-day training course in "cloud security" is a preposterous idea. The industry needs to stop making these mistakes.

With cloud migration, resources are moved away from your private network to a shared infrastructure, and access to the shared infrastructure is over a public network. Since 2002 onward, security departments did not involve themselves with matters such as network architecture and data flows, but if they did, a knowledgeable analyst would see the migration to the cloud as merely a change in network architecture, and there would be the same review process that comes with any project for which there is a significant change in infrastructure and architecture.

The bottom line with clouds is that whereas before the IT operations team had autonomy over IT resources, now they do not. In the precloud days, there was accountability with information assets and applications; now there is none. With the cloud, the keys to your empire are passed to a cloud provider that promises governance, accountability, and service level agreements (SLAs). Is the IT environment now more secure because critical assets were migrated to the cloud? The commonsense answer is that it depends on the security of the cloud provider and also on how much control the cloud client's IT staff have over the configuration of their migrated application(s) and data. But the path to the answers for cloud security is not different from the precloud infrastructure security path.

The same questions will be asked in performing a cloud risk assessment as with the precloud days, except now there are fewer answers forthcoming from in-house staff because of the loss of autonomy that comes with cloud migration. Where there are risk assessment variables that can only be evaluated by the third party that manages your cloud resources, an overriding principle exists that is about financial penalties and accountability. The greater the business criticality of migrated resources, the greater the need for a watertight financial/legal structure. The way of things is that the cloud provider will not care about security unless they face a clear undeniable risk of severe financial penalties in the event of an incident. Of course, I do not need to state the obvious: in the event of an incident that came about as a result of cloud provider infrastructure failure, in many cases, it could be difficult to prove responsibility on the side of the cloud provider.

Is the security model significantly different with clouds? Well your network is now split over the Internet. What do we do when we need to communicate over a public network? Depending on the sensitivity, we encrypt the data, right? And with this comes more questions: how are we going to do the encryption and how are we going to manage keys? This is the same sort of conversation that takes place when connecting small office/home offices and VPN-linking geographically diverse offices.

I have seen some comments from experts in the field to the effect that with SaaS situations, there is a reduced risk from application vulnerability. The noncloud application may be one that is distributed on storage media and sits on the hard disks of many thousands of PCs around the world. Bad guys (hopefully) do not have access to source code, but they can (and very often do) find security vulnerabilities with binaries. If the application is in the cloud, it may be only accessible with a Web browser. But it is not the case that the application vulnerability issue is dead and gone. Vulnerabilities with complex Web applications have been the bane of many a firm, especially over the past two years or so. For the developers of these applications, rigorous testing is critical in most cases (depending on the nature of the app). For example, maybe a Structured Query Language statement is formed as a result of client-side user input; so the server-side has to validate the input to ensure that the possibility of unauthorized access to data is reduced to an acceptable level. Because of the cloud migration there is perhaps now a need to perform a vulnerability assessment on a Web application. But Web application security assessments are not a new area of security that came about with the cloud. Web application security ideas came about long before the cloud became a buzzword. The risk assessment game has not changed as a result of the use of the cloud word.

Is there some new brand of security topic that is introduced as a result of cloud migration? There is certainly plenty of scope for CASEs to document future-proofed policies and to be involved in the drafting of legal agreements with cloud providers, but in terms of the technical IT intellectual capital, there is nothing that I can imagine that is actually new here. Cloud security is not a new field; it is just a different architecture, and not even a new brand of architecture.

If one party shares a cloud with other parties, then of course there is some concern over unauthorized access to applications and data from within the cloud, but neither party has any control over these factors. There are reports about vulnerability with control software, but as a customer of a cloud service provider, what can you do about this?

Organizations need to keep in mind that much of the security over their cloud-based resources is out of their control. If you take the case of a VM-like (IaaS) implementation, the cloud client organization needs to consider that if their cloud resource is compromised, will there, for example, be an exploitable trust relationship between the cloud and the rest of their network?

There is no obvious conclusive answer to the question about relative security postures between cloud and noncloud. Just like everything else in security, it depends on the business risks involved on a case-by-case basis. No sweeping generalization can be made apart from the fact that just because resources are moved to the cloud, the organization can forget about the confidentiality, availability, and integrity of their migrated assets. They are not obviously more secure after a cloud migration.

Clouds and VPS farms are juicy targets for bad guys. The bad guys and bots are constantly port-scanning and vulnerability-probing the IP address ranges owned by cloud providers and Internet hosting firms. Maybe they can compromise a new virtual host while it is being built and the defenses are down, install a Trojan, and come back later to wreak havoc when the virtual host is in production. The difference between an IaaS implementation and a VPS is that in many cases it is only corporate source IP addresses that need to access the cloud resource. This makes it possible for cloud providers to firewall off access to all source addresses other than those specified by their client. However, when the situation becomes more complex, for example, diverse geographic locations need access to the cloud resources, there is the distinct possibility for chaos to reign in firewall rule-bases, and then the door that was presumed shut may have accidentally been left open.

There are many concerns with cloud implementations. There is a list of valid concerns that can be discussed until the cows come home. But I am not saying that clouds are bad. In fact, the change to a cloud architecture should not be seen as a major new headache in terms of security—as I have been saying, cloud security is nothing new. Many CASEs and cloud marketeers would want the world to think that cloud security is a whole new ball game. It is not. Do not believe them.

If an organization has the appropriate general security analyst skills under their security umbrella, then it will become clear that migration to the cloud does not require thousands to be invested in training staff or bringing in external "cloud security consultant" resources. If the organization feels the need to train security staff in cloud security, then they need to review their hiring criteria.

Cloud-based computing overall has to be a sound business proposition for many organizations. There are risks and the risks need to be assessed. But because of a myth created as a result of the need for self-validation with many security pros, many organizations will be investing excessively or just being deterred from cloud migration altogether.

Summary

As I have discussed previously in this book, many security professionals feel somewhat vulnerable in their corporate seats because others in the organization, and they themselves, do not see any significant value in the wares sold by the security department. Because of various management mistakes made since roughly 2002 onward, most security departments are only in a position to parrot-fashion recite checklists of best practices and remind other departments of their compliance obligations to corporate information security standards.

Some ideas have been born in security over the past few years that came into being at least partly because of the need for security pros to find validity and a reason-for-being. One such idea is the creation of a global database of information pertaining to security incidents. This database can theoretically be used for the provision of absolute proof of security threats and therefore also prove the business need for a security department. The other validation concept is that which comes with new fads in security such as with major new IT initiatives. One such example is cloud computing, and many folks in security would have the managers believe that cloud security is a new concept—a new source of intellectual capital that requires massive investment in cloud security training and potentially even bringing in external "cloud security consultant" resources.

On the first point with regard gathering incidents data, there are several practical difficulties with both categorizing and recording incidents. Apart from the fact that the skills currently do not exist in security to be able to perform effective incident analysis, in many cases, the mechanisms that are necessary to record information pertaining to incidents are not in place. Many organizations do not even implement logging of events (and they sometimes have good business reasons not to do so), let alone aggregate and correlate the events. The hard reality is that many incidents go unnoticed by organizations, and when they are noticed, it is often the case that there are uncertainties over what actually happened in the incident.

Then there is the question that needs to be asked: at what point can we actually *rely* on the information in the global incidents database? After two years or 10 years? How about 20 years? Realistically "never" is the answer. If there is a numerical answer to this question, the number will be several degrees of magnitude more than the lifespan of popular software and hardware products.

Take the following brief example scenario to illustrate a problem with the global incidents database idea: a security analyst may have unearthed a vulnerability, and after further analysis, the security team recommends that the vulnerability is addressed. There might be a cost associated with the risk mitigation, but there is no evidence forthcoming from the global incidents database to suggest that the threat is real (i.e., there are no previous cases where this vulnerability was successfully exploited). Your in-house Hacker is telling you that there is a threat; they themselves have personally exploited the vulnerability in question in penetration tests, but there is no evidence from the incidents database to corroborate the Hacker's story. In this case, the decision maker owes it to the organization to go with the Hacker. If there is an easily exploitable vulnerability, it goes without saying that if there is a serious associated business risk, the risk needs to be adjusted to an acceptable level, and just because there is no prior history of that vulnerability ever having been exploited, this fact should not weigh in favor of sweeping the issue under the carpet.

Many have proposed an incidents database that also records the financial impact that came with a specific vulnerability exploit (and again, how does an organization measure this?). The problem is that corporate business models and networks are just too complex for this idea. The same vulnerability can be exploited in 10,000 different firms, and it will have a different business impact on all 10,000 of them. The financial impact of a specific exploit depends on so many factors.

Overall, even if such a thing existed, would you bet your business and base any decision-making on the historical gems presented by a global incidents database? Such a strategy would be extremely inadvisable.

With cloud computing, there is the question as to whether or not organizations should adopt it, and there is also the question as to whether or not cloud security is a whole new field unlike any we ever encountered in the relatively short history of corporate information security. I will deal briefly with these two questions.

The cloud is nothing more than an abstraction of the existing legacy infrastructures. These are being cobbled together by large corporations like Microsoft and Google to entertain economies of scale.

The good news is that in a pure cloud implementation, if all of the components are secure, then the implementation is secure. The bad news is, as a customer, you have absolutely zero visibility into the actual implementation, regardless of the architecture deployed, and the original rule of computer security still applies: the infrastructure is as secure as the weakest link.

Without visibility into the cloud, customers must assume that there are one or more weak links somewhere in the implementation. Even in a pure cloud implementation, there exists the possibility of a design flaw, implementation mistake, or configuration error that could expose the entire implementation to compromise.

No third party is going to value the confidentiality, integrity, and availability of the customer's data as much as the customer. The value of the paper of legal agreements and so on is of little value if an incident happens.

As bad as infrastructure and staffing costs are, cloud is not a panacea. All customers *must* do a risk assessment of their own prior to considering a cloud solution.

Although I may have come over as being heavily pessimistic on the cloud, I do not rule it out. If the cost benefit exceeds the calculations for a worst-case scenario loss, then the cloud may be given some consideration.

Then there is the rationalization of cloud security as a whole new ball game in security that requires firms to spend massively on training in-house staff and potentially even acquiring dedicated cloud security human resource.

Cloud computing is very far from a radically new model of corporate IT architecture, and the security concerns are really the same as those we have always had. Moving resources to an Internet-based cloud provider is nothing new to a skilled security analyst; it is just a change of architecture. Data flows need to be analyzed, and there is the bitter pill that whereas in cooperation with IT operations, the customer previously had some control over their information assets, now the migrated assets are under the management of a third party whose security posture the cloud customer has no firsthand knowledge of.

So a critical Intranet application has been moved to the cloud. Now it is on the Internet. The thinking and discussion that goes with this migration project is similar to the thinking that goes with piping in a VPN connection to your data center from a new office in a geographically distant location. You need to consider encryption of communications and a whole host of other matters; but is there anything unique in the IT security space, as in particular to cloud security? The answer is most certainly no, apart from the creation of some new policies and legal agreements.

There is no need for firms to be spending zillions on training existing security staff in cloud security. If they are spending more to hire cloud security "expertise" or train in-house staff, they need to review their hiring criteria.

Can cloud security be seen as a source of self-esteem improvement for security professionals? It is seen as such, but it should not be seen in this way. It is amazing how much is written about cloud security. I mean cloud security blog space, Websites, forums, and so on must occupy petabytes of valuable information real estate, along with the power requirements for keeping it available and backed up.

It is also amazing that security service providers have been given licenses to do business that have come into being just because of cloud security. They allegedly specialize in cloud security and charge out consultants at huge day rates.

Many firms will have voted against cloud migration just because of the extra spending required in training and getting outside help. This is a tragedy of misjudgment and mismanagement, but it is a tragedy born out of the same source as all the other information security tragedies to date. It is a tragedy born of the de-engineering of security.

If information security skill sets were significantly closer to where they should be, there would be no need for any discussion about a global incidents database, and security staff would not need to be scrambling for evidence of a threat in order to convince decision makers to sign off on meeting the challenges posed by the threat.

Also with the deployment of appropriate skills, the security professionals' need to find self-validation would be null and void. Nobody in security should feel the need to pretend that cloud security is a whole new field of information security, unlike anything in history. Security professionals need to understand that when they wake up each day, there are sufficient challenges that await them in their professional lives; it is just that without solid analytical experience, it could be difficult to see the challenges, or there could be a management barrier to meeting those challenges. Certainly educated people do not feel challenged by parrot-fashion quoting of checklists, best practices, and corporate information security standards.

There is no need for any fabrication of new security fads and hype-shows, although I can quite understand why this whole "cloud security" charade came into being.

SECTION 3
SECURITY PRODUCTS

By now, there have been extensive comments from industry experts about some of the security products in active business usage and how some of them offer little or no return on investment.

John Viega's comments on antivirus products in his book, *The Myths of Security* are succinct and based on reason and his own personal experiences as an employee of McAfee (now Intel—one of the more famous antivirus software vendors), and I certainly cannot find any differences with what he has to say. Even if issues such as performance (CPU and memory hits) can be addressed, it is clear that the advanced persistent threat world is moving too fast for pattern-based recognition, and the "heuristic" features of these products were and always will be just good old-fashioned plain nonsense.

Some of the more well-known and older product genres such as firewalls and anti-virus have been the subject of much discussion over the years, and I will not focus on these products here. I will first paint the intrusion detection picture from my perspective and then I will cover two other product genres for which customers of the security industry part with great deals of cash: identity management and SIEM.

9

INTRUSION DETECTION

Network intrusion detection systems (NIDS) monitor events on a network and analyze them to determine if they indicate an incident. If it is determined that there is an incident, an alert may be raised. Network intrusion prevention systems (NIPS) are essentially the same animal except that they will also block the potentially malicious network activities. NIPS, as a packaged commercial product, came after NIDS, although it should be said that even some of the earliest open-source NIDS software packages could be configured to send a TCP layer Reset packet to shut down the potentially malicious transaction in progress.

There are glitzy well-marketed products available today that perform any kind of intrusion detection, including some, which can be installed on servers, that act as a hybrid host intrusion prevention system (HIPS) and also perform some network detection function. Another modern trend is to include HIPS as part of commercial anti-virus software packages.

My narrative here is about NIDS as opposed to NIPS. For those who are interested in hearing about NIPS, given the similarities in their functions, the diagnosis of NIPS can easily be deduced from the diagnosis of NIDS. Anyway, I will give a few words about NIPS at the end of this chapter.

Since the early 2000s, during audits of client networks and servers, I would notice a sorry-looking, redundant, powered down box in data centers that turned out to be a dedicated NIDS hardware product. Such a sighting was actually common. In fact, I can bear witness to a grand total of only 10 working NIDS (that were being used in a production capacity) in all my long years.

I would routinely ask clients, all large companies, if they had deployed any kind of NIDS, and in 90% of cases where a commercial

NIDS was acquired, it emerged that the IDS was not actually used in anger at all. Were those clients wrong to turn their IDS off?

There were a few other cases where companies were using Snort (an open-source NIDS), although there was no staff deployed in actually monitoring and tracing generated false positives or doing any kind of security analysis. Having said this, the network operations team found Snort to be an extremely useful tool for diagnosis of networking problems. The open-source versus commercial software debate will rage on for many more years with no obvious conclusion, and there will be some who will feel quite nauseous after my comment about Snort. Whichever religion you subscribe to, however, Snort is a versatile and very reliable tool.

The idea behind detection is an alluring one when the check-signatories first start thinking about it. Detecting an attack, or malware outbreak, before it becomes a problem sounds like a major tick in the pros column. However, after the on switch is flipped, the actual practicalities involved in making some return on investment with IDS come as a shock to most IT staff. The firm that sold the IDS never informed their beloved clients to the effect that turning on NIDS would be like something from Frankenstein. Luckily with IDS boxes, there is an "off" switch.

John Viega makes several points on IDS in his book *The Myths of Security*. His major theme is that it makes more economic sense for large companies to deploy IDS solutions. With IDS, there is an initial "tuning" period where floods of warnings are produced, most of which are false positives. It takes some time to figure out which alarm triggers are good to set and which are best ignored. There is a cost associated with the "tuning" time, and then there is a management cost associated with the on-going investigation into alerts. John Viega's point is that these costs are more easily absorbed by larger companies, as in the ease of justification for having 6 (for example) employees monitor 40,000 users as opposed to a smaller company of 12 users.

On deciding whether or not to deploy NIDS, nothing in security is ever a sure-fire yes or no when it comes to decision time. The cost versus benefit analysis will be different for all companies. All organizations face different challenges in terms of business and risks with information assets. All organizations have different risk profiles, and so much depends on the actual physical, spatial deployment of information assets and the network architecture. So an information security strategy that says, "we will deploy NIDS because our competitors do" is extremely inadvisable, and as I will explain, in most cases it will be an expense that cannot be justified.

Again to quote Bruce Schneier, "security is complex." When we think about possible attacks and whether or not NIDS is going to be useful, we do not immediately arrive at an answer—in fact, far from it; we certainly cannot accurately put numbers to probabilities and attack scenarios. However, I think there are some observations and comments that can be made that I hope would be useful and help bring some sort of clarity to the situation.

One of the main themes of this book is about the shift in balance in security away from the practical side. Before we actually itemize some cons of NIDS, there is something that needs to be pointed out. One of the most useful questions to ask when looking at NIDS is "how do attacks or malware outbreaks typically manifest themselves?" The answer to this question cannot be found in the pages of Certified Information Systems Security Professional study guides or infosec risk management standards. To answer this question, we need to ask the experts, as in those individuals who actually know how intrusions (note that we do not differentiate between internal or external attacks—they are one and the same) are manifested—the Hackers. Whereas network activities during intrusions cannot realistically be itemized into an exhaustive list (at least not in one human lifetime), some generalizations can be made.

Another useful skill to possess in NIDS deployment is usage of packet sniffers. As I explained in an earlier chapter, packet sniffing allows one to gauge the network's "species," and even a one-hour sniffing session permits one to learn a great deal about a network and its pattern of normal behavior. This is very useful practice for anyone seeking to deploy a NIDS. However, most security professionals these days would not consider that use of any packet-sniffing tool is even a useful or required skill. I can say that the skills required to perform analysis of NIDS output are rare in security departments, not so much because of a lack of ability but more because in most cases IT is not even seen as being a critical part of the mandate of the security team.

Some potential alarm bells, problems, and other hopefully interesting points regarding NIDS are as follows.

Tuning/Initial Costs

As pointed out by John Viega, the initial tuning costs are going to be high; then in order to make the investment useful, several tech-savvy, highly skilled employees will be needed to actually analyze events to filter false positives (of which there will be many) and attempt to correlate information in the NIDS logs. At least such staff will have to be familiar with TCP/IP to a very detailed degree, and they also need to know how attacks are propagated in real life.

Even with a NIDS in full production with six staff members working full time, the time it takes to establish a plateau of noise levels could be several weeks. Then of course, how do you know who has the necessary skill to perform this role? What I have seen quite often is network operations staff engaging in information security roles. This is just wrong. As explained in Chapter 4, operations staff do operations; it is not in their mandate to understand security threats and vulnerabilities, and if it is, it should not be. Unfortunately though, it is usually the case that the security team does not have the skill or experience to take on-board the NIDS operational tasks, and the NIDS events analysis is performed by IT or network operations staff, who have no actual information security experience.

Overall, the noise of false positives will never go away. The administrators responsible for monitoring and investigating events will face a period of a few months wherein they get personal with their NIDS. But there will never be a situation where administrators can immediately diagnose every event.

Belt and Suspenders?

An oft-mentioned principle in security is about defense-in-depth, or layered security, as in a belt-and-suspenders approach. But what if the suspenders are not strong enough? They are unlikely to provide backup support for your britches if they are made of some weak material with no tensile strength. The principle of belt and suspenders is fine to a degree, and it works in some areas; but budget signatories will still want to see some justification for the cost of the suspenders. We talk a lot about "layers" in security, but when budget signatories hear the word "layers," they will think layers of cost.

We in security religiously, with extreme prejudice, point out that local logging on network devices and operating systems (e.g., syslog on Unix and Cisco devices) needs to be turned on and configured according to some stringent guidelines. In most cases, this is good advice. So then are there many types of unauthorized activity that a NIDS would capture whereas host logging would not capture? The answer is that there are not many events that only a NIDS would be able to record. The following is an example: a brute force attack on a Secure Shell port of a Linux system will be logged by the target's syslog daemon, thereby making the network event "sniffing" of the NIDS redundant.

There are other types of activity: for example, an attacker has compromised one system in a network, deactivates the host logging on that system, and then deploys a port scanner to enumerate other potential targets in the network. This is an example of an activity that a NIDS could capture, which would not be captured by individual host logging. But generally how unique is NIDS in its capabilities? "Not very" is the answer.

Security information and event management (SIEM) systems gather logs from all systems and then attempt to detect incidents based on correlated events. Certainly organizations that have deployed fully working and operational SIEMs should find even less reason to deploy NIDS. As even the most rudimentary audit programs dictate centralized logging, it seems more sensible to progress my narrative along the following lines: companies *do* log stuff.

NIDS and Denial of Service

If internal or external sourced attackers are going to stage some sort of party, they can easily cover their tracks just by flooding the NIDS with false attacks. NIDS administrators will find themselves herding cats in order to establish the real attack, if indeed there is actually an attack.

The whole area of IDS evasion techniques is a science in itself, as in the paper from 1998 by Thomas Ptacek and Timothy Newsham titled "Insertion, Evasion, and Denial of Service: Eluding Network Intrusion Detection" (http://insecure.org/stf/secnet_ids/secnet_ids .html).

Hidden Costs

In order for NIDS to work effectively, promiscuous mode "nodes" are needed around the network.

While working with IT and network operations client-side staff, I realized at an early stage of my career that there can be considerable costs with any security safeguard, apart from the basic materials cost of hardware and software. As I previously mentioned at various points in this book, what may seem like a minor network change to a security staff member actually can turn out to present costs in many forms. For example, if a NIDS is to be at all useful, we would want to log NIDS events. So then how much disk space is required, for how long are the logs retained, and how much complexity is involved with maintenance and operations of the new NIDS nodes, plus the management station? Sometimes a factor such as the added time required for operations staff to become familiar with the NIDS devices can be prohibitive.

Whereas the aforementioned hidden cost factors may seem like common sense to the reader, let me assure you that some or all of them are usually overlooked with disastrous consequences, which inevitably end up in heated political debates and short cuts that can severely reduce the effectiveness of the new technology (or lead to the NIDS being turned off, as was witnessed many times).

Return on Investment

Whether or not all senior parties were in agreement when the purchase order was signed for the NIDS, there will still be a need to show something to somebody at some stage that demonstrates the cost effectiveness of your NIDS. At the time of writing, we are in the midst of a severe economic recession from which the world has far from recovered. At times like these, even the highest echelons of the food chain can scrutinize the smallest expenses.

Maybe, as often is the case, technological purchases are made just to use up an available budget (if the department's budget is not fully utilized, they will be given a lower budget for the next year or quarter). In this case, the decision to acquire a NIDS may seem like a no-brainer. However, always expect that someone somewhere "up there" may later ask why the expense was incurred. Certainly through the height of the recession in Q2 2009, I heard of some costs analysis horror stories from my friends in the U.K.

In terms of NIDS then, how can we really justify the expense? How many attacks were actually thwarted by analyzing NIDS events? How many attacks were stopped automatically (or autotragically in the case of some false positives)?

During an attack, given the time frames involved, it is more likely that the NIDS is just acting as a kind of advanced packet sniffer. In any case, unless the NIDS nodes are thoughtfully located (which, from my experience, never happens), it is unlikely that all pertinent events are captured. With some subnets, it is likely that administrators would need to use local software packet sniffers (e.g., wireshark or tcpdump or even the open-source IDS program called Snort) in order to diagnose what is happening. I have heard administrators say something along the lines: "why do we have NIDS if we are still using packet sniffers everywhere?"

In 100-Mbps networks, there will be a backlog of events and therefore a delay in the analysis of the events by the NIDS. This is a further chronological issue that may lead to a very late detection of an attack.

Commercial information security practices these days may be flawed in many ways, but one positive trend is the increased use of encryption to hide sensitive, plain text network traffic. This trend, however, presents a downside for the NIDS cheerleaders in that use of encryption at the application layer (e.g., SSL'd HTTP connections), whereby only the TCP and IP header information will be "visible," renders the technology less effective. This does not rule out NIDS as being effective against all attacks, but certainly those attacks that are detected by analysis of the application layer will not be flagged when the traffic is encrypted.

A growing trend (and already a commonplace finding) is for automated and manual attacks to deploy some kind of encryption. A common first-stage attack scenario is to get someone, like a discerning employee, to follow a malicious link that results in some nasty code being installed on his or her corporate computer. The compromised computer then becomes a bastion from which the real damage is done, after having established encrypted links. This causes a problem for application layer security technologies in general—not just NIDS. Unless your NIDS can deduce an attack just from patterns of ports used and IP addresses, the attack will not be detected.

So then in the majority of cases, NIDS will not actually help administrators to thwart an attack, but rather just record some information in logs that may be pertinent in an investigation of what actually occurred (although I refer the reader back to my previous comments on "belt and suspenders" and layered security: is there any information recorded in NIDS logs that will not be recorded in firewall, switch/router, and/or operating system logs?).

Some attacks are staged over several months, as opposed to quick in-and-out jobs, and the different stages of the attack would most likely be dismissed as a false positive if they were even flagged at all. Even taking log retention periods into account (a factor not unique to NIDS), with NIDS, it can be difficult to try and correlate events across diverse systems and across extensive time periods.

Overall, it is far more likely that NIDS is more effective post eventus. NIDS output is more likely to be useful as a means of piecing together the parts of a jigsaw that make up an automated or manual attack, rather than actually allowing the good guys to thwart an attack.

Network Intrusion Prevention Systems

NIPS is thought to be more effective by many, as compared with passive NIDS. A wide variety of colored box products exist that perform NIPS, in some cases along with some other functions (such as VPN gateway and firewall).

In this chapter, I have already described some problems with NIDS and false positives. Now do we want to extend the function of the NIDS to automatically block an innocent network transaction? How many of the attack signatures reliably indicate an actual attack and not a potentially disruptive false positive? Some commercial software packages such as Skype will behave in an "intelligent" way behind corporate firewalls, attempting to "find a way out" with behavior that may seem like someone on the inside attempting to learn more about the internal network.

At most, NIPS should be used to detect and block only the most obvious attack patterns such as full internal port scans and authentication password challenge brute force attempts in network subnets where you would not expect such activity to be there. In reality though, network operations teams do have a need to make frequent internal port scans in problem diagnosis, and automatically blocking their tests can have an unexpected economic impact. When you analyze the case, and actually talk to network operations teams, you realize that some attack patterns that you thought were unmistakable signs of attack can actually occur in networks as part of business as usual.

I noticed an increasing trend for hosting companies to use NIPS instead of firewalls to protect their clients' public Internet-facing Web servers. When you perform your port scan on these hosts, you will get confusing results at first. Ports will seem to be "open" (as in, a service is bound to that port, represented by a number between 1 and 65535, and it "listens" for incoming connection requests from clients), but then at a second connection attempt, the port seems to be closed or nonresponsive. This is usually an indicator of an active IPS somewhere between you and the client's target computer.

Port scanning tools such as nmap allow the user to alter the timing of their scans, and it is relatively easy to bypass NIPS. But nonetheless, the IPS may slow down an attacker, block some malware connection attempts, or even completely deter a casual attack attempt.

How about testing for Structured Query Language injection or cross-site scripting attack attempts on Web applications? Well, if it is a sensitive application, as was mentioned in the previous section, the traffic will be encrypted, and the application layer will be hidden to the NIPS.

Another type of NIPS blocking activity is to link the detection with firewalls, and this idea has been around for quite some time (Snort had firewall integration as far back as 1999). When a suspected attack is underway, the detection system signals the firewall to change its firewall rules to block the attack attempt. Again, for scientific and financial reasons, this is a bad idea.

Overall, given the science and thought that goes into planning NIPS deployments, the financial risks associated with blocking critical false-positive traffic, and the nonnegligible material costs, in most cases it should be preferable to try and use other safeguards. NIPS do have some potential benefits, as described above, but are they enough to justify the associated costs?

Summary

In terms of what is needed by corporations, the workings and effectiveness of NIDS can be understood by skilled professionals with an enthusiasm for network security, in particular, "packet sniffing lovers" and penetration testers. There are research papers from the 1990s that go into deep statistical analysis such as using conditional probability models and Bayesian statistics. Those studies belong in research and not offices.

Different implementations for NIDS have been researched. Some ideas such as anomaly-based IDS are not signature-based systems, and certainly in the heady days of the 1990s, there was enthusiasm about this idea. Anomaly-based IDS is a heuristic, self-learning IDS that "learns" what is normal network activity and then flags anomalous activity. In reality though, the false positives (and false negatives) dilemma never recedes, especially given the nature of networks and the fact that normal *is* anomalous.

Usage of NIDS may by itself, in some rarefied cases, actually help to thwart an attack and save an organization a considerable sum of money. The probability of this happening is infinitesimally low (one does not need to produce numbers and spend hours devoted to statistical research in order to justify this statement—it just is), but in a few business cases, with very large networks, this could be seen as justification for the considerable expenses incurred in personnel, training, material costs, and on-going costs.

Managed service providers (MSPs) can configure NIDS nodes in client networks and then have "sniffed" network events information sent to their network operations center for correlation and analysis, on behalf of their clients. This transfers the aforementioned costs and makes it all more sensible in terms of scalability.

APT type of attacks is more common now, where the source of the attack is more likely to be from user devices such as laptops and PCs as opposed to from "outside" the private network. Increasingly also, the attacks do not fit previously known "attack patterns"—undisclosed vulnerabilities and previously unknown malware are used in attacks, making patches and antivirus somewhat useless as interactive blocker defenses. All these trends make detection more important—but the technology does have to actually work. It is not sufficient to stamp the word "heuristic" on the product. Bruce Schneier emphasizes detection a great deal in his book *Secrets and Lies*, and indeed, I would go as far as saying that the overall principle of detection, if it can be detection in the way of early warning, is something we cannot ignore in security.

John Viega makes the valid point in his book *The Myths of Security* about how it makes more economic sense for small- and medium-sized enterprises to use the services of an MSP as opposed to deploying their own in-house NIDS.

There are severe practical details that work against NIDS as a cost-effective safeguard for any company regardless of size. However, if there is a business case for use of such technology, I would venture that use of an MSP's services is a more sensible road to take regardless of the size of the organization.

A Final Note

This is a final anecdote from my time as a consultant with a large logistics firm at their Europe and Middle-East regional data center based in Prague: we did have a few worm outbreaks within the said company—all of which, we later discovered, emanated from regional offices. There was one outbreak from Algeria, another from Estonia, plus a few other regional offices, the locations of which escape my memory.

Obviously, implementation of appropriately configured internal firewalls between the data center and regional offices would have reduced the economic impact of the malware outbreaks, but for political reasons, our advice was not adhered to, despite the presentation of a concise business study on the case for regional internal firewalls.

My team in Prague was the local information security team with no budget for any specialized hardware and a very small software allowance. I had a special understanding with the local IT operations team in Prague, and with their help, I managed to "acquire" my Linux PC that was officially destined for another department. There was an overall budget for NIPS in the company, but it had not yet been put into production (and still to this day, from what I hear, the hardware is still powered off).

At my desk, I had my regular standard build Windows PC and then another PC on which I installed Red Hat Enterprise Linux. When I was not using the Linux machine, I would leave the open-source packet sniffer tcpdump running with the machine configured in VGA console mode with no screen saver. The Linux machine would be to my side but still within my peripheral vision.

I used the Linux machine for a variety of different purposes, but when I was not at the console, it was effectively a poor man's passive NIDS, with no logging or even automatic alerting. However, when there was a flood of traffic, as in a worm outbreak, I would perceive a different scrolling pattern on the screen out of the corner of my eye.

I could have installed Snort, but given time constraints and the fact that IDS was never one of our "business objectives," I settled for software included with the Linux distribution. Actually, in this case, my tcpdump scenario worked better than Snort.

The early warning of the worm outbreak did not prevent the worm from flooding the network, but it did give my line manager a heads up before the inevitable political war started, along with the flood of calls from various different departments. He had more time to gather information from network operations and prepare a carefully worded speech before shots were fired.

10
OTHER PRODUCTS

The security service provider world changed dramatically since 2002. The industry did not hold professional service offerings in the same value as they did in the good old days of the late 1990s. Penetration testing services were severely challenged by boutique security firms that crawled out of the woodwork offering radically cheaper and fully automated services (see Chapter 5). Many firms stepped back from professional services (consulting/manual penetration testing) altogether. As I have stated previously, the penetration testing space became a compliance-only show in that the only penetration testing engagements sold were for organizations that needed to show auditors that an independent third party had assessed their perimeter security.

Also from 2002 onward, security service providers dumbed themselves down along with the rest of the industry. Reasons for this were various and have been explained at different points in this book. So there was a growing problem for service providers: how to keep generating revenue while their customers were paying considerably lower prices for consulting and professional services.

The response to this problem by service providers was to lay off members of staff who could deliver services with a high degree of quality, that is, Hackers, deliver cheaper, more competitive services with less experienced analysts, and also supplement their income by reselling security products from vendors such as Symantec.

As a final point before the first section, to do with software quality, a common scenario rears its ugly head in the commercial software world and that is the accountant-driven acquisition. Occasionally there are good offerings from the open-source world. These ventures usually start out as a bunch of Hackers coding some software on the fly. For example, their commercial Web autoscanner (see Chapter 4) fails to do even the simplest things. So, *perhaps even during a testing engagement*, they will kick off a design project that *actually achieves* some automated bug testing to improve the efficiency of their tests. Later, this "project" turns into a boutique commercial venture with the same Hackers on-board. The software starts to enter into viral territory and pops up on the radars of big security software. The acquisition goes ahead: managers who were formerly accountants go through a list of the most expensive employees and either offer them a 50% pay cut to stay on or just fire them on the spot with no explanation. The quality of the software goes downhill over a number of months. After three years, various folks will have thrown in their ideas for redesign or "remodeling." The end result is a piece of software that costs US$25,000 and does exactly nothing for information risk management strategies.

Identity Management

From an IT systems support and administration viewpoint, managing huge numbers of user accounts across multiple applications, servers, databases, desktop PCs and laptops, and so on is a hugely complex task, and the more complex it is, the more room there is for administrative errors such as failing to remove dormant user accounts or allocating excessive privileges for users (even today, the former of these two crops up frequently, and my VPN access was still active at TSAP three years after I had left the company).

Identity management (IdM) started becoming a buzzword from 2004 or so onward. By 2005, U.K. organizations were mistakenly (but unsurprisingly) creating openings for "identity management experts." Skilled security analysts can quickly familiarize themselves with these products, after which they are entitled to carry the tag of "identity management guru." If security staff are IT-oriented and skilled analysts, a week-long training course should be enough. Companies do not have any need for dedicated IdM security analysts. If they have IdM, then they do have a need for well-rounded security analysts who understand IdM, but if they are presented with a hiring choice, for example, security analyst with wide cross-technology and risk experience versus security analyst with 6 months experience but who has seen an IdM product, I would strongly advise going with the former.

Some of the more popular products on the IdM shelf are from vendors such as Microsoft, Oracle (IM 11g), IBM (Tivoli IM), Computer

Associates Technologies IM, and Novell IM. These products are quite complex software suites, and some are actually "programmable" with their own configuration features.

Are IdM products and application layer protocols such a new concept? Even as far back as the 2005 heyday, IdM was far from a new idea, although the buzzwords were previral. Firms realized for years that they could reduce some of their headaches by keeping user access and role information in one centralized repository that was accessible over the internal network, and the driver for this user management function wasn't primarily a security driver, it was just to reduce errors and prevent situations where new hires didn't get their logon credentials for four weeks or more (just about every firm I ever worked with failed to have a login ready for me on my first day on the job. In one case it was three weeks before I could login! They shall remain nameless, but not shameless). From my perspective, firms gave no attention to matters such as access revocation until such time as access revocation became an audit metric (around 2005), although six years later, this remains a frequently occurring problem.

The products are referred to as being of the "identity management" type because this is better than referring to them as "user accounts management" products. IdM sounded like something new. The mid-2000s period was roughly when *identity* management products started becoming mainstream, and this was also the period where *identity* theft became viral as a buzz phrase. IdM products cannot directly be said to alleviate identity theft risks. I am sure this naming situation was purely a coincidence and had nothing to do with marketing.

Continuing on the history of user accounts management, the first breakthrough into modern electrical telecommunications came as far back as the 1830s, and telcos have been on their game with telephone directories for 70 years or more. Directory services came to information technology and computer networking first in the form of the X.500 specification in the 1980s and the X.500 Directory Access Protocol (DAP), which required the Open Systems Interconnection Protocol stack.

Lightweight DAP (LDAP) was first created for access of X.500 over TCP/IP networks, which were becoming more widespread from the early 1990s onward. The Internet Engineering Task Force came into play around 1996 in support of LDAP version 3, which included the Simple Authentication and Security Layer, and this was published in 1997.

Many commercial enterprise level products include support for LDAP. Linux and other major flavors of Unix include features to link user management to LDAP, and I have seen this feature deployed in several different firms on a fairly small scale (less than 100 Unix support accounts).

Microsoft's Active Directory (AD) is their version of LDAP, and it includes support for both LDAPv3 and Kerberos. AD is now called Active Directory Domain Services and was first unleashed on the world with Microsoft Windows 2000 Server. LDAP and AD servers both support replication of directory information between servers. Larger organizations that deploy a predominantly Microsoft server base will usually have a small team dedicated to AD administration.

Sudo does not exactly have user account management functionality, but nonetheless it is worth mentioning here because it can achieve some of the same things that IdM products are supposed to offer, and can in some cases be used as a considerably cheaper alternative. Sudo is bundled with some Unix distributions, or the binaries or source code can be obtained for free under an ISC (Internet Systems Consortium)-style license. The next four paragraphs cover the functionality, plus some disadvantages, of sudo.

Sudo is used to grant administrative rights for lower privileged users who need to perform some functions as the root user. For example, there can be situations where junior operations staff are responsible for configuring new user accounts. Their user account will be configured in sudo to enable execution of specific commands under root privileges (as is necessary in configuring new accounts), but they are blocked from using all other commands with root privileges.

Sudo is only suitable for smaller numbers of Unix accounts in non-critical situations (I would not condone using sudo on something like a critical database server that hosts the crown jewels), and it was not designed to be a centralized facility (it is not a network service; it is only a local binary plus a configuration file). Some firms such as HELL will maintain a sudo user configuration file centrally and sync out the file to Unix machines over the network.

Overall, use of sudo is inadvisable. Ideally Unix administrators should be either fully privileged root users or regular account holders that are blocked from performing such actions as opening the password shadow file (i.e., actions for which common sense dictates super user access only). Access to the Unix machine should be first by use of their own unique user account, and then if they need root access, they use the "su" command and be subject to a root password challenge. Direct access by root should be disabled.

HELL's case is an example of what can go wrong with sudo. In 2005, HELL were still using some ancient text-based applications and required non-IT skilled personnel to log in and access. There were large numbers of users, and also helpdesk staff were responsible for setting up new user accounts. You can imagine the mess. Several thousand Unix user accounts were configured under sudo. Inevitably in this situation, several dozen helpdesk accounts (with passwords such as "password") were configured to access all servers with full root access for all shell commands.

I mentioned potential difficulties with sudo previously, but in fact, if we are talking about even a largish number of Unix servers and as many as 200 administrators, then sudo can work in some cases (at least it should not be automatically dismissed as an idea). But you will often see an expensive IdM solution (plus hours of expensive post sales "consultation") sold to firms whose Unix support requirement meets the aforementioned criteria. At least one IdM product is a glorified interface for sudo anyway; it interacts with sudo to handle user account configuration (so the client is required to install sudo if they want this particular breed of IdM solution).

To round off this topic of IdM, I will return to the rationalization of IdM in terms of its value offering: is there a business case for IdM if the customer's only concern is operating system accounts? These days, there is no great requirement for configuration of lots of user accounts on Unix or Windows servers. The shell accounts are only for support/administrative IT staff. The requirement for a thousand or more shell accounts goes back to the days of text-based enterprise applications (accessed by users over plain-text telnet), although you will still see some of these in active usage in offices today.

From my observations of IdM product sales efforts, there is often a lack of interest or ability to sit down with potential clients and actually discuss their user management numbers and dynamics. If a firm is going to sell an IdM solution promising "integrated role and user administration to accelerate return-on-investment and improve user productivity," then they had better be ready to actually look at the benefits in the light of the nasty IT details of client infrastructures. Not *all* larger firms have a user management problem—they will be using LDAP/AD as it is. Certainly, not every business will see a significant financial benefit from use of an IdM product.

The IdM drumbeaters talk endlessly about integrating user accounts across "multiple sites and applications," but the reality is that not all applications can be integrated under the IdM umbrella. Unfortunately, many buyers of IdM solutions only discover this *after* their IdM product acquisition. So end users have an IdM package that integrates access to a subset of apps, but they still have to use something else to manage access to unsupported apps.

I mentioned in Chapter 4 about organizations taking a compliance-driven security strategy approach. There can be situations where internal security staff are under tough deadlines to meet audit requirements. Perhaps there is an audit finding that speaks of failings in user management. Security managers can often be tempted to go down the road of using a software solution as a quick fix, regardless of the return on investment numbers. The thing is there needs to be an LDAP/AD architecture in place anyway. IdM solutions are not a replacement for these layers. The IdM sits "on top" of LDAP/AD and is not a substitute for directory services. But this point likely does escape the attention of many auditors. As long as the IdM system takes on a vague appearance of a working product, then the auditors are happy.

Organizations that buy software purely as a compliance panacea are their own worst enemies, and of course it is not limited to IdM, as will become clear in the next section that covers security information event management (SIEM) solutions.

IdM solutions are expensive. They are big, complex software packages that require significant resources to manage/support. IdM *is* more than a nice graphical user interface (GUI) for LDAP/AD configuration, but those organizations considering investment in this area need to ask themselves firstly if they do really have such a complex provisioning/user accounts environment, and secondly, if the IdM really does offer so much on top of their existing directory management infrastructure. Certainly if there are a few applications here and there that cannot be integrated under the IdM (I still see many ancient text- and mainframe-based apps in wide production usage, and AD/LDAP integration was overlooked in the case of many custom-developed applications), then in most cases the IdM migration will not make sense, and it rarely makes economic sense to implement a commercial IdM solution in cases where there is a requirement for only operating system shell accounts to be managed centrally. "Legacy" application layer protocols such as LDAP may be legacy, but they also serve their purpose and will be sufficient for many user management architectures. IdM solutions are not a replacement for so-called legacy protocols.

Security Information Event Management Solutions

This section covers first the functionality of SIEM and then rational-izes the business case with some occasional anecdotes to illustrate a point.

First up, I will cover some of the names of the products in the SIEM space and what SIEM is supposed to do for customers.

SIEM is another product bandwagon that was jumped on by the service provider sector with great enthusiasm. Examples of products in the SIEM space are Symantec SIM, AccelOps, ArcSight (now a part of Hewlett Packard within the HP Software Division), BLUESOC, Cisco Security MARS, ImmuneSecurity, LogLogic, and SenSage.

These SIEM products were launched with the promise of being able to correlate network log events and in some cases autoconfigure the event detection based on real-time global activity. Such a product supposedly "enables an effective incident response strategy."

The security principle behind network log aggregation is that it is better to send event log messages to a box somewhere else for the rea-son that it makes it harder for attackers to hide their tracks (by tam-pering with the local message logging on their current attack target), and also having the network logs in one central place allows for better incident detection and effective log/audit management. SIEM offers a grandiose, centralized way of handling log aggregation.

I first noticed SIEM as a buzzword around latish 2006 or so, and I will first cover a little of the history of this genre of product. Some of the earlier offerings in the log management and correlation space were hugely expensive, requiring agents to be installed on every device and a central management system that looked like something out of Star Trek but was actually just a Hewlett Packard PC with a postmodernistic dark gray cover, carrying an overall price tag 10-fold that of the PC. The vendors realized they could not get away with such exuberant prices for long, and the offerings started to move in a cheaper and agentless direction.

The requirement for a local agent to be installed on each monitored device always seemed strange to me, and each agent came with a disproportionate price. It is not as if Unix device syslogs cannot be configured to log to a network syslog server. Microsoft Windows could also be configured to send event log messages to a domain controller. Agents may be low-footprint, but each additional piece of code on a computer comes with an additional cost in maintenance and an overall impact on reliability.

In the next few paragraphs, I cover the rationalization of the business case for SIEM in terms of some potential advantages and disadvantages, and I also cover some common mistakes that are made in the acquisition of SIEM products.

I mentioned in the previous section about service providers dumbing down into product sales shops. Many SIEM "solutions" I came across were poorly conceived. So often there is little thought put into the product acquisition from either side (the seller or the buyer). On the seller's side, they do not seem to care much about the actual benefit for their client. They have a sales target and give a pitch (for example, "designed to deliver proactive security protection, helping organizations demonstrate compliance and reduce overall security risk" and "security threat response and IT policy compliance via integrated log management and incident response solutions").

As with IdM, SIEM can be used to appease auditors. Plenty of purchase decisions were based on use of a SIEM product as a demonstration for auditors that the firm is aggregating and correlating event log messages. This is a quick solution for regulatory compliance but not necessarily a solution that makes business sense. In order to deduce the business benefits and risks, unfortunately, some thinking needs to be done. SIEM boxes and software cannot be just shoved into an empty shelf on a server rack, and then an effective incident response solution magically appears, especially not with a price tag that could reach US$300,000 for the "whole solution."

Many organizations were already performing network log aggregation before they acquired a SIEM solution; so what does the SIEM give them on top of this? Interoperation between the Microsoft and Unix world was never something that was easy to achieve especially as the former always seemed to paddle in the opposite direction of integration and open computing efforts.

A SIEM solution (well OK, at least some of them) does allow firms to aggregate event records across Windows and Unix environments [plus also intrusion detection system (IDS), firewall, database, router, and switch logs can be integrated], which before was not readily achieved. I have seen efforts by some organizations to build their own solution for scripted monitoring of aggregated network events, and some are effective. Problems with this usually revolve around ownership and accountability (e.g., the solution was poorly developed and/ or not documented—the developer leaves the firm, and it becomes a challenge to maintain and scale the solution). Nevertheless, if there is sufficient enthusiasm in-house for such a solution, it can pay to keep an open mind.

There are some other cosmetic benefits with different SIEM packages, but personally I cannot attest to the effectiveness of these. For example, one vendor claims to "know what's happening in the world" in the way of malicious activity. They have packet-sniffing nodes in various places around the planet, and supposedly they can pass on early trouble warnings (such as warnings about malware outbreaks) to their clients. The warning is passed to the client in real time as a correlation configuration item that will theoretically enable their SIEM to alert them of a malware outbreak before it becomes a serious problem.

Aside from the lack of business risk analysis in a SIEM acquisition, there are cases where organizations have paid for a solution and then realize postsales that they are not at all well prepared. Not only do they not log event messages to a network log server (in some cases, they have gone as far as totally disabling logging), but they also have never approached the incident response and management problem before.

As a consultant, I came across several large-sized clients that had acquired a SIEM solution with no support or effective presales analysis. Such clients are easy to "acquire" as a service provider; in fact, there are a few easier sales for a consultant who can help clients with incident response at a technical level. Basically you have a situation where a potential client has had a SIEM box dumped on them by an unscrupulous service provider/snake oil consultant, and they need to show their boss that the purchase was a wise decision as promised. So the consultant pitches a "return on investment" speech to the client as delivery of man-hours of consulting in development of an incident response strategy. In all such cases, clients are never very well prepared technically or logically for an incident response strategy.

When I left Q in London, they were well down the path of acquiring a SIEM solution, but as with many purchase decisions in security, the key plus point was one of compliance. Auditors do not dig around and check the nitty-gritty configuration of the SIEM solution. Usually, just the fact that there is a physical SIEM station (not necessarily powered up) is enough to tick off the "network logging" box (as well as some under the incident response category) even if there is not one single network-logging enabled device. The thing is Q was predominantly a Windows house, and event logging was completely disabled on the Windows servers, with some excuse about incompatibility with the virtual disk arrays. What was the likelihood of Q seeing any return on investment from their SIEM solution if the majority of their production servers were not configured to generate event logs?

The SIEM solution only *enables* (or supplements) an effective incident response strategy. Out of the box, with no postsales consulting, it is worthless. When firewalls first started appearing in machine rooms in the 1990s, there were many firms who thought you could just connect the thing up, turn it on, and that was it—the magic intelligent firewall. With SIEM, this same naivety that went with firewall acquisitions was repeated a decade later.

After my initial rambling on SIEM, I will now attempt to bring together/summarize some of the concerns with SIEM, starting with some more details on the prerequisites for a successful SIEM implementation.

With a potential SIEM procurement, what needs to happen in order to get the SIEM to a point where there is even the *potential* of return on investment? First there is the basic requirement to be able to capture log messages (with accurate time stamps—so something like Network Time Protocol is required) across the *whole* network (or at least most of it)—what is the point of a SIEM solution if some parts of the network are off-limits to log capture? The idea is that if an attack is under way, the organization can detect it and potentially even avert some of the impact of the incident. If some parts of the network are blind to the SIEM, the chances of enabling an effective incident response strategy are reduced. If log capture is only enabled for the top 10% most critical devices, the chances of being able to respond in a timely manner are dramatically reduced.

What does network-wide capture of log messages entail? It entails network logging to be enabled on all networked devices that will be monitored. This can pose an operational or practical strain on some firms. When we brought up the subject of network logging at HELL, operations responded to the effect that half a million euros would be needed to meet the storage capacity requirement.

Some SIEM solutions require "gatherers" or log collector agents to be installed around the network (depending on the organization's architecture and size). So in terms of computing hardware, it is not just the SIEM station that is required; there will be additional boxes in the proposed solution with the associated maintenance and machine room real estate requirements, and totally the project cost can run into six digits of U.S. dollars.

A lot of questions arise with these projects. Usually what happens is the security team will have some discussions with the product provider, and everything seems to go smoothly until representatives from IT operations and architects are brought into the project. Aside from political issues, other IT departments will have a string of valid concerns (e.g., how many events per second the management station can handle, and what is the requirement for disk space and redundancy?) Many projects will be canned after the first few "extra-security" meetings because the scale of the project resource requirement becomes apparent.

Then of course there is the requirement, as I have mentioned, that an organization needs to have an effective incident response strategy. The organization needs an effective incident management structure, plus incident response plan (IRP) and incident response philosophy, and IT staff need to be aware of incident response issues. Incident response is more about people and preparedness than technical controls. To enable effective incident response, there are some technical systems and network features that need to be in place, but the key is the preparedness of IT operations and security, and of course there has to be a management/organizational structure in place.

So thus far, I have said that first the network needs to be technically ready for a SIEM procurement, and also there has to be an incident response strategy, but these requirements should not be seen as a barrier. Indeed with the majority of larger organizations, these factors are mandatory anyway, regardless of the SIEM project requirement. I only mentioned these requirements here because the majority of firms who undertake a SIEM project do not meet these requirements.

Then in the presales scenario, we need to look at the final result with SIEM, as in once we have all the prequalifiers in place, do we see return on investment? Well just like everything else in security, there is no easy answer to this. The discussions about false positives and false negatives with SIEM are remarkably similar to those with regard network intrusion detection systems (NIDS) (see Chapter 9).

If we do have comprehensive log information across the network, integrated across the whole organization, then we do have a decent source of information for incident investigation. But then if our interest is purely in investigation/diagnosis, why would we want an extra SIEM product layer on top of just plain-old vanilla network logging from separate syslog and Windows Event Manager sources? If we are concerned only with post eventus analysis, the timing is not the most critical factor here. It is enough to merely correlate "manually" across separate Windows and syslog silos in cases where microsecond responses are not required.

When something bad is happening on a network, can the associated network events really be so readily associated with malevolent activity? With social engineering and malicious sites, users can be conned into revealing passwords, but when the password is used, to the uninitiated there is nothing obvious to link this event with an unauthorized access. Brute force attempts with user logins or Web applications are usually signs of malicious activity, as are port scans, but if we look at some of the recent media-covered incidents, it is not likely the majority of events in these attacks could be associated with what is obviously malicious activity.

The discussion about the hypothetical benefits of SIEM is quite long-winded, and I apologize in advance. It turns out we have to think quite hard in order to try and visualize the possible benefits of SIEM.

As an illustration, and hopefully to help bring some clarity to the discussion on the benefits (or not) of SIEM, picture a network where devices are configured to log events. Effectively each device is then a kind of sensor of malicious activity. Each device can be configured with a local commercial or open-source means of analyzing the local logs and alerting on suspicious activity. Alternatively, the devices can be configured to send their logs to a network log server that is configured with a commercial or open-source intrusion detector (for example).

With the architecture as described in the previous paragraph, we are not so far away from a SIEM solution – effectively this is one "layer" away from a SIEM solution. Thus far, we have either local or networked pools of event logs, with software that alerts on suspicious activity. SIEM is when all of these event logs are gathered in one single place. Supposedly the benefit in doing this is that by centrally gathering everything, the SIEM has total vision over the network, and the software can somehow link events from different hosts to reveal suspicious activity that would go undetected if we did not centrally gather event logs and ask our SIEM software to "correlate" diverse events.

SIEM technology is allegedly unique in the potential for incident detection, but when you think about it, what is the difference between a SIEM system and multiple pools of aggregated log silos around the network? According to the vendors, it is the correlation factor that distinguishes SIEM. There will be other benefits mentioned such as manageability and operational benefits such as "being able to see everything from one place," but from the security perspective, correlation is the key point with SIEM.

Theoretically if you have an attack situation as follows: event A followed by event B, then event C . . . , in some scenarios, each of these events in isolation is a decent indicator of an attack. How many scenarios are there where all three events together indicate an attack, but each separate event in isolation would seem to be innocuous? How many attacks will only be detectable with correlation?

Is it feasible to see a benefit from correlation? If we take an example of Structured Query Language injection with a custom-developed application, there is at least the potential for a SIEM system to detect the issue before the exploit was successful (unless the exact injection string is already known to the bad guy *before* the attack; perhaps the application has been around the block a few times). But the key here is the *correlation* part, as in the whole purpose of a SIEM is not really just to aggregate messages; it is supposed to be able to analyze network events from multiple different sources on the network in order to detect patterns that could indicate an attack is taking place—and the timing is everything (the time windows need to be short, as in seconds and minutes; it is true that some attacks are staged over weeks or months, but how do you connect these time-disparate events and decisively conclude a connection between them? Attackers do not usually use the same source IP address for multistaged attacks.)

Furthermore on correlation, how many real-life attacks involve diverse targets all being attacked within a shortish time window? One of the few things that NIDS can do well is detection of (some) worm outbreaks; a well-configured SIEM could do this also. How about brute force attacks? Usually the target is one device, and we can configure detection of brute force attempts without use of SIEM, but yes it is possible that several can be attacked simultaneously. The SIEM can detect brute force attempts, but is correlation necessary? Does it actually help? I mean when one device is compromised by malware, the malware may start looking for other targets by port scanning, and the port scanning event could be captured and an alert raised; and we can configure detection of brute force attempts without use of SIEM, but overall, I'm not sure if the "centralized, network-wide correlation" side of SIEM is a benefit that the customer can really expect to see from the product, and in this case, why expend considerable resources in the implementation of such a solution?

The more recent media-covered incidents we have heard of all involved attacking by one specific channel. If an external-facing host is compromised, then privileges are elevated by use of a local exploit, and then the attacker enumerates other potential targets by port scanning; it is possible that the initial intrusion is detected by the SIEM, and then the port scan event could be captured (if internal firewalls log dropped packet events). However, is network-wide, centralized correlation necessary in order to deduce that an attack is underway?

Anyway, would the events in an incident be so clearly connected with malicious activity? With recent public-declared incidents, in the few cases where technical details emerged of the attack, most stages of the attacks would either not trigger a log event on the host, or if an event was logged, it would not be associated with malicious activity (a false negative situation).

So in summary, it would seem that the decision making on SIEM depends heavily on whether or not correlation of events is actually feasible in real situations. If we can say that correlation is possible, then there is an "economy of scales" decision to be made. Larger end users with 10,000 or so nodes are probably justified in acquiring SIEM if we can say that attack detection by correlation is feasible rather than mythical. If correlation is only theoretical and not practical, then there is no need whatsoever for a SIEM, unless the organization is happy to have a central logging authority with all the bells and whistles that maybe can alert in isolated attack cases such as a brute force attempt on a database service. If there is no realistic potential for correlation and/ or no realistic expectation that attacks can be detected and stopped in their tracks, then organizations need only do network event log aggregation, while steering clear of a commercial SIEM solution.

Open source tools exist (although I do not have firsthand experience of their effectiveness) and considerably cheaper monitoring and detection tools are available. In some cases, usage of a host intrusion detection solution can suffice. Such a solution has the potential of detection of something like a brute force attempt on a critical database server, and alerts can be configured.

With small- and medium-sized enterprises (SMEs), there is probably a lower chance of seeing return on investment with SIEM mostly because they have a smaller footprint, they generate fewer log messages, and the correlation effort is unlikely to yield sufficiently good results to justify the considerable investment. SMEs can probably live without correlation and just aggregate network log messages from their syslogs and Windows devices, especially if they engage a managed service provider (MSP) to handle IDS.

With MSPs and ISPs that have large client bases (200 or more), there is a slightly clearer cut case for SIEM. It seems more likely that correlation of events can yield beneficial results in this case (such as with malware or other widespread attacks that affect more than one client simultaneously). If MSPs/ISPs can set up centralized logging with routers, proxies, switches, IDS nodes, and other infrastructure, then they are possibly in a position to proactively alert their clients of potential trouble.

Summary

Increasingly from the early 2000s onward, security service providers were on a mission to replace their lost professional services revenue with reselling of security products; however, there were many cases where little thought was put into the product pre- or postsales. Many times, service providers were interested purely in selling a box without seeing the delivery through, while leaving clients somewhat helpless.

There is an unwritten code of conduct for service providers when engaged in product sales. In recent times, the two main product genres for which there were numerous violations of said code were IdM and SIEM solutions.

IdM is not a new idea in that organizations had been *managing identities* prior to the buzzword, just not by use of a specialized product. Organizations with a few hundred IT users and more will have implemented LDAP or AD or both; these are used for managing user accounts, and both have been on the face of the earth for more than a decade.

Sudo is a Unix program used for allocating super user rights for nonsuper users. An example of where this is useful is where lower privileged users such as junior admins need to set up user accounts without being granted full access rights. The shell commands for user account administration are configured in sudo such that the operations staff can perform their job function as root. Sudo is also a relatively ancient facility, and it can be suitable in some cases, although it should be avoided because it does open a door for local privilege escalation. The best situation is one where system admins log in with their own unique account and then enter a root password when they need to "su" to root. Nonetheless, sudo does permit some level of user management only for Unix, although it goes without saying that in large user base situations, the complexity and difficulty of managing large numbers of sudo accounts is certain to lead to huge security holes being opened.

The promise with IdM is one of "integrated role and user administration to accelerate return-on-investment and improve user productivity," but in reality, the service provider is only interested in making a fast buck, or clients are only interested in a quick easy compliance fix (there are compliance criteria related to user management). In other cases, the service provider and/or the client were not in a position to perform the necessary pre- or postsales support.

"IdM consultants" talk about integrating user management for "all applications across multiple sites," but in most large organizations, this is more of a theoretical than a practical concept. Many organizations will acquire an IdM solution only to realize that few applications can be integrated under the IdM umbrella. One of the promises of IdM is for the IT architecture to become simpler rather than more complex, but "more complex" is exactly what the buyer gets when they have multiple IdM solutions, and complexity leads to the increased potential for security issues from misconfigurations.

IdM solutions are expensive. The software package is a big jumbled mass of add-ons, modules, and so on, and significant resources are required to manage and support IdM. It could take a very long time to fully migrate to the IdM, and the integration process is a further drain on resources.

Organizations should first ask themselves if their user management is so complex that they need IdM, and then if the answer to this first part is yes, then they should ask themselves exactly which applications can be integrated into the IdM matrix. If it emerges that only production server operating systems can be integrated under IdM, then the argument in favor of IdM is a tough one to make.

SIEM is another product box type show that the security service provider sector got very excited about. It is basically to do with logging at its core, and it pays to remember this fact and not allow oneself to be hoodwinked by marketing speak such as "enables an effective incident response strategy," "designed to deliver proactive security protection, helping organizations demonstrate compliance and reduce overall security risk," and "security threat response and IT policy compliance via integrated log management and incident response solutions."

The part about "IT policy compliance" is interesting. Many compliance programs such as Payment Card Industry Data Security Standard do have requirements for network-based logging. However, the compliance requirements do not mandate use of SIEM as a metric. It is up to clients how they meet the logging requirement. Operating systems have standard configuration options for both Network Time Protocol and network logging, and there is no requirement for a third-party product in enabling network aggregation of event logs.

Boutique security service providers armed with vendor reseller agreements zipped through end user markets, leaving behind them a wake of disgruntled former clients. The core function of SIEM is one of event log aggregation and event correlation to detect signs of potential unauthorized activity. It is not the case that sliding the SIEM management station into the rack and turning the thing on provides an effective incident response solution.

In some situations, the SIEM can detect signs of an incident, but after the fact, what are you to do about the incident? Incident response is more about people and less about technology. An incident response team and IRP need to exist. Systems need to be incident-ready (configured with appropriate logging and Network Time Protocol), and IT staff need to be aware of their responsibilities and also the technical aspects of incident recognition and first response strategy.

There is some distance between the magic box of SIEM and return on investment with the said box. Things need to be done, and thinking needs to happen. First of all, there is the obvious requirement for network logging to be enabled with time synchronization. I used the word "obvious" there, but currently, many organizations do not have even local logging enabled for more than 50% of their IT estate, and there can be some challenges with enabling network logging; one does not simply turn it on with a giant switch. There will be support, maintenance, and physical storage media overheads.

Many companies will only enable the SIEM for the top 10% of critical devices in their network, but among other problems, this reduces the effectiveness of the SIEM. If there are only critical devices in your event logging field of vision, chances are that in an incident, the damage will already have been done before you can respond to alerts from the SIEM, or the incident will go completely unnoticed.

The more one thinks about it, the more complex is the discussion over the benefits of SIEM. What does SIEM have that most firms do not already have? Network aggregated event logging and intrusion detection is possible without use of SIEM. Network transmission of event logs is a standard configurable option with popular operating systems, and open source detection solutions are available. At worst, compared with the cost of a commercial SIEM, there are some considerably cheaper commercial detection solutions available. There is never any mandate handed down from some authority that says that network-wide event logging has to be achieved with one central logging system, with real-time correlation of events.

Some firms actually had no interest in proactive detection of attacks when they purchased their SIEM. They use SIEM data only for investigation, and operations had a login account for diagnostics. But if our interest is only post-incident diagnostics and not prevention, then why bother with SIEM? We can simply aggregate syslogs and Windows events with no additional third-party software element. After all, what does SIEM actually do on top of just gathering event log data from diverse hosts around the corporate network? The SIEM is supposed to be able to correlate network log messages and alert on signs of potential unauthorized activity. Without the *correlate*, organizations may as well just set up a network log server for silos of Unix, Windows, and other devices and technologies.

The "correlate" word is the key word with SIEM then. But exactly how realistic and practical is it to be able to correlate event log messages from diverse sources and detect signs of suspicious activity? This is where the complexity comes in. In fact, these discussions are similar in nature to those with regard to the benefits of NIDS.

How likely is it that the *correlation* of log messages by itself will result in positive detection of a malfeasance? In a theoretical attack in which there is first an event A then an event B, and then an event C, in some scenarios, each of these events in isolation is a decent indicator of an attack. How many scenarios are there where all three events together indicate an attack, but each separate event by itself would seem to be innocuous?

In summary, the *correlation* is the key with SIEM. Decision making depends an awful lot on the potential for correlation. Without correlation, organizations may as well just implement their own solution for monitoring of disparate silos of logs around the network. Do not forget that there is also host intrusion detection system (HIDS) and NIDS to consider. If a firm has these types of solutions in place, then they become a factor in the pros versus cons decision making with SIEM.

If correlation is actually effective, then it adds weight to the case for a SIEM purchase. If correlation is not effective, then SIEM does not make a great deal of sense unless the organization is happy to host a central logging authority with all the bells and whistles that maybe can alert in isolated attack cases such as a brute force attempt on a database service (as I mentioned in this chapter, there are certainly more economical ways of achieving this goal, other than parting with a six-figure sum of cash for a commercial SIEM offering).

Then of course there is the question of false negatives and whether or not a malicious event can be easily recognized as such. If you look at recent public-declared incidents, there are scant technical details divulged by the victims, but there were some details about the attack methodology in a few of the cases. For some of the events, it is unlikely there would even be a log message generated (with a default logging configuration). For others, there may be a log message but not necessarily a message that indicates malicious activity. SIEM would be of little use in these cases.

With MSPs and ISPs that have large client bases (200 or more), there is a slightly clearer cut case for SIEM. If MSPs/ISPs can set up centralized logging with routers, proxies, switches, IDS nodes, and other infrastructure, then they are possibly in a position to proactively alert their clients of potential trouble if they use a SIEM system. Whether or not the financial numbers work for them is of course subjective.

The general principle with all of these product acquisition shows is to go back to basics and figure out what the product offers at the most base IT level first, and then if there is a technical need, figure out if there is a business case. For example, SIEM provides centralized logging and correlation, but we already do network logging and we have IDS. So what actually does the SIEM do for us on top of this? Then think through some actual scenarios based on real-life incidents and ask if the associated events would even be flagged as malicious if they were detected at all. Then how about correlation? Is it actually going to help us or does it just sound like a nice thing to have?

If organizations want to buy security products and see some actual return on investment other than mere compliance, then some thinking is needed. As lamented by many a seasoned security professional, the marketplace for security products is full of what is quite frankly rubbish. But how will the organization identify the good from the bad? They need an experienced security manager or architect to work with security analysts (as opposed to IdM or SIEM consultants or self-proclaimed "subject matter experts") with deep technical skills to look at the tech side of the products (as in do the products deliver what is promised by the vendor, and what is the potential resource requirement for the company?), and then armed with the necessary tech info, some thinking can be put into the business case. The security products industry is only as big as it is because the aforementioned product evaluation activities are rarely undertaken on the buying side of the equation. The reason? The major theme in this book is about skills in the industry. If the buyer cannot tune into the technical or business need for a product, the odds are of course with the confident-sounding seller, who will happily have a magic heuristic box of snake oil delivered to the client for a huge price tag. The misleading message from the salesperson will be something along the lines: "all that's needed is to find a slot on a server rack, plug it in and fire it up . . . problem solved." This was the promise with firewalls, and the buyers swallowed it. Fast forward a decade later and we find that the security industry's customers are still making the same mistakes with other products.

SECTION 4

THE
RE-ENGINEERING
OF SECURITY

Many will read this section and believe it to be a simple take on the security world, but the solutions do not have to be complex in nature. We are not reworking networks and corporations here, or taking the world back in time to the start of the industrial revolution—the powers-that-be do not need me to do this; they are doing a pretty good job of that by themselves.

In my planning of the content for *Security De-Engineering*, the decision as to whether I should include details of potential solutions was a tougher decision to make than I could have imagined. From one side, I do not really want to write a book that purely talks about problems and discusses nothing about solutions; that would be so "negative." But also, in order to justify my assertions on the solutions, a significant portion of the discussion needs to be technical in nature. However, the technical breakdown is another book in itself. So there was a dilemma here.

Eventually I decided to talk about solutions and this is the raison d'être for Section 4, and the main drive is about professional accreditation and skills in security. In the final chapter of this book, I hope to be able to give a representation of my thoughts in the area of solutions. Of course, I am not pretending for 1 second that if the security world follows my suggestions, we will all live happily ever after. However, I do think we need to evolve rather than regress (as we seem to have been doing for the past decade), and hopefully what I cover here will at least help the security world to take a step forward and halt the state of free fall we have been in for a decade now.

The overriding principle of this book has been about the growing distance between security practices and the information they are trying to protect. By removing the information technology bias from security, we have effectively thrown away the weapons we might use to keep bad guys at bay.

Checklists and best practices in themselves are not the problem. The problem is the lack of accompanying analysis. Checklists are a reminder of bases that need to be covered in information risk management, but as a list of items in the hands of a non-IT oriented security professional, they are less of a help than a hindrance to businesses.

Lest it has not been emphasized enough: in the 21st century, businesses hold their most critical information assets in an electronic form (it is reckoned that most businesses hold at least 80% of their information assets in electronic form on storage media), and it is therefore with electronic countermeasures that we protect said information. How can we protect confidentiality, integrity, and availability of information assets if we as security analysts are not at all versed in the language of information technology?

There surely *is* a place for checklists. Management standards such as ISO 27001 are checklists. The principles of standards such as ISO 27001 are ideal for forming a high-level document (a baseline security standard) that guides us in the management principles of information security. Someone in security must be aware of these high-level policies and standards; usually that person would be the security manager, and they should be familiar with this higher level of abstraction. But as we move from higher to lower levels of abstraction, we get more detailed, and there is more information and intellectual capital to take on board. As we move to lower levels of abstraction, we get closer to freezing machine rooms and nasty command shell prompts that sit in wait for us to do our jobs as security analysts. At the lower levels of abstraction, there is too much work to do for just one person, so more people are needed who understand the environment "down there" at the coal face. The problem we have had for the last decade in security is that very few professionals will venture down there to the coal face because they cannot see their way and do not have the tools to do their jobs down there in the nether regions. Security has been in a state of "too many chiefs and not enough Indians" for too long. There has been an oversubscription of security managers in the guise of security analysts. Over 95% of security pros to this point have actually been security managers, and it does not take a whole department full of security pros to handle security management. In all honesty, it takes precisely one person to do this job.

So how do we get back to where we should be? Please do not expect to see Earth-shattering brilliant new ideas here. I think these ideas have been tumbling around in the subconscious of a handful of industry folk for some time now, but for whatever reason, I do not see them being laid out in black and white anywhere. Moreover, I do not see that the problems with the industry are well known. At least the problems are not well documented—and the first stage of solving a problem is realization of the problem in the first place.

Humans will solve all of our problems in security, and so we need to cultivate the right skills for the humans in the industry; from such a vantage point, the problems may be solved.

There are other issues I thought of covering in this final section. There are many microissues, but as the basis of all problems, if we can solve the skills problem, we enable at least the potential for the solution for the other problems. There are two aspects of the skills issue solution: first is the composition of the security knowledge base, and then having identified key areas of knowledge, we need to think about the details of an accreditation scheme for validation of a security professional's command of the required skills.

One of the microissues I thought of covering was the area of operating system security controls, and it is worth a brief mention here. Operating system security controls are an area that most organizations overlook today, but by thoughtful application of operating system security controls, we may reduce our "attack surface." We cannot defend against all attacks of course, but we can make attack efforts more time consuming, and we can better defend ourselves against malware. For example, with the new so-called advanced persistent threat, we may be subject to an attack effort that exploits a previously undisclosed vulnerability, in which situation software patches are useless. But if we have configured our operating system to make it harder to elevate privileges, we reduce our vulnerability and therefore also our risk.

There are security standards and policies that tell Security Analysts how operating systems should be configured, and by synergy with other IT departments, security can be applied to operating systems depending on the level of criticality of the device. Also, changes in operating system build images enable the new security controls into the future. I briefly mentioned operating systems controls here, but to a Security Analyst with extensive IT and security exposure, the point is intuitive. Even if there were no specific directive in the security strategy about operating system security controls, it is unlikely skilled Security Analysts would overlook this point. There would be policies and standards, which were implemented, and maintained, and systems would be monitored for standards compliance.

Perhaps we have all got jaded with the state of the industry. Maybe nothing will change because the people who make the decisions in this game have a vested interest in keeping the truth hidden. This might be the case, but I am going to throw in my bob's worth anyway. As I said, there are no great miracles here. We just need to take some simple steps toward being able to offer value as security professionals, and in so doing, we facilitate trust—trust between the decision makers, other business units, and also among ourselves.

11

ONE PROFESSIONAL ACCREDITATION PROGRAM TO BIND THEM ALL

I believe issues with the current framework of accreditation are relatively well known and well documented, which is why, thus far, I have not covered this topic in any great depth. In Chapter 6, I briefly covered the (ISC)² Certified Information Systems Security Professional (CISSP) accreditation because at the time of writing, it is the most widely accepted/recognized accreditation in security.

In information security, we do seem to have lost our way somewhat with accreditation, so it seems apt to bring some sobriety back to the situation and remind ourselves of the basic tenets of professional accreditation. Professional certifications from a professional society or major vendor are supposed to at least indicate a level of proficiency in a subject area. Ideally, the accreditation qualifies the holder to perform a certain function.

Most engineering programs at the undergraduate level include intensive study in applicable areas such as mathematics and physical and life sciences. Practical and computer lab sessions will also form a major part of engineering courses. External bodies perform an accreditation function with engineering programs to determine if the courses meet applicable standards. The writing in large text at the top of the accreditation section of the U.K.'s Institution of Civil Engineers Website goes "If you hold a degree which is shown as being accredited, this means that the University offering this programme has been subject to a formal visit by Institution of Chartered Engineers (ICE) to ensure that the degree programme is of an appropriate standard and covers the appropriate core civil engineering subjects such as surveying, geotechnics, fluid mechanics and structures." So basically, if you hold an ICE-approved degree, you have a recognized professional qualification.

Furthermore on civil engineering, some tasks (such as designing a bridge) need to be carried out by a licensed engineer. In the U.K., such an engineer is a "Chartered Engineer" who carries letters after his or her name ("CEng"), which actually do mean something.

Of course, throughout history, there have been failures in civil engineering (one of the more famous for its spectacular visual effects was the Tacoma Narrows bridge collapse from wind resonance in 1940). But generally, when a new building goes up or a bridge is finally completed, even the first "guinea pig" user is not afraid to cross the bridge, unless he or she is of a particularly nervous disposition.

The civil engineering field has succeeded in creating that level of trust where new users automatically have the belief that the bridge will support their weight and they will not fall into a precipice unless they are extremely unlucky. But of course, if there were no such trust, there would be no bridges or tall towers. The Manhattan skyline would look very different, and the population of Hong Kong would be a few digits less. This goes back to the "measurement of failure" that I mentioned when talking about automation in security in Chapter 5. In aeronautical engineering, if a plane crashes, people usually die and the reputation of the airline is severely impacted. There is no choice but to build stuff safely—and the uncomplicated system of accreditation effectively enabled the society that we are currently a part of. A U.K. civil engineer cannot design a bridge unless he or she is a Chartered Engineer, and other countries have something equivalent to this.

There has always been a high level of discontent with accreditation in security, but with the spate of recent incidents, there have been growing numbers who question the applicability of certifications such as CISSP and CEH *ad infinitum*. The most recent (reported) major incident at the time of writing was the intrusion on Sony's gaming network whereby 70 million identities were stolen. The immediate effect on equities was a drop of 4% as of 10th May 2011 (although there is no solid proof of the link between the security incident and the stock price), but customers were offline for more than three weeks, and there has to have been a negative effect on customer and game developer levels of trust.

The Stuxnet worm from 2010 targeted industrial software (in particular, the Siemens Supervisory Control and Data Acquisition that was used in a wide variety of industrial systems) and equipment and included a programmable logic controller rootkit. In 2010, the main target was apparently Iran, and allegedly some industrial facilities (including some associated with Iran's nuclear program) were knocked offline. In case the threat posed by cyberwarfare to whole nations was not respected, here was a reminder.

Certainly through 2009 into 2011, more than ever before, there were a growing number of incidents that affected the bottom line of the victims, and if there was ever any doubt as to the lack of value of security accreditations, the events of 2010 onward certainly helped to confirm the dire state of affairs.

There are little pockets of security pros here and there who create their own fantasy world where current-day security accreditations matter. There was a service provider boss I met in London who used the term "seesers" [Certified Information Systems Auditor (CISA) is the Information Systems Audit and Control Association (ISACA) accreditation that is by their own accord a "globally accepted standard of achievement among information systems audit, control and security professionals"]. By his way of thinking, if you were a "seeser," you were a security professional; if you were not, you had nothing to offer (of course, he was a "seeser" himself).

CISSP is by far the most widespread security certification in the industry (as of July 2010, there were allegedly more than 67,000 people holding the accreditation), and it forms the basis of a very profitable business for (ISC)². How applicable is the certification to the needs of the industry? I think the answer is "not very" because like so many other accreditations (CISA included), the study content is high level and more closely akin to information risk management principles. In the few niches where the content becomes more detailed, the relationship to business practices is questionable. The CISSP Application Development Security domain is a good example. The content of this domain comes as common sense to seasoned pros and newcomers (newcomers pass the exam with flying colors on a regular basis) alike; moreover, most of the material has theoretical rather than practical value. Business environments often do not support the kind of practices laid out in CISSP study guides, but this is not a critical issue. The most challenging aspects of developing secure applications are ground-level and architectural issues, and the whole field is more than can be covered in any one syllabus, let alone one that covers the whole industry in one pass.

The premise of CISSP is that the whole industry is covered in ten domains—but it goes without saying that security is too wide and deep a field to be covered in one fairly short swoop. In that swoop, one can only expect to skim the surface while going a little deeper in some areas, and the areas that are covered with more depth have scant applicability in everyday business security practices.

Overall, security managers are likely to find more value in CISSP course material as compared with security analysts and architects, yet CISSP is the only certification that is widely recognized in the industry—and that is most certainly a problem.

C-Levels Do Not Trust Us

With security accreditation, where are the challenges? What are we trying to achieve? In my way of thinking, what we need to do is create a level of trust between security staff (of all levels) and the more senior decision makers, and the implementation of an accreditation program that is in sync with business needs is going to help get security closer to where it should be. We need security managers to interface with C-levels and give a message that leads to C-level support of effective and cost-efficient information risk management.

From what I have seen, the trust between C-levels and security is at best flimsy. I mentioned back in Chapter 4 about the minimization of security programs down to bare regulatory compliance levels; one of the drivers for this was (and still is) the top-down driven strategy where C-levels got tired of listening to requests for budgets with very weak justifications, delivered with almost zero confidence by security managers. The accompanying loss of patience by seniors resulted in speeches that start off as something like "just get us through this audit and don't let this stuff get in the way of anything that makes us money," and get progressively louder. The problems with the bare compliance approach to security were explained in Chapter 4.

We can say that if a firm has experienced security incidents after a security manager has given assurances over the risk posture, then this will clearly have a negative impact on C-level trust, but even if there has been no severe incidents (or as is often the case, the incident went unnoticed or was deliberately obfuscated by the security team), there is still going to be an issue with C-level trust in many organizations.

I have also mentioned previously in this book about confidence, and by this I mean the levels of confidence that security managers have in their own message. Up to now, security managers have not been delivering a message to C-levels with any confidence. The management levels of security will bleat endlessly about vulnerability management programs that autotragically produce reams of pie charts and graphs with green colors that say everything is fine in the world of information risk. But inwardly, the managers are aware that realistically they have very limited visibility of their organization's security posture, and this is very difficult to hide from C-levels who reached their lofty heights by being masterful politicians.

Also as explained in Chapter 4, many of the functions of security were passed to IT operations, and the graphs and charts from vulnerability management and security information event management (SIEM) suites actually come from them. But how much are the IT operations heads vested in security? In most cases, they were reluctant to take it onboard because they were aware of the huge security holes, their resources were already strained, and they were aware that just because their team is more IT-oriented than the security team, it does not mean their skills are appropriate for information risk management. Usually the security manager rather than the IT operations manager will handle the security line reporting. So the security manager is delivering a message from people outside his or her own team. This also does not help to boost the levels of confidence.

Generally, even though they campaign vehemently that security does not need to be a technical show, security staff are in most cases inwardly aware that it needs to be a technical show at the lower analyst levels, and it also cannot be just fobbed off to another department. They are aware that security cannot be just a checklists and standards evangelist (CASE) show, and this realization undermines the confidence that a Security Manager has in their own value to the organization; it also adds to the lack of confidence they have in the quality/accuracy of their line reporting.

Before we can cover professional accreditation in security, we need to cover more details about management and tech roles; but first I will talk about the job classifications in security.

Infosec Vocational Classifications

We do not do ourselves any favors in security by creating so many different job titles. I have already covered the ill-advised practice of overspecialization of security and also covered industry sector specialization.

The industry has a need for people who specialize as security analysts, security architects, and security managers (the particulars of this role are covered in the subsequent section), and it does not need to be more complicated than this. There could also be a categorization that is "security consultant," but really this position is effectively Security Analyst plus communication skills.

Is there a need for a role titled "penetration tester"? Not really because security analysts have to have at least a good understanding of the tools and techniques in penetration testing if they are to understand risks. Certainly penetration testing is not mutually exclusive with security analysis. How about "identity management consultant?" No because a skilled security analyst has the core knowledge that enables him or her to easily pick up on the requirements of identity management—in fact, the two areas are only different when it comes to identity management *products*. There is a bucket of buzzwords that the vendors create in tandem with these products, and these need to be learnt; but is there a requirement for an "identity management specialist"? As an absolute maximum, if an organization is going to acquire an identity management product, they might need to send a couple of security or operations folks on the vendor's training course.

"Security architect" is a role that not every organization would need. I see the skills for this role as being not so dissimilar from those of the security manager, except there is no people management or reporting as such. There is no team of security analysts reporting to a security architect, although there is some level of seniority that an architect has over an analyst. Architects can "mentor" analysts, but they are not involved in setting objectives, key performance indicators (KPIs), and so on.

The architect role is particular to larger companies that roll out significant numbers of changes or new applications, which is the majority of large-sized organizations. A security architect is a dedicated tech role but requires understanding of "mature" stuff such as business objectives, information risk management principles, network architecture (data flows and so on), and security policies, standards, and guidelines. Security architects review new changes and projects with respect to security requirements. They are involved in projects from a design phase. They have a deep technical understanding down to operational level matters, but they can also empathize with business goals and project team members. They are in a position to make balanced calls on security (i.e., they review project IT requirements, and each aspect of the project specifications is reviewed in terms of risk; changes to the design are advised in light of potential risks versus the business benefit or cost).

Requirements of an Infosec Manager

There has to be an infusion of trust in the security industry, which starts at the bottom. If security managers have faith in their team, and also themselves, then they in turn have confidence in their message, and they can go to C-levels with ideas of how to restructure the management of information risk for the economic benefit of all concerned. Of course, it helps if the security managers come from a technical security background themselves, even though their day-to-day job is not at all a hands-on role.

In order to understand the requirements of security managers, we do need to understand something about the requirements of security analysts because the managers' role is influenced by the skills in the team they manage.

Security managers who lack a technical background will need to be constantly filling in their void of knowledge by back-and-forth communication with security analysts, and this has a negative impact on the team's efficiency. Take the following as an example: say the team needs to communicate the findings of an application security assessment to the developers. If managers know the nature of the vulnerabilities and how they are manifested, they can handle the presentation by themselves, and there is no need to tie up an analyst for a two-hour meeting. Likewise with reporting, analysts are notoriously bad in this area, and a lot of correction will be needed before sending the report to the relevant department. Can you imagine the nightmare (for both managers and analysts) if there is no tech understanding on behalf of the reviewer?

Take the following as another example: if security managers are discussing a new project requirement in a meeting with the design team, they can figure out the security resource requirement easily if they can visualize handling the risk assessment themselves. If not, then they need to tie up an Analyst potentially for hours in explaining every aspect of the project before a resource requirement can be estimated.

Without at least a few years behind them in a tech-oriented security role, the security manager role is almost redundant. The analysts in the team will be filling in constantly, carrying out "mature" tasks that they find boring, and the team will not get to achieve a great deal. This was actually the real scenario I encountered in both TSAP and Big Four, and it led to friction in a few cases. For all intents and purposes, the team ended up being almost nonfunctional.

Although the main drive of this book has been about the loss of analytical skills in security practices, I do realize that security is not all technical. I have also lamented on the blind usage of checklists and security standards in the industry, although it goes without saying that checklists and information security management standards are imperative as high-level guides.

In Chapter 2, I discussed the Hacker paradigm in detail and celebrated the technical genius of my former work colleagues and the older genus of security pro in general. However, as can be gleaned from that chapter, I do not believe that a return to the late 1990s is in any of our interests.

However, if we look at the late 1990s, the skill sets of the security professionals of that era are what are needed today, but that is not to say that we need teams full of Hackers doing analysis work (I discuss the requirements for analysts in the next section). The missing ingredient back then was of course management. Just as artists have an agent to represent them and sell their work, Hackers need a manager who understands their lingo and behavioral quirks, and can wield the Hackers' skills like a weapon to be used in information risk management programs.

Fast forward to today, do we need technical Hacker geniuses in every security analyst seat? Actually no, and moreover, I doubt the security industry could get the Hackers to come back into corporate environments unless it sold itself extremely effectively. Maybe 10 years from now, it could be possible to see some Hackers coming back and working for "the good guys," but in the meantime, I would say we could get by in the short term without them—we are looking for skills rather than a specific mold of a person, and if that means we have to hire more analysts to cover the bases that were previously covered by the Hacker, then so be it; but we are not talking hugely significant differences in security department headcounts (more on that later).

What about managers in security? What are the required deliverables from security managers? The manager should understand the network and the business architecture, and with knowledge of how applications and information assets relate to dinars, pounds sterling, dollars, rupees, renmimbi, yen, baht, rupiah, and euros, the manager is in a position to carry out his or her role as a leader, rather than just a dictator.

As a problem not unique to security, most managers these days are bosses more than leaders. To be a leader requires the people under the leader to *want* to be led by their leader. That means the leader has to be acting in the best interests of his or her team, without selling short the folks higher up in the food chain. So managers have to understand the requirements of the business, plus find the respect and trust of the security analysts in their team. How do they do this? They have to have "graduated" from a security analyst role themselves (to enable themselves to be empathic with their team members), rather than, as so often happens these days, they come from IT operations or even an entirely nontech background. And for the people above them in the reporting line, managers have to understand their concerns. These usually revolve around business objectives.

The security industry these days is like so many other areas of IT. The only requisite of a security manager is that they are "mature." Perhaps they have some project management history, although it is not mandatory that the projects were even remotely related to security.

A common scenario in modern-day security departments (and also witnessed in my time at TSAP) is one where security managers perhaps have a tech background, but their vocational experience in computing dates back more than five years. The manager is unable to speak the same language as the analysts, and in some cases, there will be some level of intimidation felt by the manager. Conversations will be purely at the level of following up on team objectives, and when a deadline is missed, the manager will not really understand why there was a problem, and mistrust results. What usually unfolds is that the manager virtually divorces the team, and whenever you hear stories about Hackers being "difficult to manage," the background narrative will often be something similar to what I have just described.

Of course, managers are not hands-on techs; that is not part of their jobs. After some years, they will forget some aspects of security analysis, but if they can converse with techs and show some understanding, they have the potential to be a winner as a manager. Even if security managers have no tech experience, they can usually get results just by at least pretending to be interested in their team's work. From my experience, techies are not so difficult to motivate.

Security managers do not need to be business analysts. The understanding of how information assets and applications relate to business objectives does not require an MBA. Although so many security managers in the industry would have us believe otherwise, the story here is a simple commonsense story. Anyway, security managers will be in touch with project managers, and when someone in the business hatches an idea for a new application project, security managers should be able to talk to the business and understand the drivers behind the idea. What is needed here is really just common sense and what TSAP managers would call "maturity."

The Requirements of a Security Analyst

Before we can talk about the requirements for security analysts, we need to talk about the requirements of the security team. In this regard, the idea is not so different from that in existence today. The bigger part of the role is basically to create and maintain security policies and then ensure compliance with the policies. The functions of the team can be generalized at a high level with a glance over ISO 27001 (or the organization's baseline security standard, if there is such a thing) to include ensuring that the controls implemented are not forgotten on a dusty shelf and are carried forward into the future.

Some departments (it is irrelevant which department; as long as the skills are there, it does not matter about the name on the label) should be carrying out risk assessments such as penetration tests and application tests for new and existing projects and infrastructure. Other functions can include vulnerability management, business continuity/ disaster recovery, wireless security, war dialing (there is a blast from the past, perhaps not so applicable in some places), identity management, incident response, and security awareness training.

The difference between what security teams do these days and what they should be doing is to a large degree about access to resources. If security analysts are skilled IT professionals with accreditation to prove it, there is no reason why they cannot have direct visibility of policy compliance. That means Unix security staff are granted root access to Unix resources (with full accountability of course), network security staff are granted Cisco enable access, database security staff are granted full privileges for databases, and so on. Security analysts should have visibility and full access to all areas of an organization's infrastructure. This enables them to take control of security and investigate incidents without hindrance. Naturally, before they are allowed such universal access, they need professional accreditation to facilitate trust.

The other big differentiator between current-day practices and the proposed model is a lessening of dependence on security products that either do not work or have no business justification. Areas such as vulnerability management are (in the majority of cases) entirely dealt with by use of a software product and operated/maintained by IT operations. Total faith is held in the functionality of the products, but to date, I am yet to come across one that gives even remotely accurate results and also covers all of the security bases. Taking vulnerability management as an example, most of these packages are based on the same flawed autoscanner technology that I covered in Chapter 5.

Products are fine if they work, and a business justification can be found in terms of return on investment. The thing is if you have a department full of skilled security analysts and an able security manager who understands something about the network architecture and business objectives, the organization is in a position to make educated calls on product acquisitions. Taking SIEM as an example, very few of the people involved in product evaluation have any visibility (i.e., logging configuration and analysis experience) with Cisco, Unix, databases, or Windows logging. Is this is a small point to make? I can assure you it is not. Visibility from ground level up allows organizations to make educated calls on the effectiveness of a product.

All this outer world talk of highly skilled security departments is all well and good. It sounds nice. But coming back down to Earth with a bang, where are we going to find the people to fill these highly skilled Analyst roles?

The British Broadcasting Corporation (BBC) Website (my attention is always caught by articles about security from sources other than IT and security sources) ran a story on the 26th July 2010: "UK Seeks Next Generation of Cyber Security Specialists." "The challenge is being run to help fill out the numbers of skilled computer security workers Britain can call on." So there have been problems in recruiting people with the type of skills necessary for the profession. There is another comment: "A lot of people that came in through to 2000 have moved on." Whereas I would agree, there is a typically polite British aspect to the statement. The reality is not "moved on"; "moved out" would be more appropriate. Certainly the vast majority of the pre-2000s Hackers I knew were moved out. Some did resign, but most were just fired or laid off.

There is another comment in the aforementioned article: "Defending all of our interests in cyberspace is a relatively small cadre of talented and highly skilled public sector and private sector cyber security professionals." Problem is here, how do they know whether or not the current breed of professionals is talented, or were they just being nice with these words? Are they talented because they are CISSP certified? The article implies there is a lack of skilled people in security, but the private sector (and especially the public sector) has never actively tried to recruit more security people in any significant numbers. The number of currently employed security staff is entirely determined by the requirements of regulatory compliance. Private sector companies need to show auditors that they at least give an illusion of interest in security (see Chapter 4), and the minimum number of staff required to do that will be the security head count. As is always the case where you get politically correct dialogue, the real meaning of the article is unknown. Are they talking about a recruitment drive for cyberwarfare? Are they saying there are not enough *skilled* people in security, rather than not enough people? Certainly it is not the case that private sector bosses have come to the government complaining that their head counts are too low, and they cannot find enough people to do the jobs.

In another article on npr.org titled "Cyberwarrior Shortage Threatens U.S. Security," funnily enough also from July 2010 (is this coincidence or was the BBC not prepared to talk about "warfare" as in cyberwarfare?), there are some choice comments such as "There may be no country on the planet more vulnerable to a massive cyberattack than the United States" and "The protection of U.S. computer systems essentially requires an army of cyberwarriors, but the recruitment of that force is suffering." James Gosler, a veteran cybersecurity specialist who has worked at the Central Intelligence Agency (CIA), the National Security Agency, and the Energy Department, was interviewed for the article. He says, "You can have vulnerabilities in the fundamentals of the technology, you can have vulnerabilities introduced based on how that technology is implemented, and you can have vulnerabilities introduced through the artificial applications that are built on that fundamental technology," and he goes on to say "It takes a very skilled person to operate at that level, and we don't have enough of them." You know what? He is absolutely right.

In another article, you guessed it, from July 2010, ChannelNewsAsia.com was reporting something on a similar vein to do with problems in finding skilled people for cyberwarfare "defense" in Singapore.

In a wider context, *Forbes* magazine ran an article titled "Danger: America Is Losing Its Edge in Innovation" by Norm Augustine. According to Mr. Augustine, and I tend to agree, scientists and engineers are seen as geeks and misfits in the United States, whereas in some other countries, they are celebrities, and this is one of the reasons why kids do not choose engineering or science as a career in the United States. Although the vast majority of the current information security workforce would care not to agree, this lack of graduates coming through with an engineering-type mindset (which would include subjects such as computer science or computer systems engineering) does not help us in security.

I can tell similar stories about negative perceptions of techs from my time in Asia. There is a negative perception in society about engineers, and especially in Thailand, there is a really offensive job title that is "programmer." Several times I heard of stories where new hires came into firms as programmers but requested to have the word "manager" on their name card instead of their real job title. The drive with most engineers and IT staff is to get an MBA as soon as possible and then get into management.

So by now we all get it (although perhaps not admit to it)—we are short of skilled people in security. The focus with articles lamenting the lack of skills is usually defense/cyberwarfare, but really it was cyberwarfare that made some sectors of the public wake up to the skills shortage factor in the security world at large. In case it was not clear, cyberwarfare *is* about security—from reading these articles, you could be forgiven for thinking that there is a band of government employees out there looking for specific cyberwarfare experts, and when their keyword searches draw blanks, they report a lack of cyberwarfare skills in the country. Cyberwarfare recruitment efforts I am aware of involved getting a bunch of vaguely enthusiastic hobbyists together, the majority with no vocational IT experience, and getting them to solve puzzles. There was no focus on IT knowledge as far as I am aware.

Are the skills needed to help cyberwarfare efforts somehow different from the Hacker skill set I described in Chapter 2? Not really. The activities may be slightly different from those of a security analyst working for a big bank, for example, but Hackers can be cyberwarfare experts, and indeed they are perfectly qualified for this function.

In Chapter 2, I painted a picture of the Hacker ethic and tried to give a ground level view of what a Hacker's CV may look like. I noted that because of the Hackers' boundless enthusiasm for technology, there are a few core technologies with which they are not well versed. Moreover, they tend to be able to learn new technologies on the fly, perhaps during risk assessments or remote penetration tests.

In Chapter 2, I also drew some reservations with Hackers, mostly to do with a lack of willingness or ability to fit into the corporate robot mold. However, these cosmetic issues are easily solved if the industry did one day agree that Hackers are not so bad after all (as if this fact was not already known). I picture a scene where there is a sealed-off lab area in corporate office spaces, something like a secret research facility. Food and drink are shoved in through a cat flap in a door. The Hackers are not allowed to speak to other employees directly by voice. In fact, why not go the full ten yards? Potentially all human–Hacker communication could be banned mainly because mere humans find the Hackers' nature to be offensive, sarcastic, toxic, and generally demoralizing. The security manager is the input/output (IO) port interface to the rest of the organization. Ideas and reports come out of the off-limits Hacker zone through the security manager only.

But humor aside, are there enough Hackers to go around? If we are to believe reports about a lack of engineering mindsets leaving our universities, then it seems we may not be able to find them even if we want to. Hackers come in various guises though. Some are hobbyists who never worked in a regular IT job. Perhaps they could come in for an interview? I don't see why not, as long as the right person conducts the interview. The chances of finding a person with no IT vocational history, who is also suitable for the analyst role, are slim, but it could pay to keep an open mind.

Then again, is there a need to have actual full-blown Hackers in every Analyst seat in the corporate world? I don't think so. It is just that we need more non-Hackers to achieve the same results as we can achieve with Hackers. We are looking for specific skills in security. Because of the vast portfolio of skills held by Hackers, organizations could save an awful lot of money by hiring them (as long as they are well managed), but it does not have to be the end of the story if the good guys cannot find enough Hackers.

Really what we are looking for in terms of security personnel are sufficient numbers of people to come into the industry who have at least some relevant corporate IT experience with some relevant core technologies such as Unix, Windows, Cisco, Oracle, and so on. What I am leading toward is I do not think we should necessarily be looking to rehire actual Hackers in security straight from the streets (although of course, if we can get some, it would be good).

The path to the analyst role can be one of graduation from other IT roles such as IT or network operations, development, database administrator (DBA), and so on. When IT operations staff read my previous comment, based on their knowledge of current-day security departments, they may laugh, and I would not be surprised at this reaction. The idea that security is somehow a "step-up" from operational roles such as support and administration may seem totally ridiculous, and when you consider the current skills portfolio of modern-day security departments, it is indeed ridiculous. But there is security where it is today, and there is security where it should be today; sufficed it to say they are almost 180° degrees different.

I think it was some years before I got into security vocationally that the area had me in awe. I recall hearing some of my more enthusiastic colleagues speaking of the challenge of security. Security, more specifically hacking, was seen as the ultimate test of an IT geek's ability. Although it may not have been thought of in such formal terms, there was an intuitive sense that security was indeed a step-up or a branching out from a regular IT administration or programming job that forced an employee to focus on one product such as a specific Unix flavor or Oracle- or Cisco IOS-based devices, or one task such as writing Pascal or C programs. Security was the IT geek's heaven because of the possibility of getting one's hands on so many different technologies. The technical challenge was seen as greater in security, and if security is being handled properly, it *is* greater.

I commented in Chapter 4 about the differences between the required skills for IT operations and security. In summary, to be an effective security analyst requires deeper understanding of operating systems and applications as compared with the IT operations type of role. A DBA, for example, uses certain functions of the database administration interface for their daily role in support and maintenance. However, bad guys have no such boundaries. Big and complex software packages such as operating systems and database management suites come with a whole bunch of functionality that IT operations staff will never use, but which bad guys may play with in order to gain unauthorized access. IT operations staff may know something about their particular flavor of Unix and file systems permissions and so on, but deeper knowledge of security and attack vectors with their OS is not included with their training course material.

The point about moving "up" from other IT functions to security is actually irrelevant. If it offends people to talk of "up" or "down" or whatever, then it can be "sideways." The point is though, if an IT admin (for example) has an enthusiasm for IT and has also demonstrated excellent competence and professionalism, he or she may be considered for a role in security.

There has to be a bridge between security and operations (one that typically does not exist today). They have to speak the same language, and it is very beneficial to firms if security understands the challenges faced by operations. How apt would it be then if security analysts were once operations staff themselves?

Personally, if I were a security manager and I was looking for new recruits for my team, I would consider "private time"/hobbyist programming to be a good sign of enthusiasm for IT, and therefore a good sign of potential as a security analyst. Because of the demands of the role, enthusiasm is essential. When I am in the U.K., United States, and Australia, for various reasons, I do not see a great deal of enthusiasm from operations staff (this has a lot to do with shoddy people management), but there are often one or two who always look for ways to improve things, perhaps with little Perl or Shell scripting ventures here and there. These folks are usually "somewhere near the top of the class" also in terms of KPIs and deliverables, although they may not fit in so well socially—they do not win at away-day go-karting or bowls events. Such a profile is ideal for security.

Staying on programming, one of the activities of the security team will be assessment of Web application security for in-house or third-party developed custom apps. Although this role does not have to be exclusively handled by a former Web application programmer, for sure, firsthand knowledge of how these applications are developed certainly helps a great deal in security assessment of the apps.

Any analyst can go to the Open Web Application Security Project (OWASP) site for example, read the material there, and play around with the Webgoat sample application. But there is no substitute for knowing the mind of the programmer when assessing Web apps. After I had actually written PHP/MySQL applications, I found it much easier to understand the actual implementation of queries on the server-side and make better guesses as to where SQL injection issues may be lurking. Terms get thrown around in Web application security such as "session" for example. If analysts have never written any server-side code that involves user authentication, they may not really grasp what a "session" is in this context. There are many such examples along these lines.

Actual programming as such is probably more applicable for security service providers rather than end users, but nonetheless, scripting (Perl, Ruby, or Shell with Unix and batch file type efforts with Windows) is a very useful skill to have for Security Analysts. DBAs will usually be proficient in SQL scripting, and this skill will be essential for many security teams. There are some nice tools from companies such as Red Database Security (http://www.red-database-security.com) for Oracle, but no amount of products and tools will ever alleviate the need to run queries and manually check aspects of database configuration completely.

With regard database security, the "crown jewels" are often held electronically in a database at the higher level of abstraction. At least one person in the security team will need to understand what goes on with databases "under the hood," and who better to perform this role than a former DBA? Again, as with IT operations and operating system security, a database security expert who has been a DBA will understand the everyday challenges in the DBA's world, and this enables empathy and a balanced approach to database security controls. For example, a security analyst needs to look at the security controls on a database host. They have a need to remove setuid permissions from the database software package binaries, or better still completely delete the binary files (reducing the "attack surface"). If the analysts (or someone in the team) were DBAs, they will know what is redundant and what binaries are used for what purpose. Of course, they check with the existing DBAs on these matters before making calls on changing server configuration—but they will not be completely clueless on the matters at hand. The same goes for roles and privileges with user accounts. The analyst who specializes in database security is in a position to know which accounts can be removed and which accounts can have some privileges removed.

Ramping up tech skill levels in security departments is going to address so many of the problems faced by the business world today. So often I came across IT operations teams who systematically wrote off the security department and felt they could be bullied into anything (in Chapter 4, I covered a case with a London insurance firm where the IT operations department initiated a remote user support project that involved tunneling the support connections through an untrusted third party's network). If security better understands the challenges faced by the IT operations department (and the organization as a whole), and they can all speak the same language, everyone can row in the same direction. Operations staff should be inspired by security analysts rather than annoyed by them.

So many of the ill-founded practices found in large organizations can be exorcised by deployment of the appropriate skills in security. Another example is JavaScript in Web browsers. It is usually someone other than an analyst who questions the enabling of JavaScript in Web browsers (disabling JavaScript can alleviate the risk from Web-based attacks such as cross-site scripting), and when the security department is not sure of the risks involved, the default action will be to issue a decree to the effect that client desktop and laptop builds must have JavaScript disabled. Corporate policies are updated, but they will later be revised, probably within three months.

The problem? The Internet is built with JavaScript. It is so widespread, and it is really the *de facto* means of performing operations such as client-side input validation. The security team needs to take an educated look at the real risks with cross-site scripting. What can happen? Session cookies are stolen? Firefox saved passwords are compromised? How about implementation of a JavaScript keyboard sniffer? There are means of dealing with these to some extent such as "noscript" whitelisting. JavaScript has its own security mechanisms also such as the "same origin policy." Without going into detail, developers should be aware of these features, even though they do not help as a blanket risk remover across the whole Internet for every application. "Noscript" is one that will get administrators chasing their own tails. Developers do need to be aware of these features though, even if the game with secure application coding does not seem to be one we will win in our lifetimes.

But should JavaScript be disabled altogether? How about just turning off Internet access? Turning off JavaScript has the same effect. What will happen if the organization disables JavaScript is that increasing numbers of requests will come for JavaScript to be enabled based on "critical" business needs. So all that disabling JavaScript does is to succeed in helping the security team lose whatever credibility it had left, remove Internet functionality for employees, and act as a barrier to application development.

There can be very few cases where the risks to the organization of enabling JavaScript outweigh the cost of disabling JavaScript. If all relevant parties are aware that JavaScript is enabled in corporate client Web browsers, then the information risk strategy can be formulated with this in mind. For example, application security assessments can be performed with the knowledge that the default client install image has JavaScript enabled. If IT staff are aware of the risks, the risks can be taken into account, and they can be mitigated or worked-around.

Because of the way application security is going (it will get worse before it gets better), organizations need to plan for successful exploits against their own Web applications; problems such as cross-site issues and SQL Injection (SQLi) will exist, and they may be exploited. The key is not to allow these exploits to lead to more financially damaging exploits.

Regaining the Trust: A Theoretical Infosec Accreditation Structure

Thus far, I have spoken of the roles and responsibilities for security managers and security analysts. I have already implied that it might be a good idea for security analysts to "graduate" from other IT roles such as IT operational roles, network operational roles, DBAs, application developers, and others. Also, as I mentioned earlier, security managers will be more effective if they have some history as a security analyst.

If you look at the vocational IT scene in larger organizations in the developed world, you will see professionals in boxes. IT administrators are in Windows, Unix, DBA, network (predominantly Cisco), messaging, and other boxes. So there would be one "channel" from which IT operational/administrator staff could move into security, and their function as a security analyst would then be closely related to their former lives in their operations or development capacity.

Taking Unix security in a predominantly Unix house, when you consider internal testing and other security functions, there is certainly enough workload to keep one person busy. The same can be said for all of the other popular core technologies. Larger firms with 10,000 or more globally networked nodes can easily justify employing more than one network security specialist who deals with Cisco gear, firewalls, intrusion detection systems (IDS), and so on. A firm that is focused more on Windows than Unix does not need a certified Unix security analyst and so on; the makeup of the team is very much down to common sense.

There are reputable certification programs for Microsoft admins from the vendor themselves. Microsoft Certified IT Professional certification is one of the newer accreditations from Microsoft that covers Windows Server 2008. Some firms still swear by the older Microsoft

Certified System Engineer (MCSE) certification. Likewise with Unix, IBM issues an AIX certification, and other vendors such as Redhat have their own programs. Cisco has a modular program of certification that is quite complex (there are five levels with seven different paths).

The subject is a little too detailed to cover here, but the content of the study courses for the aforementioned accreditations is not enough for an effective information risk management program. I mentioned in Chapter 4 about differences between operational and security skills, and some of the missing content can be gleaned from there. Almost all of the vendor administration courses have a security element. Microsoft has some security content in their accreditation paths, and Cisco has first Cisco Certified Network Associate (CCNA) Security and then Cisco Certified Security Professional (CCSP).

I am unfamiliar with the Cisco security accreditations. But from what I have seen of vendor courses in general, they do not cover areas such as attack vectors or local privilege escalation. There is no emphasis on how attacks are manifested, so the holder of these accreditations will not be necessarily aware of threats, or for want of a better phrase, "how stuff is owned." With the security offerings from other vendors, they tend to go overboard while missing the salient security points that actually should matter to businesses. Really it is enough to cover the IT administration skills and leave the security offering as file system permissions and so on.

Taking Cisco accreditation as an example, I do not believe there is enough security coverage of areas such as network architecture/data flows, IDS, or firewall configuration. I mean the points covered do not relate to actual real-world threats. So can network administrators jump straight into a security analyst role just because they have the Cisco security certifications?

How about Microsoft administrators? They have covered NTFS file system permissions and other areas such as Kerberos and Active Directory security; is this enough for entry-level security analysis?

I believe there has to be some sort of general security accreditation program that consists of precisely *one* exam for which one certificate is awarded in the event of a pass. Effective security analysts are a different kind of beast from IT administrators. They need to be able to put themselves in the mind of an attacker, and I believe there is a common, shared body of know-how that bridges all popular technologies in use by organizations, and also one that all security analysts should find familiar.

I do not think the path to security analyst from IT admin should be one of, for example, MCSE and then some advanced Microsoft-only security certification. Why? It is because the candidate security analyst has already proved his or her worth as a Microsoft person with his or her career track record to date. There are some areas of Microsoft security that need to be covered on top of what a 5-year Microsoft veteran will know from his or her professional lives; but there is no real justification for a dedicated Microsoft security accreditation program as a prerequisite for entry as a security analyst.

What I think would be a useful approach to security certification would be something like a penetration testing accreditation, but it is not called penetration testing. The idea is something like penetration testing, in other words, a field of knowledge that covers all popular technologies to a level that demonstrates competence and previous exposure to the technology. Additionally, areas such as basic Web application testing, attack vectors and exploits should be covered. I again need to apologize because to go into detail in discussing this subject is a book in itself; clearly I cannot jot down the details of the course material in this book alone, but to some extent, it may be necessary to do this in order to explain my points.

What I think we need to test is candidates' ability to be flexible and their ability to solve puzzles (this is effectively what attackers are doing when they are gaining unauthorized access and writing malware), and also we need to test their enthusiasm for IT. So a Unix administrator needs to show some interest in something other than Unix. Unix folks usually do have some deep-seated revulsion for Microsoft Windows, but this does not really work if they want to be security analysts. The Unix administrator would need to show some good knowledge of Windows, Cisco, Oracle, Microsoft SQL Server, firewalls, IDS, mail servers, and a few others in order to pass the security entrance exam. There should also be some sort of programming challenge, although which programming language is tested is not so important. All this sounds difficult? Well, this is security unfortunately. We need security analyst candidates to show the kind of enthusiasm and raw talent that is needed for the role, and a good way to do this is to set a multidimensional exam such as what I just described.

With regard to becoming an accredited security analyst, I do not believe it is so much about the technical content of the exam study material. Being an effective security analyst is not so much about being a brilliant penetration tester or a reverse engineering guru; it is about the attitude. This also does not mean that all security analysts have to be Hackers, but they do have to have some real enthusiasm for IT and an ability to learn fast and be flexible. People who have such abilities do not necessarily need to be a Microsoft SQL Server guru before they perform a risk assessment on an SQL Server database; if they know how an attacker thinks, this is enough because the base security knowledge will be easily acquired for this particular product, and also if an organization has Microsoft SQL Server deployed in production, then there should also be an Microsoft SQL Server security policy somewhere. If this document was thoughtfully and conscientiously drawn up with peer review, in itself it will be a very useful Microsoft SQL Server security guide.

Security is a wide and deep subject. The focus should not be on specific products because there are too many of them, and there are always new ones, but then there are products that every company has such as Windows or Unix; the exam can test the candidate's knowledge in these areas, but it is not important that the candidate has very deep Unix *and* Windows experience. There are some bases that need to be covered (by the security department as a whole) that include operating system knowledge, databases, network gear and so on as I mentioned before . . . but it is not the case that a candidate has to be a very senior Windows admin, plus also a very senior Unix admin and so on.

I discussed these points with people in the U.K. and Australia before, and what usually comes out, after some initial reservations (the unwritten rule in most big firms is that you stick to one Operating System or Oracle or Informix or DB2 and you cannot deviate from this), was enthusiasm for the idea. There are plenty of people out there in IT jobs who love IT. Maybe their work environment gets them down, but they got into IT vocationally because they studied computer science as a higher education subject; there was some enthusiasm for IT in the beginning of their careers. I doubt there would be a shortage of people knocking on the security door.

What about more advanced security accreditations? It depends if the subject area deserves it. I would think application security is an area that would require a further "module" to be gained. Penetration testing would be another such area. With other fields of security, it could be enough to get people channeled in as Security Analysts and let them find their way, as long as they have a good aptitude for learning (which they will have proved in their security entrance exam); they do not need to have passed an exam in incident response, for example.

So then what will be the makeup of the security team? If the company has a lot of Unix boxes, then ideally at least one Security Analyst will have come into the team from a previous life as a Unix administrator. If there are a lot of Oracle instances in production, then the ideal person is one who was working as an Oracle DBA in the firm. Security managers can make their own call on this, and it depends on the proportion of databases. It is not the case that a company that has an estate of 80% Oracle and 20% MySQL needs two security analysts: one from an Oracle DBA background and another from a MySQL DBA background; the Oracle expert can also handle MySQL security. If it is the other way around, then clearly the security manager should be looking for an ex-MySQL DBA. It is hard to be specific on the numbers as it depends on the size of the organization, and of course multinationals have geographical variables in the equation. Most firms will have a need for an application security guru, but if they do not have in-house accredited personnel, they need to outsource this work to a service provider that does have accredited personnel.

The quality of the accreditation program depends on the quality of the board that makes up the questions, but if the examination contents are technically biased, there is less room for nonspecific, airy-fairy content. With certification programs such as CISSP, CISA, and so on, there is almost an entirely different language used for each. Different terms and phrases are used to describe the same underlying principle. These accreditation programs are high-level, low detailed programs that are more suitable for managers, and they are radically different from each other. But with analyst exams, there is a real need for the content to be technical, and although there could be some disagreements over the exact content, at least there is no room for misinterpretation and invention of new terms. Many of the questions will be vendor-specific, and therefore vendor terminology and ideas will be used.

The security manager position is one that ties itself with management-level accreditations and these I have already discussed. The CISSP and CISA type of exam is more appropriate for managers, but then with CISSP in particular, there is a lot of material that would need to be weeded out. The British Computer Society ISEB Certificate in Information Security Management Principles (CISMP) is a good course for managers, and no, I have not been sponsored to make this comment. I speak from my own experience of having taken the exam.

So overall, I believe the following path would be appropriate for the industry: security analysts are IT professionals who enter the field after a minimum of five years or so of vocational work in some other IT department, preferably from the same company (to facilitate the relationship with their previous department—this is especially important for security departments). They should also have gained a professional accreditation particular to their role such as MCSE.

Before entering into their new life as security analysts, they need to have gained security accreditation. This accreditation currently does not exist. It needs to be invented with input from ground-level technical experts in the field, with some rationalization by reputable senior folks. I have given some ideas as the content of the syllabus for this exam.

The security team is made up of security analysts who have "core" expertise areas related to their previous position in the company. Take the following as an example: a company has around 1000 nodes (roughly a medium-sized firm) of predominantly Linux operating systems. They have MySQL databases in production, Lotus Notes for internal communication/collaboration, and so on. The network is not surprisingly made of mostly Cisco gear. So the security team in this case could be made of at least four security analysts who came into the team from each of the four areas I just mentioned; but that does not mean that in their security roles they are dedicated "Linux security analysts," "MySQL security analysts," and so on.

There will be one security architect probably, plus of course the security manager. Security managers and architects "graduate" from having been security analysts for at least five years, and they must have gained accreditation in security management.

So with all this, many readers will be thinking along the lines "there are hundreds of accreditations out there, what is so special about this one that makes it the one certification program to bind them all?" This is a good question. I do not know what the history behind the U.K. acceptance of the Chartered Engineer accreditation is, and even if I did, I would not bore the reader with it; but I suspect that in this story, there are similarities with the way that security will eventually go.

I guess, overall, I cannot say for sure that if a security program of the genre I am describing in this chapter is adopted that it would be widely and universally accepted—it could perhaps need some sort of government or big four auditor impetus if this is to happen; but I would not rule out the potential for humans to "know the right thing when they see it, and then do the right thing." It is basic intuition that tells us that security is an information technology discipline. If an accreditation program comes along that puts security pros in touch with the security aspects of core technologies, then it is not so obvious that the idea would not go viral. There could be different programs in different countries, but just as with civil engineering, the same basic structure is adopted, pretty much because it just makes sense. It starts with one company recruiting people for security out of IT operations and so on, and if the idea works, it will build momentum, but it takes an open mind to take the first steps.

Thus far, CISSP has been the most widely accepted accreditation to date, and over the past five or six years, there have been a growing number of CISSP program critics. Certainly these days, whenever you come across forums that talk about CISSP, there are more folks in the "nay" camp as compared to the "aye" camp. But also, is there any alternative? The others have not been adopted because they carry a more or equally negative perception with the masses. This has nothing to do with exam costs or other cosmetic features. At the end of it all, the thing that matters is the syllabus. What is the knowledge base that is under examination and what does it really mean (through the smoke and mirrors) to be certified under that particular examination program? The private-owned organizations that spawn these accreditation programs can use whatever marketing techniques they want to create an image of "professionalism" or "ethics" in the eyes of prospective exam-takers and employers, but in the end, although it can take a few years, the real value of the credential will become apparent.

Finally in this chapter, there is the matter of finances and the whole business case for changes in security personnel. Not surprisingly, there is no case study out there somewhere to show cost benefits, but one thing is for sure, this proposed model for the reengineering of security departments will absolutely not lead to massively higher costs, and would in all likelihood lead to significantly lower costs.

Security departments these days make huge investments in areas like SIEM and IDS that require not only six-figure sums to get up and running but also for "operations security" staff to monitor and fine-tune the systems. Qualified security analysts that are able to perform technical analysis and product evaluation are in a position to give a tech pros versus cons argument to the security manager who can then weigh the business case. In most cases, these product acquisitions will never have happened had the analysis been carried out with the appropriate tech and business case/return on investment input. In fact, in such a futuristic model, the security products space would change beyond recognition.

The general security strategy premise of bare compliance I described in Chapter 4 is one that would change quite radically. No longer would the firm just acquire products as short cuts to meeting regulatory requirements, for example, the organization buys a six-digit SIEM system because an auditor tells them they need network logging. Now, with the new makeover of the security team, there would be an on-going cost for the security team (which is composed of just the soft and hard costs for any employee), and compliance would occur almost transparently with "business as usual" costs. There would no longer be the annual scramble to meet audit requirements, whereby the business spends in a reactionary way to pass the audit. Under this new model, businesses have seamless compliance, plus they also get some return on investment in the way of reducing risk down to business-acceptable levels.

Overall, when things are done right, they are done cheaper. Security managers no longer need to tie up their team members because they have more independence in the way of being able to answer more questions themselves, do presentations and reports without tech support, and so on. Revenue-generating business processes are no longer shut down because of security regulations where the actual risk did not justify such an action.

In terms of head counts in security, intuition tells us that if we increase the levels of intellectual capital and skills held by security analysts, then we need fewer of them to achieve the same goals in information risk management.

Summary

In this chapter, I have laid out how I think the information security world can get back in touch with the information. I have lamented greatly in this book about how a loss of tech skills in security has led us down the dark alley in which we now find ourselves. Basically I think the ground levels of security, as in security analysts, need to first get skilled up and then be able to use those skills to gain visibility in areas such as policy compliance, for example. When I say "visibility," of course I mean visibility of data, configurations, networks, firewalls, and applications.

Many of the problems have resulted from security detaching itself (and being detached) from the rest of the company, and in particular, IT operations. The keys to all information resources are currently held by departments other than security because of a lack of IT skills. Which operations manager in their right mind would hand a root password to a security analyst who has never even logged into a Unix computer before? But what if security analysts were once themselves IT operations staff? Then they could all speak the same language and understand each other's requirements. If security analysts are to help bring the organization's risk profile down to an acceptable level based on business risk, then it helps a great deal if they first have IT skills themselves (as I mentioned in Chapter 4, there is a big difference between the required security skills and IT operational skills), and then they have full unadulterated access to information assets and applications.

In summary, I would like to see a very simple accreditation structure in security that consists of precisely two levels of accreditation, and also I would like to see precisely two or three security positions/titles as a maximum: Security Analyst and Security Manager. Potentially there could also be such an animal as a Security Architect. There are so many certifications out there from start-up private ventures, and who is to say which one is the best? There are also so many position titles. It does not help to create self-proclaimed position titles such as "subject matter expert" because the reputation of the industry is so low, and this business of creating new titles for self-promotion reasons has grown thin: people see through it now. Self-proclaimed "evangelists" are less likely than ever to have any advantage over plain old security analysts.

The idea with accreditation is to put the security world back in touch with ground-level IT operations and other IT departments. So this means that the only path to security should be from other IT departments. An IT operations member with five years of experience and a vendor certificate such as MCSE can get training to study for a generic security exam.

The security exam tests knowledge to at least a basic level in all popular technologies such as Windows, Cisco, firewalls, Web application security, penetration testing, and databases (SQL), and there has to be some sort of programming test. What we need in security are enthusiastic IT people who are also flexible. The content of the test is designed not so much as a test of IT knowledge but rather a test of flexibility and enthusiasm; but it is still in touch with the reality of technologies that are likely to be found in most large organizations. A candidate who does not see an issue with covering several different operating systems (other than their usual comfort zone operating system) is a flexible and enthusiastic candidate. The focus on products and specific technologies is not so important because there are new ones popping up regularly; we cannot keep up if we want to test employees on every technology known to man. Scripting rather than programming is an important skill for Security Analysts; moreover, if the candidates have got into coding at some point in their careers, it is a good sign of enthusiasm.

The security manager's role is to know the business and security management principles, and he or she should be able to wield the security analysts as a weapon to be unleashed at strategic points in the information risk management cycle. As a team, they create the cycle and then maintain it into the future. The structure that is followed can be that of the firm's baseline security standard, which in turn is based on ISO 27001. What we have today is a security department full of security managers who specialize in security standards, whereas really there should only be one such person, even for a largish-sized company.

The security manager has been the part of the puzzle that was always missing from security. The security analyst skills were present in the 1990s (the Hackers), but what was missing was the IO interface between the security analysts and the rest of the organization, sort of the artists' agent who sells their artist's work and speaks to customers on their behalf.

You need a security manager who both understands their team and can talk at the same level as the security analysts, but also understands the needs of businesses.

Security managers must have "graduated" from a security analyst role, and they must have been in that role for at least five years. To become security managers, they need to have passed a security management principles exam, not unlike the British Computer Society ISEB CISMP exam. I have no vested interest in the BCS—I am not being sponsored.

If I go back through all of the problems laid out in this book thus far, I can relate all of them at least partially to a lack of any decent level of proof of knowledge/experience on behalf of security professionals.

In Chapter 4, I commented on migration of security functions to operations teams. With appropriate prerequisites for entry into life as a security analyst, there would never be any need or intention to move security functions away from the security team.

Chapter 4 also discussed autoscanners. Use of autoscanners created a void of technical knowledge that spread through the industry in the early 2000s. With verifiable (by accreditation) and appropriate levels of knowledge in security, there would be acute awareness of the shortcomings of an automated-only approach to vulnerability assessment.

With regard to checklists, they are still going to exist of course. They serve a purpose. Personally when I am engaged on security assessments of infrastructure, I do not trust myself to remember everything I am supposed to *check*, and this is why I will use a *check*list. It is just that with propagation of certified IT and then security skills, the checklist will not be followed minus application of thought. Security analysts, as the name suggests, are supposed to analyze things, not parrot-fashion deliver security services with checklists and "best practices."

How about the "audit-driven security strategy" as I covered in Chapter 4? Again, with the population of suitable skills in analysis and management, organizations will move away from this approach slowly over a few years. There will still be audit and regulatory compliance requirements for a long time to come, but it will no longer be the case that the security strategy is geared up to just about creep over the line in barely passing the audit. However, once regulators realize how bad their audit quality has been all these years, the audits may well start getting more rigorous and detailed, also covering more real estate.

Does a move away from an audit-driven security strategy mean that firms will be spending more for security? I cover this aspect in greater detail at the end of this section.

As I covered in Chapter 8, the security industry yearns for IT innovations such as "cloud" in order to find new ways to be appreciated. In the future, the accreditation structure of security will be sufficient for security professionals. There will be no more creation of virtual banks of intellectual capital that lead firms to spend more on specific expertise and products where they are not needed.

Chartered Engineers in civil engineering do not cry out for the world to respect them. Why? Because they are Chartered Engineers, that's why. Likewise, there will be no more talk of incident databases in connection with proof of a security threat. There could be incident databases, but the information in the databases will not be used to support decision making or decision breaking. With proper accreditation and skills in security, Security analysts and managers will be able to plant their feet in the ground, look the decision maker in the eye, and confidently give their message—and the message will be received and understood. What happens after that is up to the decision maker, but we in security will have given a correct, verifiable, confident message, and if people choose not to listen to us, we have done our bit. However, I would not mind betting that they *will* listen to us.

With the adoption of correct skills through the chain of analyst to manager in security, the perception of management will be that security is an IT department; it is part of IT, except it does not carry so much overhead. Security will carry the image of offering genuine value because it is more "in touch" with the business as compared with other

IT departments. This has always been the intention with security, but thus far, so little of the potential of security has been realized.

So far, security has always been a radically too much or radically too little show. Either security backs off from projects and the holes are discovered later, or security blocks innovation that can save money or generate revenue. Striking the balance is a qualitative process, and it is impossible to find the *correct* balance point of costs versus risks; but to date, so many decisions have been horribly out of whack because there has been little or no technical risk assessment, apart from the use of automated tools that do not work.

There is a doubt that many will have about the futuristic security accreditation program I have described in this chapter. What is the unifying factor here? What will lead the security industry to adopt this scheme? Well, I would not rule out the capacity of humans to do the right thing, and intuitively people know that information security is an IT discipline predominantly. CISSP has been the biggest security certification known to man thus far, but more and more people are questioning the relevance of the CISSP syllabus to everyday ground-level security requirements. Currently there are no real alternatives to CISSP. There are many similar types of accreditation programs that are higher-level management type of shows. Currently there are no certs that come even close to meeting the needs of the industry, at least not at a security analyst level. So who knows? Perhaps it could take a while, but there could be a domino effect of firms using a "security graduation scheme" such as the one I have suggested in this chapter.

And what of costs? How will the proposed revamping of security skills affect the bottom line of business costs? Well, one thing is for sure: the costs would not be significantly higher. The industry currently has several ways in which it hemorrhages cash with security—most notably in product acquisitions that not only have huge initial integration costs but also require head count to be brought in for monitoring and fine-tuning. Where proper analysis is conducted with product evaluations and managers have access to accurate tech diagnosis, they are in a position to make the right call on products based on return on investment. Many of the huge product acquisitions going on in firms today would never happen under this scheme, and some product families would perhaps cease to exist. The overall market for products would shrink a great deal.

Generally when you have more highly skilled Analysts and Managers, there is the simple fact that fewer people are required to perform the same function. At the moment, especially in markets such as the U.K., there are issues with overspecialization where you have security staff who specialize in one small part of a large task, whereas with skilled Security Analysts, the whole task can be performed with one head count and very often in a shorter time frame (because they can "just get on with it"). The thing is the security analysts out there today may be lacking in skills, but their salaries are usually consistent with national average IT salaries. So what do you choose, a team of five analysts to perform a task who get paid US$6000 per month each, or a skilled analyst who can do it all by himself or herself, certainly not five times slower (the efficiency through teamwork thing is a myth; in practice, it does not work in most offices), with the same salary?

Especially in the case of security managers, there will be economic benefits. Their increased efficiency and interdependence lead to benefits across the whole team mainly because they do not need help to do things like write reports and deliver presentations. There will be fewer questions asked and less use of team resources, which enables the whole team to focus on their own jobs.

The other cost-saving area is that of compliance. Currently organizations base their entire security strategy on crawling over the line and just about meeting audit requirements. So what happens is every year, there will be reactive spending to get through the audit, and employees are scrambling around trying to meet their audit obligations. This audit-driven security strategy (as I also explained in Chapter 4) leads to major disruption for all IT departments. Organizations will often buy products as a short cut to meet some critical audit point (such as SIEM to meet the network logging requirement).

With the deployment of appropriate analyst and manager skills, compliance will be seamless. There will be no annual scrambling around, putting everything else on hold. The security team can focus on security rather than just focusing on passing the audit (they are not the same thing). So effectively the company is spending to pass the audit, but the costs are the usual on-going costs. The money that goes into passing the audit can finally be used to pass the audit and, as a bonus, buy security also!

Index

A

AccelOps, 231
Active Directory Domain Services,
    228
Advanced persistent threat (APT),
    55, 149, 180
    attacks, 222
Anomaly-based IDS, 222
Anti-Hacker, 51
Apache, 126
Apple iMac, 22
Architect, 149
ArcSight, 231
Arms-crossed approach, 77
Audit-driven security strategy,
    99–105, 281
Automated vulnerability scanners,
    25, 83–89, 111–141
    CHMOD test, 123
    corporate information security
        practices, 114
    cutting labor costs, 114
    disadvantages of full automation,
        112, 131
    erroneous vulnerability checking
        by, 124

exploit of software bugs, 127,
    138–139
false-negative, 135, 138
false positive testing revelations,
    121–125
final section on, 129–132
functionality, 113
glass half full scenario, 139, 140
methodology, 121
negatives of, 117
publicly disclosed vulnerabilities,
    127
quality issues, 118–120
reliability, 129
scanning target IP address, 115
TSAP management support for,
    120
vs. manual penetration testing,
    121
in vulnerability management,
    114
and Web application, 115, 132–136
    custom, 133
    ineffectiveness of, 134
    vs. autoscanners, 135
    vulnerability, 133
Autoscanner modus operandi, 138

Autoscanners. *See* Automated
    vulnerability scanners

B

Banner issues, 118, 119
Baseline standard, 52
BC/DR. *See* Business continuity/
    disaster recovery expert
    (BC/DR)
Belt and suspenders principle, 216
Berkeley Internet Name Daemon
    Domain Name Server
    (BIND DNS), 126
Berkeley Internet Naming Daemon
    (BIND) issues, 174
Bernanke, Ben (chairman of the
    U.S. Federal Reserve), 4
Best practices, 193
    in incident response and
        management, 93–98
    in security service provision,
        98–99
Big Four, 7, 50
    security team, 154
Big Four consultancy
    audit activities, 100
    hiring policies, 101
Black box network penetration
    testing, 173
Black box security testing, 136
Blacker-than-black category, 20
Black Hat Briefings, 19, 20
Black hat Hackers, 19, 20
Black Hat Technical Security
    Conferences, home page
    of, 19
BLUESOC, 231
Bounce.exe program, 172
Bounce method, 172
BP, offshore oil drilling disaster,
    12–13
    financial impact on, 13

British Broadcasting Corporation
    (BBC) Web site, 262
Buffer overflow/programming error
    testing, 126–127
Burp Suite tools, 136
Business continuity/disaster recovery
    expert, 148, 149
Business ethic, 24

C

Careers in information security,
    143–167
CASEs. *See* Checklists and
    standards evangelists
    (CASEs)
Certified Ethical Hacker (CEH)
    certificate, 17–18
Certified Information Systems
    Auditor (CISA), 253
Certified Information Systems
    Security Professional
    (CISSP), 17, 253
    accreditation, 144
    study guides, 215
Change management system, 33
Chartered Engineers in civil
    engineering, 252
Checklist, 89–93
    key management issue, 89–90
    problems with, 107–108
    security analyst's, 90
Checklist ethic, 107
Checklists and standards evangelists
    (CASEs), 49, 143
    common assertions, 67–68
    culture, 51
    ethic, 53
    and Hackers, 65–66
    modus operandi, 60
    and network security, 60–61
    -oriented team, 51
    role of, 70

security professionals, 71
skill set, 68
survival guidelines, 58–60
Chief information security officer
  (CISO), 14
CHMOD, 123
CIA triad, 164
Cisco accreditation, 271
Cisco Certified Network Associate
  (CCNA) Security, 271
Cisco Certified Security Professional
  (CCSP), 271
Cisco Security MARS, 231
CISSP. *See* Certified Information
  Systems Security
  Professional (CISSP)
CISSP accreditation, 193
CISSP Application Development
  Security, 253
CISSP Code of Ethics, 17
CISSP exam study guide, 91
C-levels
  concern over security threats, 103
  and information security, 11–12
C-level trust, 254–255
Cloud computing, 200–206
  architectures, 201
  criticisms of, 201
Cloud implementations, 206
Cloud migrations, 194, 203
Cloud risk assessment, 203
Cloud security, 200, 202, 203, 205
  consultant, 206, 207
  experts, 202
  rationalization of, 209
  as source of self-esteem
    improvement, 210
Cloud systems, classes of, 202
Compliance-driven security strategy
  approach, 230
Computer Associates Technologies
  IM, 226–227
Creative programming, 24

Credit crunch, 4
Criminal organizations, 48
Critical security project, 195
Cross-site request forgery problems,
  41
Cross-site scripting, 41
  problems, 133
Crypto algorithms, 65, 66
Cryptology, 65
Custom (zero-day) exploit, 27
Cybercop Scanner, 85, 117

D

Database administrators (DBAs), 147
DBAs. *See* Database administrators
  (DBA)
Deepwater Horizon, 13
Denial-of-service (DoS), 198
DES3, 89
Distributed denial of service
  attacks, 11
DoS. *See* Denial-of-service (DoS)
Dot com boom, 11
Double dip scenario, 4

E

Early warning system, 113
Economic security, 19
Enterprise certification, 116
Ethical penetration testing, 18
Ethics, 17–20
Evangelist, 149. *See also* Security
  Evangelist
Exploit-testing restriction, 175–179
External audit, 53

F

Facebook
  clicking on wrong link, 41
  and Hacker, 40–42

security in, 41
server-side issues, 41
False negatives, 88
False positives, 85
testing revelations, 121–125
File inclusion bug, 27
File Transfer Protocol (FTP), 28
Financial Times, 11
Firewall configuration, 60, 61
Forensics experts, increase in
requirements of, 62
FTP bounce, 172
FTP CHMOD vulnerability, 123
FTP vulnerabilities, 122–124

G

GFI LANguard, 85, 111
Global security incidents database,
195
Great autoscanning lottery, 125–129

H

Hacker
clashes between managers and,
24
defined, 24
element in security, 29–35
ethic. *See* Hacker ethic
and Facebook, 40–42
informal dress code, 37
in IT operations, 25
misconception, 17
in network operations, 25
and nuclear fusion reactor, 30
in penetration testing, 25–29
in remote security testing, 25–29
reports, communication problems
with, 35–36
as security analyst of late 1990s,
38
traits, 40

unethical, 18
Hacker ethic, 21, 23. *See also* Ethics
and business ethic, 24
report findings, 31
skill sets, 24–25
Hacker/penetration testing, 25–29
documentation, 26
exploiting services, 29
in late 1990s, 26
older style of, 43
quality analysis of report, 35
real-life scenarios, 26–28
recoding/patching open-source
tools, 28
rules on methodology, 26
skills, 29
Hackers' computers, 22
programming code, 22
resource utilization and efficiency,
22
VGA console mode, 22, 23
Hackers' goals, 21
*Hackers: Heroes of the Computer
Revolution,* 21
freedom of access to information,
21
Hackers overstating security risks,
38–40
Hats in security, 19
HBgary SQL injection, 133, 134
HELL, 9, 50
security departments, 54–58
HIPS. *See* Hybrid host intrusion
prevention system (HIPS)
Hong Kong Monetary Authority
(HKMA)
information security requirements
of, 31
Hybrid host intrusion prevention
System (HIPS), 213
Hydra, 29
Hypertext Markup Language
(HTML), 27–28

I

IBM AIX systems, 28
IBM (Tivoli IM), 226
Identity management experts, 226
Identity management (IdM),
    226–231
  products, 226–227
  product sales efforts, 229
  solutions, 230
  value offering, 229
IdM. *See* Identity management
    (IdM)
IdM consultants, 241
IdM security analysts, 226
IDSs. *See* Intrusion detection
    systems (IDS)
ImmuneSecurity, 231
Incident management and forensics,
    61
Incident response and management,
    8, 93–98
Incident response plan (IRP), 97
Incident response strategy, 96
Incidents data, gathering, 195–200,
    207
Industry sector comparison, 9
Informational vulnerabilities, 122
Information security, 143
  corporate life, 60
  incidents, 10, 11, 13
  in infancy, 50, 69
  in mess, 3
  poor state of, 48
  problems, 3
  specialization in, 146–151
  spending, 7–9
    driving forces for, 7–8
  and strange attractors, 145–146
  top-level managers and, 10–12
Information security department, 61
Information security professionals,
    19

Information security risk
    management
  IT operations staff and, 70
  strategy, 52
Information security strategy, 215
Information Systems Audit and
    Control Association
    (ISACA) accreditation, 253
Information Technology Service
    Center (ITSC), 57
Informix DBAs, 147
Infosec accreditation structure,
    theoretical, 270–278
Infosec manager, requirements of,
    257–260
Infosec risk management standards,
    215
Infosec vocational classifications,
    256–257
Infrastructure as a Service (IaaS),
    202–203
Instant manager, 151–154
Institution of Chartered Engineers
    (ICE), 251
Intelligence gathering, 121
Intelligence vulnerability, 118, 126
Internal audit, 53
International Information System
    Security Certification
    Consortium (ISC)², 17
International Standards
    Organization (ISO), 44
Internet Engineering Task Force,
    227
Intrusion detection systems (IDSs),
    61, 214
  anomaly-based, 222
IP address range(s) restriction,
    testing, 173–175
(ISC)² CISSP accreditation, 251
(ISC)² CISSP certification, 17, 165
ISO 27001 and IT governance, 153
ISO 27001 Standard, 92

IT administrator, 150
IT change management system, 147
IT operations, 57
IT operations skills
    and security skills, 77, 106
IT policy compliance, 241

J

JavaScript, 269

K

Key performance indicators (KPIs),
    25, 105, 159
    targets, 110
KPI. *See* Key performance indicators
    (KPIs)

L

Law of diminishing enthusiasm,
    115–121
Layered security, 176
Levy, Steven, 21, 22
Lightweight Directory Access
    Protocol (LDAP), 28, 56,
    227
Linux machine
    base install of, 23
    VGA console, 23
Linux platform security in HELL,
    54–58
    development of security standard,
    55
    network architecture problems,
    55–56
    root/super-user login, 56, 57
    security initiatives, 57
    security program, 56
Linux security analysts, 275
Linux security program, 56
Listening services, 89

Local exploit, 23
LogLogic, 231

M

Malware attack, 181
Managed service providers (MSPs),
    222
Management, attributing blame to,
    3–5
Management accreditation, 165
Manager/secretary password issue,
    5–7
Manual penetration testing, 85, 89
Massachusetts Institute of
    Technology (MIT), 21
Microsoft, 226
Microsoft Certified IT Professional
    certification, 270
Microsoft Certified System
    Engineer (MCSE)
    certification, 270–271
Microsoft Internet Information
    Server (IIS) version 4.0.,
    118
Microsoft's Active Directory (AD),
    228
Mitnick, Kevin, 6
Modern security practices, 68–69,
    70
Monetary Authority of Singapore
    (MAS), 37
MS SQL Server security guide,
    273
Mutt, 23
MySQL security analysts, 275
The Myths of Security, 214

N

Nessus, 85, 111
    test patterns, 126
Nessus Project, 84

Network access control (NAC), 115
Network address translation (NAT), 64
Network intrusion detection systems (NIDS), 213
  as advanced packet sniffer, 219
  belt and suspenders, 216–217
  and denial of service, 217
  deployment, 214–215
  and false positives, 214
  hidden costs, 218
  implementations for, 222
  open-source, 214
  output, 220
  problems, 220
  return on investment, 218–220
  tuning/initial costs, 216
Network intrusion prevention systems (NIPS), 213, 220–222
  blocking activity, 221
  diagnosis of, 213
  vs. NIDS, 220
Network penetration tests, 30, 84
Network Security Assessment (Chris McNab), 28–29
Network segmentation, 9
The New School of Information Security, 89
NIDS. *See* Network intrusion detection systems (NIDS)
NIPS. *See* Network intrusion prevention systems (NIPS)
Nmap, 112, 117, 129, 221
Noscript, 269
Novell IM, 227
NULL sessions, 64

O

Open network architecture, consequences of, 55
Open Source Vulnerability Database, 99

Open Web Application Security Project (OWASP), 137
  site, 267
Operating system (OS)
  security controls, 107
  security of, 31
Oracle DBAs, 147
Oracle (IM 11g), 226
Oracle security assessments, 58

P

Packet sniffing, 215
Packet Storm, 63
Paros, 136
Pass-the-audit strategy, 109, 110
Payment Card Industry Data Security Standard (PCI-DSS), 92, 148, 194
PCI auditor, 202
PCI-DSS. *See* Payment Card Industry Data Security Standard (PCI-DSS)
PCI-DSS expert, 147, 148
Penetration tester, requirements of, 28
Penetration testing
  bigger picture, 179–186
  costs, 184
  misconceptions, 170
  modern-day, 173
  need for, 183
  renaissance for, 179
  restrictions, 170–179
    client-driven, 171
  return on investment from, 189
  teams skills, 190
  TSAP engagements, 187
  zero-days in, 176
Platform as a Service (PaaS), 202
Port scanning, 117, 129, 132
Post-2000 penetration testing, 25
Potentially disruptive exploits, 178

Pre-2000s Hacker era, 75
Privacy expert, 147
Programmer, 263
Protect and proceed *vs.* pursue and
    prosecute, 94

Q

Q2 2011, 10
Q3 2003, 47

R

Random-access memory (RAM), 22
Red Hat Linux security standard,
    52, 53
Regulatory compliance, 10
Remote network security tests,
    30–31
Remote security testing
    hacker in, 25–29
Risk assessment, 159

S

SCP (Secure Copy), 108
Script kiddy, 29, 88, 113
Script-kiddy exploit, 127
Secure shell access, 122
Secure Sockets Layer (SSL), 39
Security, 106
    complex, 70, 93
    post-2000, changes in, 75–110
Security analysts, 63, 148, 158, 256
    requirements of, 260–270
Security application, 40
Security architect, 256–257
Security awareness, 42
Security awareness programs, 6
Security challenges, 34, 44
Security consultant, 256
Security department managers,
    skilled politicians, 61

Security departments, 76
    testing for false positives, 88
Security evangelist, 149
Security expert, 144, 148
Security incident investigation, 61–62
    security professionals in, 62
Security information event
    management (SIEM), 62,
    217
Security information event
    management (SIEM)
    solutions, 231–240
    advantages and disadvantages,
    232–233
    core function of, 242
    detecting signs of incident, 242
    functionality of, 231–232
    procurement, 234
    products, 231
    return on investment, 239
    technology, 237
Security initiatives, 164
Security managers, 256
    role, 279
Security problem, 23
Security professionals
    characteristics of, 49
    lack confidence, 12
    technically oriented, 51
Security risks, 38–40
    Hackers overstating, 38–40
Security service providers, 35–38, 52
Security service provision, best
    practices in, 98–99
Security standards, 52
Security strategy
    audit driven, 99–105
Security teams and incident
    investigation, 61–63. *See also*
    Checklists and standards
    evangelist (CASE)
Security threats, ignoring warnings
    over, 12–14

SenSage, 231
Service provider manager and
    security analyst, lack of
    trust between, 87
Setuid root privileges, 80
SIEM. *See* Security information
    event management (SIEM)
Simple Mail Transfer Protocol
    (SMTP) tests, 121
Simple Network Management
    Protocol (SNMP), 27
Skype, 220
Smoke-and-mirrors approach, 76
SNMP spoofing, 27
Snort, 214
Social engineering, 6
Software as a Service (SaaS), 202
Software vulnerabilities, 63
Sony's gaming network incident, 252
Source IP address
    restriction, 171–173
    spoofing, 172–173
South Korean telco, penetration
    testing, 26–27
SQL injection problem, 133, 134
SSL certificate, 39
Standards and policies expert, 147
Structured Query Language, 56
    statement, 204
Stuxnet worm, 252
Subject matter expert, 279
Sudo, potential difficulties with,
    228–229
Sybase DBAs, 147
Symantec SIM, 231
System administrators, 147

T

TCP/IP networks, 151, 153
Technical analysis functions,
    migration to IT
    departments, 75–83

Technical security functions to IT
    operations, migrating, 144
Technical track, 154–160
Telnet vulnerability analysis, 78
Testing windows, 178
TNS listener, 32
Triple DES, 66
TSAP, 21
    firing of human resources,
    47–48

U

Ubuntu Linux test Virtual Private
    Server (VPS), 128
U.K. job market, 51
U.K.'s Institution of Civil Engineers
    Web site, 251
Underground intelligence, 99
Unix administrators, 80
Upward pressure, example of, 110
U.S. debt, 4
U.S. National Security Agency,
    121
U.S. property market
    economic crisis in, 4
U.S. Securities and Exchange
    Commission (SEC), 11

V

Variable source address, 172
Vi editor, 116
Virtual private networks (VPNs), 34
VM-like (IaaS) implementation, 205
Vmware, 201
Vulnerability assessment program,
    105
Vulnerability/malware
    announcements, 63–64.
    See also Checklists and
    standards evangelists
    (CASEs)

W

Web app autoscanners. *See*
    Automated vulnerability
    scanners, and Web
    application
Web application security source
    code testing, 136–137
Webgoat project, 137
White box network penetration
    testing, 173
White box source code testing tools,
    137
White box testing, 136
White box tools, 137

White hat Hackers, 19, 20
    U.S. federal criminal charges
        against, 20
White hat security testing services,
    20
Windows Server Message Block
    (SMB) services, 64
Windows *vs*. Mac, malware issues,
    42
Wireless security, presentation on,
    47

Z

Zero-day testing, 176